THE JOHN HARVARD LIBRARY

If any unbecoming Language it is for the want of knoledg & Larning—for I am at me prid to all
ordirs of Men & Individuals, who are frind; to true Libirty & the Rights of Man & the Meanes
I have Descibed is not a Costly one—for Comfident I am that Each penny Laid out in it would
Soon Save pounds in other needles Expences—Therefore unless you See More Dificulty in ap=
=plying it then or Less need of it then I Do—you will Immediately put it on foot & niever give
over untill Such a Society is Establised on Such Lasting foundation that the gates of hell
will not prevail against it—which May the Almighty grant is the Sonceer Desire of a
                                                                    Labourer

Constitution of the Labouring Society

Introduction

1st Whereas, it hath pleased the Supream Governour of the universe for the fall of Man Lapsd
the Irrevartable Sentance on him that in the Swet of thy face Shalt thou Eat thy Bread
It is undoutedly the Duty of Every persone who is Blesd with the facultees of a Sound Body
& Mind to apply him Selfe Industerously to Some honest Calling for the Benifit of himself & Society

2ly Although their are Many Callings, which Men May Live honestly by with out Labour
yet as Labour is the Soul paraant of all property by which all are Suported There=
=fore the Caulling aught to be honourable & the Labourer Respected

3ly And whereas not only the Constitution of our Government alows of Asociations & the
Libirty of the press—that all ordirs of Men who Live without Labour have Improved there on
Therefore we whose Names are hereunto Subscribed In ordir to Establish a Cheap Easy and
Sure Conveyance of knoledge & Larning nisesary for a Labourer to have as possable & to promote a
Similarity of Sentiments & Manner in Industry & Economy—Agiculture & Manufactory &c &c we
hereby Constitute our Selves Into a Society of frinds—by the name of the Labouring Society

Article I

Sect 1st The persons who Constitute this Society are all the free Male persons in the United States
who are 21 years of age—who Labour for a Living & are willing to join & submit to this Regu
Sect 2d Also their are admited into it—all persons of any other denomination—provided
They Subscribe to its funds & Submit to the Regulations of the Society

Article II

The Society Shall be Divided Into Meeting Like the ordir of Cincinaty Viz Clase
Town County State & Continental Meetings

Clase Meeting

Sect 1st This Clase Meeting May be formed by a Greater or Less number Just as their Situation
Circumstance or Inclinations Sute—A Single persone May be a Clase if he will be at the
Expence thereof—or twenty May join & have them a draw name So use the Magezein by turn
or Meet together & hear it read

Town Meeting

Sect 2d The Town Meetings to Include all the Clase, Belonging to Each Towne—unless they are two
Large & by that Case they May Divide as they find nisesary—& they Shall Meit anually
on the 4th of July at 4 oclock afternoon & Choose them a president—Vice president Clarke
& treasurer or Colector

County Meeting

Sect 3d

THE KEY
OF LIBERTY

———————— ◆ ————————

The Life and Democratic Writings of

WILLIAM MANNING,
"A LABORER,"
1747–1814

Edited and with an Introduction by

MICHAEL MERRILL *and* SEAN WILENTZ

HARVARD UNIVERSITY PRESS
Cambridge, Massachusetts
London, England
1993

10 9 8 7 6 5 4 3 2 1

This book is printed on acid-free paper, and its binding materials have
been chosen for strength and durability.

Library of Congress Cataloging-in-Publication Data
Manning, William, 1747–1814.
The key of liberty: the life and democratic writings of William
Manning, "a laborer," 1747–1814 / edited and with an introduction by
Michael Merrill and Sean Wilentz.
p. cm.—(The John Harvard library)
Includes index.
ISBN 0–674–50287–6 (cloth: acid-free).—ISBN 0–674–50288–4
(pbk.: acid-free)
1. United States—Politics and government—1783–1809.
I. Merrill, Michael, 1948–   II. Wilentz, Sean.   III. Title.
IV. Series.
JK171.M26   1993
322'.2'0973—dc20   92–28165
                                                       CIP

Frontispiece: William Manning's manuscript constitution of the
Labouring Society, from the 1798 draft of "The Key of Libberty."

To Jim Shenton

CONTENTS

ILLUSTRATIONS

PREFACE

William Manning—farmer, foot soldier, political philosopher—may be the most obscure author yet honored by inclusion in the John Harvard Library. For more than a century after his death, few if any persons outside his immediate family even knew he *was* an author. It is time his obscurity ended.

In 1799, Manning completed work on the first-known plan for a national association of American laboring men and their political allies—an unacknowledged landmark in American history. Audaciously entitled "The Key of Libberty," Manning's essay delivered a blistering critique of Federalist policies, along with a broader historical commentary on the social origins of American politics. It was not, however, his only notable piece of writing. From the dawn of the Federalist ascendancy until several years after the Democratic Republicans' triumph in 1801, Manning was a diligent political scribbler. To his endless disappointment, none of his efforts was published in his own lifetime. Yet better than any similar body of sources so far discovered, they describe the aspirations of the popular, egalitarian currents of the American Revolution and its aftermath. Read alongside the surviving evidence about Manning's biography, they shed new light on the ideas and values, secular and religious, that lay behind the rise of American democracy.

Manning's life and writings would have remained completely unknown had his descendants not lovingly preserved his papers and, in time, deemed his ideas worthy of publication. In 1922, the Manning Family Association privately printed a 1798 version of "The Key," along with some notes and a brief introduction supplied by the young Harvard historian Samuel Eliot Morison. The family eventually deposited all the drafts of "The Key," as well as Manning's other papers, at the Harvard College Library.

Through the 1970s, Morison's edition of "The Key" (reprinted with corrections in 1956) remained the only substantial scholarly presentation of Manning's manuscripts. Over the years, it attracted the attention of a few prominent academic historians, along with some radical writers. All cited Manning's work as an excellent introduction to what Merle Curti called the "crude but vigorous idiom" of a Jeffersonian farmer. But Manning himself remained a shadowy figure. The occasional attempts to elucidate his politics and to identify the events and ideas that shaped them were cursory and often misinformed. No one noticed just how pioneering his proposals were. Sandwiched between the classic writings of Paine and Jefferson, "The Key of Libberty" came down as a curiosity piece of American democratic thought, the product of a disembodied voice—"A Labourer," as Manning called himself—from an obscure corner of the Massachusetts countryside.

A more recent revival in Manning's reputation has grown from some basic changes in how historians approach the revolutionary era. Twenty-five years ago, calls came for a revisionary history of the American Revolution, written "from the bottom up"—that is, from the perspective of the ordinary people who did most of the protesting, fighting, and dying. Since then, a small library of books and articles has detailed the lives of artisans, yeoman farmers, women, and slaves and has shown how they contributed to building the new nation. Although rich in evidence about mentality and collective political consciousness, these new histories have had little to say about the plebeian intellectual history of the Revolution and the early republic (apart from that singular presence, Thomas Paine). Many writers have assumed that popular ideas simply imitated one or another strain of elite political thought—classical republicanism, emergent liberalism, or some combination of the two. Continuing research, however, has turned up a number of interesting plebeian writers—including such unknown figures as Walter Brewster, Abraham Clark, and Simon Hough—who espoused a distinct and powerful body of democratic ideas about disparate political topics. Of all these thinkers so far discovered, William Manning is the most rewarding.

Read closely, Manning's manuscripts illuminate a largely unknown world of plebeian intellectual life and political debate.

They also pose a series of interesting problems for those who portray the American Revolution as a triumph, not only for democracy, but also for capitalism. Gordon Wood, for example, has recently insisted on the radicalism of the Revolution. In his view, no other revolution, even in modern times, has enabled so many people to live so well or so freely. For Wood, it marked a decisive break between an older, proprietary monarchialism and a newer, entrepreneurial democracy. Other historians, notably Joyce Appleby, have described the shift in terms of a victory for liberal capitalist values—supposedly the animating force behind the rise of Jeffersonianism.

Manning's writings suggest that there is more to the story than this. He certainly welcomed the Revolution as a radical political departure, one that he had fought to achieve. And he clearly thought democracy and economic growth could be fully compatible. But he also retained an abiding suspicion of moneyed men— or "capitalists," as other contemporary writers called them—who inevitably found that their self-interest led them to use their collective power to subvert honorable commerce, compromise democratic government, and exploit the mass of ordinary citizens. Democracy, to men like Manning, involved checking that moneyed power through legitimate political action, and then sustaining that check through popular organizations. Its triumph did not herald a liberated pursuit of individual selfishness (which Manning thought sin incarnate). Neither did plebeian democrats like Manning reduce democracy to freedom for capitalist entrepreneurs. Instead, they understood it to be a system of government in which the productive majority held the preponderance of power and exercised it in their own interest.

Studying Manning's life and works has, we admit, left us with a certain fondness for the man, despite his own obvious limitations. Of the latter, there were many, quite apart from the handicaps imposed by his lack of schooling. An acerbic critic of his dissembling political enemies, Manning could also be less than truthful about himself. And his political ideas certainly leave a lot to be desired from a modern point of view. Forged in a world of household-centered production and trade, Manning's democracy did not extend beyond adult free males. He never suggested that women deserved formal political citizenship. Nor did he join with those democratic writers who attacked the brutality and moral stain of American slavery. Yet Manning should not be dismissed simply because his ideas fail to live up to our expectations. It is in part thanks to Manning and the other plebeian democrats of his day that our standards can be as high as they are—for those men helped stamp American society with a far greater degree of equality than it would otherwise have had. Their clear-headed realism about power and its uses, always alert to tragedy and human frailty, still merits respect, especially when compared to most of what passes for political thought in our own time.

Other historians will certainly offer different interpretations of Manning's life work. Although we have composed a commentary that runs nearly as long as Manning's own writings, we do not claim to have had the last word about him or anything he wrote. Quite the opposite: in making his writings more widely available, we hope to encourage more reflection and debate about the kinds of democratic thinking he proclaimed.

This book had its origins in an exploratory paper on Manning, which Professor Alfred F. Young asked us to revise and submit for a projected collection of essays on the post-Revolutionary era. The research eventually expanded well beyond our expectations, thanks in part to Professor Young's exuberant prodding. He urged us to find out more about William Manning and his world, and was the first to encourage us to undertake an edition of Manning's writings; more than anyone, it was he who illuminated our continuing efforts. We are also grateful to Northern Illinois University Press, publisher of Professor Young's collection *Beyond the American Revolution*, which includes a much shorter, preliminary version of the present introduction.

At Harvard University Press, Aida Donald immediately understood what we were up to—including the historical irony of publishing William Manning's musings with John Harvard's imprimatur. Her enthusiasm and wise counsel pulled us through some difficult moments. Also at Harvard, Elizabeth Suttell did an excellent job in helping us pare down an unwieldy, complicated manuscript and in guiding us through to completion. Maria

Ascher superbly edited the final version. In New York, Tom Wallace handled business matters with discretion and wit.

The libraries and staffs at several repositories were unfailingly cordial and helpful. Above all, we wish to thank everyone at Houghton Library at Harvard, where the bulk of the Manning manuscripts are stored. Additional thanks to the librarians and archivists at Baker Library of the Harvard Graduate School of Business Administration, the Massachusetts Archives, the Massachusetts State House, the Middlesex County Courthouse in Lowell, the Billerica Town Hall, Bennett Library in Billerica, the Massachusetts Historical Society, Lyndon Library of the University of Massachusetts at Lowell, the New-York Historical Society, Carey Library of Rutgers—the State University of New Jersey, the New York Public Library, the National Archives, Firestone Library of Princeton University, and Speer Library of the Princeton Theological Seminary.

Important financial aid came from the American Council of Learned Societies, a Rutgers Prestigious Fellowship Award, the Princeton University Committee on Research in the Humanities and Social Sciences, and the John Simon Guggenheim Memorial Foundation. The Labor Institute of New York, and the Oil, Chemical, and Atomic Workers International Union in Denver, Colorado, also provided important moral and material support. Steven Jaffe was a fine research assistant and co-conspirator. Jonathan Earle helped out during the delicate business of checking transcriptions. Karen Carver completed some important last-minute checking in the Billerica church records on microfilm in Salt Lake City. Cheryl Brooks prepared the index.

Together and separately, we delivered drafts of the introduction before several audiences, in the form of lectures and seminar papers. We are deeply grateful to our listeners and inquisitors at the Milan Group for Early American History, the Rutgers Social History Seminar, the Princeton American History luncheon seminar, Washington and Lee University, and Yale University. Barbara Karsky, Gary B. Nash, and Alan Taylor offered helpful suggestions in their comments on an earlier draft, as did Jon Butler, David Weiman, Jean Agnew, and William N. Parker in discussions of a later version. John Murrin deserves special thanks for his thorough reading of several drafts, including the final one, and for his bountiful criticism. So too does Dorothy Sue Cobble, who also followed the growth of this project closely through its many incarnations and offered important encouragement at some crucial points.

Richard and Barbara Manning, now living in Saco, Maine, happily facilitated a research trip to Billerica, answered questions, and made available the Manning Family Collection at what is now the University of Massachusetts at Lowell. Their support was an important turning point for us, and we hope we have done their ancestor justice. George H. Manning and the Manning Family Association cleared publication of the manuscripts and some of the photographs, for which we thank them. Charles Stearns of the Billerica Historical Society provided some important tips and shared his detailed knowledge of his hometown's history.

We also want to acknowledge our spiritual and scholarly debts to the late Samuel Eliot Morison and to Ruth Bogin for their excellent work in presenting earlier editions of Manning's manuscripts.

The members of our respective families never gave up hope that the Manning Folly (as one of them called it) would one day be over. For their good humor and for everything else, our love and thanks to Rena Lederman, Evan Merrill and Jayna Merrill, Christine Stansell, Jamie Wilentz and Hannah Wilentz.

James P. Shenton taught us both when we were undergraduates at Columbia College, and then served one of us as a singularly supportive graduate adviser. The experience of those tumultuous times twenty years ago helped make us historians—and no one did more to inspire our decision (and that of numerous other Columbia College graduates) than Jim Shenton. This book is dedicated to him.

Introduction

WILLIAM MANNING
AND THE
INVENTION OF
AMERICAN POLITICS

◆

You shall see men you never heard of before, whose names you don't know,
. . . rude and sturdy, experienced and wise men, keeping their castles, or
teaming up their summer's wood, or chopping alone in the woods; men fuller
of talk and rare adventure in the sun and wind and rain, than a chestnut is
of meat, who were out not only in '75 and 1812, but have been out every
day of their lives; greater men than Homer, or Chaucer, or Shakespeare,
only they never got time to say so; they never took to the way of writing.
Look at their fields, and imagine what they might write, if ever they should
put pen to paper.
—*Henry David Thoreau,* A Week on the Concord and Merrimack Rivers *(1849)*

William Manning was one of those "rude and sturdy, experienced
and wise men" whose idealized memory haunted Henry Thoreau. A middling farmer in Billerica, Massachusetts, until his
death in 1814, Manning answered the patriot call to arms in 1775
and fought at the nearby battle of Concord. After the Revolution,
he took an active interest in Shays' Rebellion, the debates over
Alexander Hamilton's fiscal program, and the other momentous
events that shaped the postwar era. But unlike the thousands of
other Middlesex County farmers, living and dead, whom Thoreau called to mind, Manning actually did become a writer. The
fruits of his literary labors, dating mostly from the 1790s, were
hardly masterpieces. Nor did his writings have any easily discern-
ible impact on his time, for none were published until long after
his death. They are, nevertheless, landmark American documents, among the richest surviving products of eighteenth-
century popular political thought.

Merle Curti once suggested that the significance of Manning's
work rests partly on the man and his idiom.[1] As his labored syntax and uneven spelling attest, Manning was one of the self-
educated citizen-soldiers of the Revolution. Caught up in the
wider ferment that defined the political battles of the 1770s and

after, his life exemplifies, in concrete and often surprising ways, what historians have sweepingly described as the democratization of American thought at the end of the eighteenth century.[2] As Nathan O. Hatch has observed, his manuscripts are "the rarest kind of historical evidence, a window on the mind of a man who would generally be considered among 'the inarticulate.' "[3]

Yet Manning was far more than an emblematic social type. His essays, raw as they might at first appear, deserve full evaluation as important literary and political statements. "The Key of Liberty," comparable in length to Thomas Paine's *Common Sense*, stands up particularly well as a sustained piece of political writing. While it lacks the full measure of originality, wit, and daring that made Paine's pamphlet the cornerstone of American democratic radicalism, it has much more of them than most of the material that found its way into print at the time.

At the core of Manning's politics was his belief that all government rested on a conflict between two broad classes. These he called, following other writers, the Few and the Many. The first consisted of a minority of wealthy, learned, polished, moneyed men—Manning included rentiers, professionals, stock jobbers, speculators, merchants, and government officers—who did not live by their own labor, and whose incomes vastly exceeded their contributions to society. On the other side was the great majority, those who lived by the labor of their own hands—artisans, laborers, and ordinary farmers like himself. This distinction between the Few and the Many was a commonplace at the end of the eighteenth century. So was the recognition that the wealth and exceptional power of the Few arose from the toil of the Many. In the aftermath of the Revolution, apologists justified this state of affairs on the grounds that only a select group of moneyed, educated gentlemen could administer society responsibly and virtuously. The peace and security of all, they reasoned, necessitated government by the Few. "All communities divide themselves into the few and the many," Alexander Hamilton declared at the federal constitutional convention in 1787. The first group, he explained, included "the rich and well born" and the second were "the mass of the people"—a "turbulent and changing" mass who "seldom judge or determine right." The public good, Hamilton believed, demanded that the unsteadiness of the Many be checked, and that the Few be granted a "distinct, permanent share in the government."[4]

Manning took an opposing view, in line with a democratic way of thinking that had emerged all across the revolutionary republic (especially among men of the lower and middling sort), and surfaced with redoubled force after 1787. Manning totally rejected the idea that the Few were uniquely fit to govern. He and his fellow democrats insisted that all free men who were old enough and established enough to be self-governing— it did not take much—also had the capacity to participate fully in the politics of the wider society. The notion that any part of the government ought to remain in the hands of the Few was, to them, simply a self-serving cover for the exploitation of the Many— exploitation carried out mainly through the agency of the government itself, which the Few manipulated to their own advantage. Only by keeping government and its laws as simple as possible, and by keeping officeholders directly beholden to the productive majority, could the Many be protected against the machinations of moneyed elites. From the start, democratic republicans believed, the whole point of the American Revolution had been to establish such a polity of the Many. As one group of rural North Carolina democrats declared in 1776, when "fixing the fundamental principles of Government," the main object ought to be to "oppose everything that leans to aristocracy or power in the hands of the rich and chief men exercised to the oppression of the poor."[5] Throughout the political struggles of the early republic, plebeian democrats like Manning resolutely kept this object in view.

The period immediately following the Revolution was a trying time for such egalitarian partisans. In state after state, plebeian democrats and their political allies among the elite lost the initiative to self-seeking opportunists and countermarching conservatives. On the defensive, they had to cast about for ways to register their dissent without crossing over into disloyalty. Some fell back on prerevolutionary tactics and organized protest petitions and conventions, which proved ineffective. Others recklessly turned to armed uprisings, which proved disastrous.[6]

Antidemocrats hoped that the framing and ratification of the new federal constitution in 1787–1788 would put a stop to this agitation, which Edmund Randolph of Virginia denounced as "the fury of democracy."[7] But in the aftermath of the ratification struggle, differences over Federalist finance and foreign policy pushed Thomas Jefferson, James Madison, and others into active opposition to the Washington administration. Thanks in part to their efforts—and to pressure from many other, more obscure Americans—this opposition coalesced during the presidency of John Adams into something roughly resembling the nation's first political party, which enabled ordinary citizens to express their discontent as part of an organized electoral movement appropriate to a democratic government, and not as a traditional mob or "the people out-of-doors." This movement helped elect Jefferson president in 1800–1801, changing the course of American political history.

Manning did his best to play a part in these events, and his writings offer a grassroots view of the nation's political transformation. Dismayed by the menacing, illegal tactics used by some popular movements in the 1780s and 1790s (above all, the uprising led by the Massachusetts regulator Daniel Shays), Manning tried to design his own democratic vehicle to combat what he perceived, in disgust, as the rising power of the Few. He began with an unshakable belief that any opposition had to respect the legitimacy of the established constitutional order. He then read everything he could lay his hands on, trying to learn how and why America's minority of moneyed men had managed to seize power and hold it after the Revolution, despite their weakness in numbers. Eventually he came up with a proposed solution, unprecedented in American history: a democratic educational and political association, the Laboring Society, that would organize and unite the Many, and ally with that small part of the Few who were genuine friends of free government. Only this association, he argued, could secure the political power supposedly won in the Revolution by the laboring majority.

Nothing came of Manning's plans. Given who he was and where he came from, that outcome is not surprising. But if his specific program went unpublished, his broader vision of the potential shape of democratic politics was both powerful and pre-scient—outlining a distinctly American form of electoral mobili-zation, foreshadowed in the Revolution, that has influenced politics in this country down to the present day. If Manning's name went unknown outside his native Billerica, his basic under-standing of democratic republicanism was widely shared, well before the emergence of a formal Jeffersonian opposition—in the petitions and protests of plebeian Americans as well as in the writings of disaffected leaders like Madison and Jefferson.[8] In the 1780s and 1790s, this democratic pressure from below encouraged all sorts of creative thinking and popular agitation, quite apart from the notorious rebellions in New England and Pennsylvania. These, in turn, helped force an epochal shift in American politics, contributing enormously to the Jeffersonians' eventual rise and victory. Historians, with their attention fixed mainly on the Jeffersonian gentry or on belligerents like Daniel Shays, have captured only pieces of this dramatic story, so basic to our history. If we are to enlarge our understanding of the rise of American democracy, we must learn more about men like Wil-liam Manning.

Early Life

Manning's ideas, like his unedited manuscripts, carried the strong imprints of his country background and of his political awaken-ing during the American Revolution. He was born in Billerica, a farming community about eight miles north of Concord, on May 21, 1747. His great-grandfather, Samuel Manning of Cambridge, had arrived to take up his father's sixty-acre allotment in the town shortly after its founding in the 1650s; a little later on, in 1662, he bought the thirty-acre estate of the late Thomas Hubbard, and there made his home. A Harvard graduate, and a successful merchant in Cambridge before resettling, Samuel served seven terms as Billerica town clerk, three as the town's representative to the Massachusetts General Court and eighteen as town select-man; he also held several positions in the church and the military. (His house was a garrison post during the Indian wars at the end of the 1690s.) When Samuel's eldest sons left Billerica as young men, the main portion of the estate fell to his fifth-born child, William; the Manning Manse (built in 1696) then descended through him to his eldest son, also named William (who started a tavern in the 1750s); and then to his eldest son, our William.[9] None of Samuel's Billerica descendants enjoyed his educational advantages, or matched his political influence. Yet the successive William Mannings did manage to sustain their status as independent freeholders. On the eve of the Revolution, our William's father held 54 acres of improved farm land in Billerica, and 160 or so of unimproved woods and swamp—a respectable if unspectacular estate to hand down to his offspring.[10]

Inheriting the family name and property would have assured Manning of a measure of economic security and a place in town affairs. But the process of inheritance, always difficult, had become even more troublesome by the time he came of age in the late 1760s. Traditionally, young men waited until their fathers released control of some land before getting married, to ensure they could support their own households while helping to provide for their parents. By the second half of the eighteenth century, however, as arable land grew scarcer throughout the region and establishing a household became more difficult, premarital pregnancy and early marriage became far more widespread. Manning was one of these impatient children. In March 1769, when he was twenty-two years old and still living in his father's household, he married Sarah Heywood, also twenty-two, of nearby Woburn. Six months later, Sarah gave birth to a daughter.[11]

In the world of the yeomanry, such precocious displays of independence could have severe consequences—for fathers could easily punish wayward children when it came time to bequeath the family holdings.[12] The elder Manning left no direct statement about his son's marriage, but there are signs of strain in the Manning household over the next few years. Outsiders—and even young William—may not have understood how deeply the tensions ran. At the time of his son's marriage, William *père* was at least generous enough to provide the couple with some livestock. Beginning in about 1770, young William kept the tavern's accounts and may have begun running it day to day. In 1775, when he was twenty-seven, his neighbors elected him as the town's highway surveyor, a recognition of his impending coming of age. Perhaps father and son kept their quarreling private; perhaps they did not quarrel at all, which may have persuaded young William that he would get his hoped-for inheritance. But whatever expectations he had in the latter direction wound up being betrayed. His father refused, until the day he died, to sell or deed over any land to his eldest son. More important, the elder William voided his will in 1772 and drew up a new one, which stipulated that the land be shared by his wife and all of his children.[13]

The trouble did not end with the old man's death in 1776. Our William contested the new will "for maney [sic] reasons" and gave way only when his siblings agreed to sell their shares for £40 each (a deal he apparently financed by selling 40 acres of his allotment to a neighbor). One brother subsequently became a housewright and another a husbandman in nearby Chelmsford; the youngest set up shop in Billerica as a shoemaker, a lowly trade; the sole surviving sister married a farmer in her hometown. As for Manning's mother, when her widow's share of the legacy was finally recorded, it came with an added handwritten clause that three designated townsmen would arbitrate "if any dispute shall arise between the widow and William Manning relating to the personal estate."[14]

Thus, the headstrong, resourceful Manning consolidated his control of the family land. Given where he lived, however, his hard-won personal independence did not presage any marked change in his way of life. Late eighteenth-century Billerica was a sleepy, secondary country town.[15] The town's population roughly trebled between 1688 and 1765, to just over thirteen hundred persons—but it was still only the eighth largest settlement in Middlesex County at the outbreak of the Revolution. Until after the Revolution, Billerica's inhabitants felt little pressure or opportunity to alter their family-based agricultural economy. To be sure, the town was not an isolated frontier hamlet. A network of simple country roads had always linked it to Woburn, Chelmsford, and other Middlesex communities; by the middle of the eighteenth century, a secondary highway facilitated travel to and from Boston, nearly twenty miles away. Billericans built two grist

Map of Middlesex County and Boston, 1774. Billerica (spelled here with a *k*) is located near the center of the county, to the north of Ledford.

mills along the Concord River before 1708, and by 1771 the town had five mills in all. Many, perhaps most of the district's farming families (including the Mannings) produced a marketable surplus of grain each year, some of which found its way to Concord, Boston, and elsewhere. Still, Billerica's commercial contacts were only of secondary importance to the local economy. On the eve of the Revolution, the proportion of Billerica farms that practiced mixed husbandry and produced enough foodstuffs to be self-sufficient was greater than the statewide average for Massachusetts towns.[16]

Once he had taken control of the family homestead, young Manning had more than enough land to support his household. Even so, neither he nor his neighbors expected to live solely off the produce of their own holdings. As farmers and as tavernkeepers, the Manning men found themselves enmeshed in a dense network of commercial exchanges and local trading partnerships—economic connections spelled out in the surviving Manning family tavern account book.[17] These relations would long shape Manning's thinking about politics and economics, so (dry as such matters are) it is important to explain in some detail how they worked.

Today, most everyday exchanges of goods and services involve commercial transactions. When we go to the store, we expect to pay for our purchases on the spot and without delay. Such promptness is the chief distinguishing characteristic of commercial exchange. The means by which we pay for what we are buying—whether with ready cash or with some kind of negotiable debt instrument (such as a check, credit card, or more elaborate loan agreement)—is much less important than the fact that payment is essentially immediate. Credit is available in such a system, but it is itself commercialized—typically a contractual promise to pay a certain sum of money at regular intervals for a given period. (Such credits are themselves commercial assets that can be readily sold in recognized markets.) Similarly, in Manning's day, merchants, especially those involved in long-distance trade, depended upon prompt payment for value received, whether in the form of country produce, manufactures, coin, or negotiable debt instruments (such as bills of exchange or paper money). Although willing to extend credit, they could not afford to wait indefinitely to settle accounts; they had their own debts to pay and could not eat promissory notes.

The local trading partnerships that characterized the bulk of Manning's relationships and those of his neighbors operated on a very different basis. Above all, they were not governed by the expectation of anything close to immediate or punctual payment. Accounts remained open for years, with items passed back and forth as necessity dictated and availability allowed. First one party would be in debt, then the other, with only intermittent, interim reckonings of who owed what to whom. The reciprocal credits that trading partners extended each other were not commercial assets: there were no ready markets for them. In most cases, creditors did not charge interest on long due accounts, although there were exceptions, as in the case of certain types of mortgages and bonds.[18] Debts in these arrangements were social obligations, to be honored, not sold—part of a dense web of interlocking local commitments, including (not incidentally in William Manning's case) the web of inheritance that bound together the different generations of a single family. They provided both the foundation of a community's prosperity—its means of exchange—and a safety net in the event of unforeseen changes in the supply of or demand for goods and services.[19]

The overwhelming majority of the entries in the Manning account book were transactions of the latter type, examples of what might be called "complex barter."[20] The Mannings did not demand goods or money every time they provided some farm service or waited on someone in the tavern; most often, they extended informal credit on the reasonable expectation that they would eventually be repaid. Among the Mannings' constant customers, for example, was one Joseph Osgood, a blacksmith. Osgood first appeared on the inside front cover of the Manning family accounts in 1753, when he was credited with £5 "old tenor" for "grandmother's maintenance." He showed up again a year later for "fetching goods," and continued to put in regular appearances over the next twenty-five years; in return for molasses, rum, cider, farm products, and fencing material, Osgood shoed the Mannings' horses, repaired their iron tools, made nails, and occasionally worked with them on the farm. Only once were the accounts reckoned, and that occasion served to record Osgood's credits, not to end the relationship. Nor was Osgood the Mannings' only trading partner; similar long-term barter arrangements tied them to the many Pollards, Sprakes, Danforths, Dowses, and other Mannings who lived nearby.[21]

The Mannings did not, of course, conduct all of their business on this basis. Travelers who stopped at the tavern had to pay immediately, as they might never be seen again. The merchants who supplied tea, sugar, and rum had to be paid sooner rather than later. The Mannings themselves no doubt expected prompt payment for the surplus crops they sold to grain dealers from Boston. Such commercial relations enabled total strangers to conduct long-distance or impersonal business conveniently and efficiently. They greatly reduced the time and energy required to ensure that payment was in fact forthcoming. And they also broke the close links between business and personal relationships so critical to the local trading networks—links that reinforced the existing unequal, patriarchal structure of the local community.

As commercial connections grew rapidly at the end of the eighteenth century, they tied once-quiet towns like Billerica far more tightly to the bustling commerce of the seaboard cities and towns. In the process, they promised to release local laborers and property holders from the material and social constraints of personalized exchange and inheritance—creating new possibilities which many proved eager to seize. However, the same expectations of immediate payment that made commercial exchanges so attractive also left them open to sudden credit crunches and financial crises unheard of in the local trading networks. The more that men like Manning turned to the opportunities presented by the commercial markets, the more vulnerable they became to fluctuations in the terms of trade, the state of credit, and government fiscal and monetary policy. In facing such difficulties, many of them would often look to the more forgiving ethic of extended obligations typical of the barter networks for inspiration about how to help offset the harsher effects of commercial exchange.

Coming of age in the 1770s, William Manning might not have

sensed these future tribulations. Like most other New Englanders, he knew how to get along in both the complex barter and commercial systems, despite the sharp contrasts in their governing conventions. He had even used the commercial system to correct what he considered abuses in his customary, personal relationships, when he sold some of the family land and paid off his siblings in order to slip the constraints imposed by his father's will. But once he had taken possession of the bulk of his father's estate, he had the means to carry on like all his yeoman neighbors. If he never stopped serving what he later called the "irreversible sentence of heaven on man . . . to hard labor during life," he did have the prospects of a secure living in return. If he never became one of Billerica's richest citizens, neither would he ever threaten to become one of its poorest. Now a full-grown man with a family of his own, he seized his independence in 1776, and might well have quietly lived out his life within the familiar environs of his farm, his tavern, and his town. But the world had changed the year before, and William Manning changed with it.

Manning and the American Revolution

In 1790, when Manning wrote his first short essay, he accused "the rich" of harboring dark designs to use their political and economic power in order to "buy up whole townships at a time and bring us into lordships." A few years later, in a draft of "The Key of Liberty," he declared that politics revolved around "the unreasonable desires of the Few to tyrannize over and enslave the Many." These turns of phrase were common in the 1790s, warning that greedy, moneyed Americans were out to accumulate sufficient wealth and power to impose an updated kind of aristocracy, undermining the economic independence and political rights of their humbler countrymen. Yet such expressions also had deep roots in the political vernacular of the Massachusetts countryside, dating back to the seventeenth century. Manning probably first encountered this talk amid the coming of the American Revolution, when the fear of lordships galvanized popular opposition to imperial Britain and its American supporters, and he and his neighbors became (as he put it) "highly taken up with the ideas of liberty and a free government."[22]

Billericans had watched the coming storm for several years prior to the battles at Lexington and Concord. Since the 1760s, the town meeting had objected to the continuing efforts of George III's government and its American agents to tighten their control of the colonies. By the mid-1770s, Billerica was among the most radical of the Massachusetts country towns, one of a handful willing to join the Solemn League and Covenant organized by Boston militants in 1774 in response to the Coercive Acts.[23] The Crown and Parliament, Billericans observed on that occasion, were attempting to "dragoon us into slavery because we disdain patiently to take the yoke upon our neck"; the town's official protest ominously recalled "the unlimited Prerogative, contended for by those arbitrary and misguided Princes, *Charles* the First and *James* the Second, for which the One lost his Life, and the Other his Kingdom."[24] This resolve foreshadowed the town's most important part in the unfolding drama—events in which William Manning was an active participant.

On March 6, 1775, the Billerica town meeting selected Manning as highway surveyor, but the meeting's attention (and, presumably, Manning's) was fixed on more pressing matters than the local elections. All across the province, towns had been making military preparations for a showdown with the royal governor, General Sir Thomas Gage. In the face of widening unrest, Gage had suspended a special session of the provincial legislature the previous October. On their own initiative, the would-be delegates assembled at Concord, and requested that the citizenry help defend the insurgency. Accordingly, Billerica followed its neighboring towns and organized a company of Minutemen. (Manning, at this time a sergeant in the militia, did not join, but his brother Solomon did.)[25]

Apprehension became fury two days after the town meeting when Thomas Ditson, a Billerica farmer, was assaulted by some British soldiers in Boston. Ditson had gone to town to buy a gun, but he wound up getting bilked of his four dollars, tarred and feathered, and then paraded around to the derisive strains of

"Yankee Doodle." In their defense, the soldiers claimed that Ditson had tried to convince them to desert. The Billerica town meeting, unpersuaded, directed its newly elected officers to prepare a formal protest, which a delegation of selectmen later managed to present to Gage in person. The governor reacted angrily to the remonstrance, considered himself insulted, and insisted that Ditson had been guilty of sedition (which was probably true). The town replied with a resolution condemning Gage, while the irregular provincial congress weighed in by denouncing the assault on Ditson and declared its approval of "the manly and resolute conduct of the town of Billerica."[26]

One month later, Gage issued the fateful order that sent a detachment of 700 troops against the patriots' military stores at Concord—and the countryside took to arms. The Billerica Minutemen, members of the militia, and other nearby farmers answered the call, arriving in Concord just in time for a bloody skirmish with the British at Merriam's Corner. Many in the company then joined in hot pursuit of the retreating redcoats. Among them was Sergeant William Manning; he was also one of the thousands of country people who, having chased the soldiers all the way back to Boston, laid siege to the city.[27] Years later, in a draft of "The Key of Liberty," Manning recalled these days as an all-important personal turning point: "I saw almost the first blood that was shed in [the] Concord fight and scores of men dead, dying and wounded in the cause of liberty, which caused serious sensations in my mind."[28] From then on, he claimed, he was deeply interested in politics—"a constant reader of public newspapers" who "closely attended to men and measures."

Remembering is, of course, an act of reconstruction and reordering. We cannot know how much Manning, looking back on these events more than two decades later, conflated his troubled rise to *personal* independence in 1776 with his patriotic service in the cause of *national* independence a year earlier—both of which surely caused "serious sensations" in his mind. Yet even if Manning's recollections included unconscious revisions, his comments jibe with what is known about common experiences throughout the rebellious colonies. There are numerous accounts of deep personal transformations during the *rage militaire* of 1775—feelings of patriotic outrage and rededication that became especially powerful once people like Manning saw the corpses of friends and neighbors who had been killed in the early fighting. These feelings, in turn, stoked new kinds of political talk and behavior behind the American lines. Habits of equality replaced those of deference; the boundaries between high and low, urban and rural, local and international suddenly blurred; a promiscuous exchange of ideas and opinions sprang up everywhere and continued over the duration of the war.[29]

Judging from his later writings, with their knowledgeable allusions to events and opinions from the 1770s and 1780s, there is every reason to believe Manning's claim that after the battle of Concord he actively joined in such conversation. Never meek or submissive, he was swept up by a radical movement that would inspire him for the rest of his life. His experiences immediately after the Concord fight had to impress him even further. According to one eyewitness, the very sight of the citizens' army laying siege to Boston—with "every tent a portraiture . . . of the persons who inhabit it"—betrayed the army's democratic temper. The restiveness of the troops, especially in the presence of senior officers, further confirmed "the great degree of equality" observed by the men. It was precisely the egalitarian habits of this "drunken, canting, lying, praying, hypocritical rabble, without order, subjection, discipline, or cleanliness," which led one Loyalist Boston surgeon to draw an obvious if inflammatory parallel: these New England Congregationalists, he reported, were literally "the descendants of Oliver Cromwell's army who truly inherit the spirit which was the occasion of so much bloodshed . . . from the year 1642 to the Restoration."[30]

Manning's tour of duty ended after only a fortnight, and he did not enlist for a longer stint. He was not one of those Billericans encamped in Cambridge on May 1, 1775, when the first of several muster lists was drawn up. Nor is there any evidence that he participated either in the battle of Bunker Hill (as a local historian later claimed) or in any of the other engagements that accompanied the siege down to the British evacuation on March 17, 1776. Instead, Manning returned home to tend to his farm, his tavern, and his aging parents, preparing to take up what he expected would be his rightful inheritance. A year later, he was commissioned a second lieutenant in the Middlesex militia, but when the regiment was sent out of Massachusetts soon thereafter, Lieutenant Manning apparently hired a replacement and stayed home to assume his responsibilities as the head of the family.[31]

Such limited military service was not unusual for an independent property holder, especially one who was almost thirty years old, and it by no means signified a lack of revolutionary ardor. Most men in similar circumstances served in the state militias, as Manning did, rather than in the Continental Army.[32] Manning's added family burdens explain why he remained in Billerica even when his militia company did not. According to family tradition, he contributed to the cause on the home front by erecting a small saltpeter works to help supply the patriots with badly needed gunpowder. His wife, Sarah, reportedly helped feed the companies of American soldiers that passed in front of the Manning homestead. Settling in amid the war, the Manning family grew large, even by the country standards of the day. (Sarah bore four children between 1776 and 1783, and four more soon after the war ended. Counting the five born before 1776, this made a grand total of thirteen, twelve of whom survived infancy.) They appear to have suffered only one direct setback during the war: in 1778, as a deranged economy played havoc with commercial trade, William cleared up the tavern's outstanding debts and closed out its account book.[33]

The next ten years of Manning's life after his return from battle were outwardly uneventful. There was no dramatic moment to rival the exhilaration and shock of the Concord fight. But the experience of war had left him, by his own telling, a changed man; even with the distractions of a working farm and a small house full of little children, he made it his business to see for himself whether the Revolution's promise was being fulfilled. Judging from his later essays, his political outlook and loyalties took permanent shape during this period of war, state making, and social reconstruction—a time in which he also began to play a more prominent official role in town affairs.

The first important series of political developments occurred between 1776 and 1780, when the patriot leadership in Massachusetts sought popular approval of a constitution for the newly independent commonwealth. None of the other rebellious colonies had undertaken to secure such a public mandate for its revolutionary government. Yet in the very middle of the war, the leading men of Massachusetts conferred with the towns for four years, hoping to replace the old colonial charter with a new, popularly approved constitution. In 1778, their deliberations produced a draft proposal, which the towns emphatically rejected. A second version, completed two years later, underwent important revisions after being debated at length in town meetings across the state. Even then its supporters had to mount a concerted effort to rally support for its ratification.[34]

The spotty Billerica sources are silent about whether Manning participated in these debates, but it is hard to believe that he ignored them. At the Billerica town meeting of June 5, 1780, the assembled citizens considered the proposed document paragraph by paragraph. At the end of these discussions they approved it in its entirety—with the proviso that, if possible, the power to select militia officers should be removed from the governor's office (as proposed) and be democratized. (Other towns raised the same complaint: the final draft had the militia officers elected by the eligible men in arms.) In 1798, Manning would acknowledge that, by common assent, the approved constitution was "the completest model of a free government of any existing."[35]

Assuming that Manning's views had not changed, they were doubly significant in light of both his personal history and his subsequent development. Many Massachusetts citizens thought that numerous provisions in the proposed constitution—notably its property requirements for the vote—were still far too restrictive and conservative. Radical democrats, centered in the western towns, objected strongly enough to oppose ratification. So, in the eastern part of the state, did many of the contributors to Manning's favorite newspaper, the *Independent Chronicle* of Boston. Manning may have sympathized—for his later writings suggest he believed that property owning ought not be a prerequisite for political activity. Yet where others were quick to see only aristocratic designs, Manning could find redeeming democratic possibilities. Above all, the constitution's inclusion of a comprehensive declaration of rights—the most important concession to popular opinion made by the framers—won Manning's enthusiasm. Thereafter, time and again, Manning showed a willingness to accentuate the available means of democratic redress under the new revolutionary governments, even when other democratic currents led in more desperate directions.[36]

Manning's concerns about orderly government largely stemmed (as we shall see) from his Calvinist view of human nature. But they also evoked a more strictly political anxiety, strongly stated in his later writings, about where overzealous opposition to authority might lead. This wariness surfaced in the early 1780s, when popular conventions assembled throughout Massachusetts to protest the high taxes and hard money policies that the state's mercantile elite had recently pushed through the legislature. Several of the conventions singled out the constitution of 1780 for harsh criticism. Manning took a different view—for he believed, contrary to the conventions, that the Declaration of Rights already provided an iron-clad guarantee that "all power lays in the people" and that "the poorest man" had the same claim to justice as the gentleman of wealth and standing. If these guarantees were ever violated, Manning insisted, the people could meet peaceably to deliberate and, if need be, "reform, alter, and totally change their constitution." But in the early 1780s that point had not been reached. He would not lightly change his mind after the struggle for American independence formally ended in 1783.[37]

Manning's refusal to let his democratic affinities outweigh his constitutional concerns may have sharpened his stubborn sense of independence. According to Samuel Eliot Morison, his neighbors believed he had an ornery streak: if William Manning drowned, they allegedly said of him, his body would not float with the stream like other people's.[38] Yet contrary to what Morison suggested, Manning's self-assurance, far from making him a lonely eccentric, seems to have been a political asset in the troubled 1780s—for Billericans increasingly looked to Manning to serve the town in an official capacity. In 1782, the town meeting put him on the school committee. Two years later, he served on the grand jury and on a committee that prepared a report about the proper conduct of church singing. In 1785 and 1786, he was chosen selectman; in 1787, he served as town constable and tax collector.[39] As he approached the age of forty, Manning, although still a man of moderate means, could have considered himself one of the fathers of the town. Suddenly, however, he became embroiled in yet another crisis of authority that would profoundly shape his political thinking.

Manning and the Massachusetts Regulation

The Massachusetts Regulation was a string of rural uprisings in the mid-1780s, the largest of which, the western rebellion led by Daniel Shays, has gained the most attention from historians. To the farmers and debtors who supported it, the Regulation was a justified response to the inflexible and oppressive policies of a conservative governor and legislature. To the government's friends, including many who would soon push for a new federal constitution, it was mob lawlessness pure and simple, exemplifying the need for a more centralized and energetic national government. Manning formed a different opinion, at once sympathetic to the rebels but also firm about "the madness and folly of rising up against a government of our own choice." His account of the Regulation is one of the more dramatic narrative sections in "The Key of Liberty," suggesting a great deal about the episode's personal impact.[40]

At the close of the Revolution, Manning reported, "the people were driven to the greatest extremity," since the economic dislocations of the war did not end with the arrival of peace. Having, in effect, won the war with borrowed money, Massachusetts (like other states) had to find the means to repay its debts and provide a reliable currency. As Manning recalled, the state's small farmers—especially debtors—unfairly bore the brunt of the readjustment. Merchants shipped off hard money "until there was but little left." Massachusetts taxes and debt burdens were among the highest in the land. Efforts to mitigate the situation through legislation, successful in other states, failed to carry in the Massachusetts General Court. The situation rapidly worsened in the mid-1780s: creditors, following the unforgiving conventions of high commerce, began calling in old debts, while refusing to receive payment in paper money. Those who had hard money to lend demanded exorbitant interest. Lawyers and other officers of the court demanded fees far above the rates established by law. Property sold at less than half its value. The jails became filled with debtors. Even worse, Manning continued, the people, "being ignorant that all their help lay in being fully and fairly represented in the legislature," refrained from voting. By 1785, "the Few only were represented at Court, with an aristocratic Bowdoin"—conservative James Bowdoin—"as governor at their head."

Under Bowdoin's direction, the legislature refused to pass any measures to relieve the fiscal pressure on the commonwealth's debtors, and instead aggravated the situation by tightening its hard money policies. Several towns in the western counties (but also including some in northern Middlesex) called a new round of popular conventions and issued public remonstrances, condemning the government and demanding reforms. Their protests got nowhere. In frustration, Manning related, some counties foolishly closed down the courts by force of arms—insurgencies that "shook the government to its foundation."

Approximately one-quarter of the Massachusetts population took an active part in the uprisings. A large number of other citizens—possibly a majority statewide—refused to support the government's effort to suppress the regulators. Even the legislature hesitated before the movement, rejecting Bowdoin's request for a declaration that the western counties were in a state of rebellion, placing them under martial law; instead, it settled for a combination of police measures and mild reforms. The governor had to act on his own to raise troops to crush the Regulation, and he managed to do so only with great difficulty and after a considerable delay.[41] A far wiser course, Manning later argued, would have been for the government to handle the hot-headed rebels more like wayward children than implacable demons, and to greet them "with fatherly councils and admonitions." Instead, Governor Bowdoin and his hard-line supporters let loose "the dog of war" upon them.

How did these events affect Manning and his townsmen? Most Billericans probably sympathized with the rebels' plight, although not to the point of joining their cause. Well before the uprising began, the town had aligned itself with the other country towns opposed to the eastern creditor majority in the General Court. As early as April 1781, the town meeting protested a major refunding act as contrary to "the principles of equality and justice." Through the mid-1780s, Billerica's representative to the General Court consistently voted against the creditor majority's measures. Likewise, Billerica's voters rejected statewide candidates linked to the eastern conservatives (although more than half of the town's eligible voters simply failed to vote). In the three-way gubernatorial election that first elected James Bowdoin in 1785, Billerica turned out for Thomas Cushing, an ally of the popular hero, John Hancock; Bowdoin did not receive a single Billerica vote. A year later, when Bowdoin received 73 percent of the statewide tally, Billerica gave him only twelve votes (27.3 percent of the total), while giving thirty-two (72.7 percent) to Hancock, who was not even formally a candidate.[42]

Once the rebellion began, however, most Billericans drew back from open opposition. Although it is impossible to be certain, very few, if any, of them, actively supported the protests. In August 1786, perhaps sensing the coming storm, the town meeting refused to send a delegate to the convention called by Groton, Pepperell, Shirley, and other northern Middlesex towns to discuss public grievances—a convention that provided the impetus for the county's main contribution to the unrest, the so-called Groton Regulation led by Job Shattuck.[43] No Billerican was among those later charged with participating in the rebellion, either in Middlesex or further west. On the contrary, once the violence started, a substantial number of the town's leading citizens sided wholeheartedly with the government. Josiah Bowers, a selectman, led a militia company of fifty-five men from Billerica and its vicinity which marched westward under the command of General Benjamin Lincoln, Sr. Twenty-three prominent Billericans also contributed to a voluntary levy in support of a second military expedition to Worcester.[44]

Yet despite this show of support for the government, another significant proportion of the town seems to have shunned participation in the repression. Some probably sympathized with the regulators' cause but disapproved of their tactics; others may simply have regretted the government's use of force. Isaac Stearns, one of the most distinguished men in town, chaired a convention in Concord on September 12, 1786, hastily called to prevent a violent confrontation between the Middlesex regulators and the county court; Stearns mediated between the two sides and helped prevent bloodshed. Shortly after Stearns's return from Concord, certain unnamed citizens convinced the town meeting to authorize construction of a gun house, but the meeting quickly reconsidered the idea and scrapped it. The town's voters also shared in the general revulsion against the government's actions that cost Bowdoin his job in the next election. Billerica voter participation in 1787 more than doubled over the previous year's figure, from 44 to 107; John Hancock received 74 percent of the ballots and Bowdoin the rest (the same abysmal proportion he received the previous year); in the contest for lieutenant governor, Benjamin Lincoln, head of the force that suppressed the rebels, received only one vote in Billerica.[45]

For William Manning, more than for most of his neighbors, the entire affair had reverberating significance. As a selectman in 1786, and as the town constable and tax collector the following year, he belonged to the machinery of local government expected to implement many of the unpopular fiscal measures enacted at Boston. But local foot dragging was something of a tradition when it came to collecting taxes—a kind of passive resistance that helped cushion people (especially poorer people) from the General Court's demands. In 1786 the Billerica selectmen, including Manning, under instructions from the General Court, ordered the previous constable to render a portion of the taxes he was supposed to have collected and asked all former constables to square their accounts with the town; at the same time, though, they specifically instructed the collectors to exempt persons "under low circumstances" from paying immediately. Not surprisingly, the order brought little in the way of practical results. Manning, in turn, proved just as dilatory as his predecessors when he served as collector in 1787. In 1788, when the selectmen once again had to order former constables to deliver their receipts or face proceedings, Manning owed over £150.[46] Like Manning the publican, Manning the tax collector was willing to let at least some of his townsmen handle their payments as a continuing obligation, payable at their convenience rather than on demand.

Given these circumstances, Manning would seem to have had his reasons for supporting the goals of the Regulation, if not its tactics. His refusal to crack down on delinquent taxpayers certainly conformed with his self-description in "The Key" as someone opposed to the government's policies and sympathetic to the debtors' plight. Yet when Manning came to reflect on his actions of 1786–1787 a decade later, he was not forthright about all of them. To say, as he did, that he "received frowns from both sides for being opposed to their measures," was to leave a decided, but misleading, impression of neutrality. Manning may have deplored Bowdoin's repression, but he supported it nevertheless—for according to a receipt in the Massachusetts Archives, he, along with other town officials, helped gather supplies for the army sent westward through Billerica in January 1787 to suppress the Regulation.[47] He ended up tendering five days of assistance to the "aristocratic" Bowdoin's army—nearly half as much time as he had actively served in the citizen's army of 1775. If, as he later observed, the government had let loose the dog of war, then he, William Manning, had done his own small part to feed and comfort the beast.

Manning's activities might seem baffling, even treacherous, in view of his later, self-appointed role as a tribune for the Many. One does not expect the friends of the people to give aid and comfort to the armies of the Few, especially when those armies are marching off to shoot at indebted small farmers, and his actions were clearly beyond the bounds of a reasonable neutrality. Manning's own view of the matter can best be described as ambivalent. In his first major essay, composed three years after he lent material support to Bowdoin's army, he took up the complaints of aggrieved debtors. And while he never explicitly mentioned the Regulation, his mind was very much on atonement: "Although I have neither learning nor ability for the purpose," he noted at the beginning of the manuscript, "yet to clear myself from the guilt of consenting or passively submitting to measures . . . glaringly unjust, I have composed, and beg that you would seriously and thoroughly examine, the following arguments and plan." Later, in a draft of "The Key of Liberty," Manning neglected to mention his own role in supplying the army, and went out of his way to attack those who had supported the government in 1787—especially the war profiteers and suppliers who, he said, helped foment the costly military response.[48]

Obviously, Manning took no pride in what he had done. He may have felt compelled by his position in the town to supply the army. As a selectman, Manning had obligations to uphold the law; if he eventually dawdled in collecting taxes, in the pressing crisis of 1786–1787 he took his obligations much more seriously. At the same time, it is crucial to be clear that his actions were perfectly consistent with his subsequent writings. Having fought in the opening hours of the Revolution, Manning could not imagine either taking up arms against the new government (however much he might disagree with its policies) or aiding those who had done so (however just their grievances seemed). Citizens, he would later observe, ought always to be prepared "to support the constituted authorities in the suppressions of insurrections, rebellions, or invasions of a common enemy." If he helped strike a blow against the Regulators, he did so not in order to attack the rights and interests of the Many but to establish them all the more firmly, and on an orderly constitutional footing.

The ultimate outcome of the Regulation only redeemed his faith in constitutional procedures, even as it dramatized what he would soon be describing as the struggle between the American Few and the American Many. After Bowdoin had suppressed the armed demonstrations and continued to ignore all appeals to compromise, the citizenry undertook what Manning called "the most zealous searches after a remedy for their grievances." These searches led them at last to seize upon their electoral rights and sweep the governor and his offending legislative majority out of office. With a full representation sent to the General Court, even from the most distant and the poorest towns, both sides of the controversy reached a mutual accommodation. In the end, "everything appeared like the clear and pleasant sunshine after a most tremendous storm"—"a striking demonstration of the advantages of a free elective government."

The Regulation's personal effect on Manning was more clouded. At the town elections in March 1787, two of the most prominent progovernment men, Josiah Bowers and Edward Farmer, were not returned to office—a signal of the town's displeasure with the government's measures. Manning, too, was passed over as selectman, and found himself named the town constable and tax collector instead. One year later, he was not elected to anything.[49] Did he salvage a political post in 1787, only to be shunned by his townsmen later on? Or did he simply tire of town politics? There is no way to tell from the existing evidence. What is clear is that, after 1788, he would never again hold a major position in town government.

There is one tantalizing hint that Manning's views made him unpopular—for in retrospect he expressed support for the federal constitution which his townsmen voted to reject in 1788.[50] Unfortunately, from this distance it is hard to know exactly what Manning was thinking during the ratification debates. Like many of those who opposed the new framework (or so he later claimed), Manning believed the original motivation behind the Philadelphia Convention had been "to destroy our free governments."[51] And he felt the document so inexplicit that "like a fiddle with but few strings . . . the ruling majority may play any tune they please upon it." Still, Manning thought the new constitution "a good one principally"—provided a vigilant citizenry insisted upon fair construction and prevented a powerful, centralized minority from perverting its manifest ends.

Perhaps it was this nuanced view of constitutional government and the new federal plan that cost Manning the political backing of his neighbors, leaving him caught between the minority, who never doubted the framers' wisdom, and the majority, who rejected the proposed new federal government outright. Perhaps his suspicions about the convention's motives only surfaced well after the fact, in which case he would have been an even stronger supporter of the Constitution in 1787–1788 than he later suggested. More likely, Manning came fully to support the Constitution only after the inclusion of the Bill of Rights in 1791, a common trajectory for plebeian democrats.[52] Such a shift would have been consistent with Manning's admiration for the Massachusetts Declaration of Rights of 1780. It would also explain the importance he attached in his later writings to the federal government's establishment "for national purposes only" and his allusions to the Tenth Amendment, which reserved to the states or to the people all powers unenumerated in the Constitution.

Whatever their political fallout, the upheavals of the late 1780s did have one clear-cut personal outcome: if the American Revolution made William Manning a reader, then the Massachusetts Regulation and its aftermath made him a writer. His public career may have been over in 1788, but his political passions were far from spent. Soon after, more interested than ever in national affairs, he started writing out his complaints about the policies of the first federal administration to serve under the new Constitution.

"Some Proposals": Manning and Hamiltonian Finance

Manning wrote at a time when Billerica was starting to open itself up to the region's accelerating commercial and cultural life. The most dramatic improvement involved the construction of the Middlesex Canal, begun in 1795 and completed in 1803—a route that promised to connect Billerica's farmers to eastern markets as never before. A regular stagecoach line linking Billerica to Boston and New Hampshire began service in 1795; two years later, the town received its first post office. Ebenezer Pemberton, the esteemed principal of Phillips Andover Academy, chose Billerica in the mid-1790s as a promising place to establish his own school. The town's Social Library, founded in 1772, enjoyed enough success that a second lending library had to be opened in 1807.[53]

This burst of activity would turn out to be fleeting: some manufacturing firms followed the canal to town, but it did not otherwise materially affect Billerica, which never advanced beyond the second rank of Middlesex communities. (When Thoreau paddled past the place in 1839 on his famous trip down the Concord River, he found it "an old gray town" where nature had "gone to decay, farms all run out, meeting house gone gray and racked with age.")[54] Momentarily, however, in the 1790s Billerica seemed poised to break out, and came to resemble what one historian has isolated as a distinctive type of democratic Massachusetts town, "at once agrarian and commercial," lacking much in the way of home-grown cultural resources but "assured of stimulating contacts with the outside world."[55] In this quickening milieu, it was not difficult to imagine, as Manning did, that Billerica might be the springboard for an entirely new kind of political association, uniting men like himself who lived in similar towns with their kindred spirits in the eastern seaports.

Manning contributed to and benefited from the town's improvements. One local history (which is not a consistently reliable source) reports that the Manning tavern was one of three Billerica establishments kept busy by the additional stagecoach traffic and the demands for staging and teaming along the line, but there is no other evidence to confirm this.[56] Without question, Manning aided in the construction of the Middlesex Canal. A section of the proposed route ran across some of Manning's land, which he appears to have sold for a nominal fee. And in December 1794 he contracted with the canal's promoters to complete digging of thirty-four rods of the canal itself, for which he was paid $238. He was the first Billerica landholder on record to have reached such an arrangement with the canal company.[57]

Yet Manning the improver could not escape persistent economic difficulties; Billerica's brief awakening seems to have added new sorts of concerns along with the possibilities of commercial prosperity. Throughout the 1790s he fell behind in his obligations and was perpetually scrambling for cash. The precise reasons remain obscure. Was he unable to pay his taxes? Did he overextend his resources (for example, by trying to reopen the tavern)? Did he, like so many of his neighbors, become caught up in the rage of consumer buying that spread in the 1790s (and that he would later mention in his writings)? Did he suffer at the hands of his creditors after the brief financial panic of 1792? Did

Jabez Ward Barton, *William Rogers House, Billerica, Massachusetts*, c. 1822, watercolor on paper. The Rogers house, built of brick in about 1807, exemplified the prosperity and the heightened expectations in Billerica during the 1790s and after. In the foreground is a portion of the Middlesex Canal at the point where it crossed the Concord River. By 1822, the canal fed into a nearby mill pond, constructed to power the Patten saw and grist mills. William Rogers, a farmer, is supposed to have earned the money to build his house by hauling dirt with his ox cart during the canal's construction—a job William Manning also performed.

some illness befall the Manning household? Or was the cost of supporting his huge family simply too much to bear? The sources are silent. They do show that in September 1798 one Jacob Abbott, a trader, won a court judgment against him for nonpayment of an unspecified debt.[58] On several other occasions—in 1787, 1792, and 1793—Manning mortgaged his land (once to a Boston bank) in order to raise money. Several times more he secured personal loans from neighbors and kin.[59] Manning may have used the funds to add scattered parcels of land to his holdings, but he was more often selling land than buying it. (Between 1793 and 1799 he parted with nearly 70 acres, some of it from his original inheritance.)[60] He was able to support his wife and children on the 137 acres that remained to him, perhaps with help from the tavern, assuming he had indeed reopened it. His three eldest sons took contracting and wage-labor work on the canal in an effort to establish themselves—successfully, as things turned out. But their father's status remained that of a farmer of the middling sort—a man, in Manning's own words, who had "a small landed interest" but who was always "obliged to follow hard labor to support a large family."

Such activity in a developing town like Billerica has sometimes been taken to imply a certain mentality—in particular, a full and unproblematic devotion to the commercial market and its ethic. The logic of this position is flawed. Manning pursued his self-interest, just as, he later observed, all men were condemned to do. He fully acknowledged the essential contributions of commerce and money making to prosperity and human happiness. In "The Key of Liberty," he would praise the new state-chartered banks, such as the one he dealt with, for helping to break the Federalist stranglehold on credit. Although he criticized the moneyed Few for victimizing the Many, none of his writings retreated into what some historians have described (mainly with reference to later rural dissenters) as the sentimental pose of the eternally virtuous, "injured little yeoman."[61]

Yet if Manning was not an anticommercial communalist, the simple facts that he helped build a canal, sold off parcels of land, and borrowed money from a Boston bank do not, in themselves, mark him (in the awkward jargon of the modern social sciences) as a profit-maximizing individualist who believed in the universal justice of commercial markets. Nor do they signal an attachment to capitalist enterprise. One could participate in local land markets or even local mortgage capital markets and still oppose capitalism (that is, a commercial economy dominated by moneyed men). Such participation could also heighten one's appreciation of the potential social dangers (as well as the personal costs) of all sorts of otherwise fruitful commercial relationships, as it might well have done in Manning's case. For markets do not simply and automatically liberate economic energies; they can also be turned to oppressive ends by powerful moneyed interests whose endeavors are not directed, as Manning would later write, to "the benefit of the community." (The same was true of local barter and inheritance networks, which could also be turned to oppressive ends—a point that Manning, with his troubled family background, might also have developed but did not.) The perils such oppression posed to free governments in the United States, and what could be done about it, were the paramount problems which Manning addressed in his writings.

Manning started his first known essay in early February 1790—an attack on the proposal by the new Treasury secretary, Alexander Hamilton, to refund the outstanding war debt at face value. The timing of the work is noteworthy. For some years, Manning had been following the newspaper accounts of what he called the "many altercations, proposals and disputes" about how to handle the country's debts. But Hamilton did not deliver his report on the public credit to Congress until January 14, 1790. Manning could have read a newspaper summary of it no earlier than the last week of the month.[62] He must have worked furiously, pulling together and elaborating ideas he had been mulling over for some time, to have them in shape by February 6, 1790, the date which appears on the manuscript. The result, although far more modest than the later "Key of Liberty," reveals just how much Manning had learned from the Massachusetts funding debates and related conflicts in the 1780s.

Hamilton had proposed to repay the present holders of wartime debts from the state governments and the Continental Congress at the face value of their notes (with accrued interest) without making any provision for the original creditors—that is, those who had actually provided the revolutionary governments with needed funds and services. The plan sparked heated controversy, since many of the present holders were wealthy speculators (including, some charged, Hamilton's closest friends) who had bought up badly depreciated notes in the 1780s at a fraction of their face value. Thanks to the secretary of the Treasury, these speculators seemed on the verge of reaping a windfall profit. The humbler men who originally held the paper—including revolutionary soldiers and suppliers paid off in government scrip—would receive nothing beyond the pittance given them when they sold their notes.[63] Manning was not, as he was quick to point out, one of the original creditors. All the same, he detested Hamilton's report and set out his objections in the form of a remonstrance to a representative in the Massachusetts legislature (presumably his own), with the cumbersome title "Some Proposals for Making Restitution to the Original Creditors of Government and to Help the Continent to a Medium of Trade."

"Some Proposals" reflected Manning's awareness of arguments favorable to paper money as a spur to productive wealth.[64] It also exemplified his lifelong experience at the border of complex barter and commercial exchange. When his father died, Manning had used the commercial system to correct the injustice he felt had been done to him in his customary, personal relationships. Now he sought to correct the injustices of the Treasury secretary's plan by applying the principle of continuing obligation that governed the barter networks. He based his thinking on a general statement of justice applicable to either system: "Strict and plain justice between debtor and creditor is that the former pay unto the latter the full value of what he received with interest therefore, and no more." (In the text, Manning illustrated this principle by describing a typical commercial exchange.)

The war debt raised vexing questions about how the government could do justice to the claims of both the original and the present holders. Did the fact that the original holders had sold their notes extinguish the government's obligation to see that they eventually received the full value of what they had originally lent? Manning thought not. If the government redeemed the debt of the present holders at its full value, without making any provision for the original creditors, the present holders would unjustly receive considerably more than they had paid for the certificates (including interest), while the original creditors would have to be satisfied with considerably less (the amount they had been paid when they sold off their holdings). Even worse, it was the original creditors, as taxpayers, who would foot the bill for paying the present holders. However, if the government compensated the original holders for their losses—Manning proposed giving them 60 percent of the debt's full value in government-backed paper money—and gave the remainder to the present holders, it could do "strict and plain justice" to both.

A larger social and political rationale lay behind Manning's position. Most of the "great men," he wrote, had either been Tories during the Revolution and fled the country, or had been sufficiently dubious of an American victory to withhold their full support from the revolutionary governments. In contrast, the vast majority of the original government creditors had come from "the middling sort of people." Additionally, thousands of local suppliers had helped provision the revolutionary armies, willingly taking in exchange for their goods and services the government's promise to pay at some unspecified future date. And thousands of officers and enlisted men had accepted similar promises in lieu of pay for their years of service in the Continental Army during the 1780s. Without their support, the Revolution would have failed. Now that peace and prosperity had returned, it was a grave injustice to overlook the claims of those ordinary men who had stood by the nation when its prospects were the most dim. Were the government to do so, Manning feared, then "no person in his senses would trust such a government when in distress a second time."

The supporters of Hamilton's plan appealed to a different sense of obligation, rooted in the conventions of high commerce. The present holders, they insisted, had purchased their certificates fair and square. Compensating the original holders, Hamilton observed, would be "inconsistent with justice, because in the first place it is a breach of contract; in violation of the rights of a fair purchaser."[65] In fact, the present holders had done the original creditors a service by giving good money for the certificates at a time when the prospects of their redemption remained very unclear. They deserved praise, not opprobrium, as patriotic men who had taken risks that the original creditors had been unwilling or unable to bear. Not to recognize the legitimacy of the present holders' claims would destroy any possibility that they might lend similar assistance again, should either the government or its financially distressed, poorer creditors ever need it.

The defenders of the original creditors, including Manning, scoffed at these arguments. "We might go on to pay the present holders a thousand times over," Manning insisted, "and then a great part of the sum would be still due to the original creditors." The present holders deserved to receive the full value of the outstanding debt if and only if the notes they purchased had been surrendered voluntarily, or in conditions over which the government had no control. But this is exactly what had *not* occurred. Instead, the state governments had compelled "the poor soldiers" and "public creditors" to pay off taxes and private debts in hard money; consequently, they reluctantly sold off their notes for what they could get. Neither impulsiveness nor poor calculation lay behind the original creditors' actions; in all cases, Manning declared, they "acted more like persons beset with robbers and prudently delivered up their purses rather than their lives."

The only just course, Manning declared, was to compensate the original holders. Others (including James Madison) offered similar proposals, but Manning criticized them as incomplete, primarily because they did not help meet the need for a secure and readily available means of exchange for the mass of ordinary citizens. Manning's own plan went beyond simply compensating the original creditors for a portion of their losses. In addition, he aimed to expand the supply of money available throughout the country, and thus to stimulate local commerce and enable productive small holders to pay their taxes and other debts without distress. Accordingly, Manning proposed to redeem the current holders' securities at only 40 percent of their face value. The remainder of the debt, he argued, should be converted into government-backed paper money, and secured by a 5 percent sinking fund financed by taxes "equally assessed and vigorously collected" (which would enable the government to retire the whole issue within twenty years). The new notes were then to be distributed among the original creditors and soldiers, in rough proportion to their initial claims, as compensation for the losses they suffered when forced by government policies to sell their certificates at a steep discount. Moreover, in order to settle any lingering disputes between people caused by the disastrous devaluation of the government's securities during the war years, Manning urged that county-wide courts of equity be established to hear all complaints against those who refused to settle disputes on reasonable terms.

These proposals led to the essay's rhetorical high points, where Manning laid out some general observations about money, class, and justice (including an informed defense of paper currency), and the evils intended by the "sharpers" who would profit by Hamilton's plan. His terminology quietly owed a great deal to ten essays by Benjamin Lincoln, Jr., (written under the pseudonym "Free Republican") published four years earlier in Manning's chief literary source, the *Independent Chronicle*. In a sweeping review of classical history and American current affairs, Lincoln had shown how all politics arose from a contest between those he labeled the Few and the Many. But whereas Lincoln interpreted this struggle as a justification for government by the Few, Manning came to the opposite conclusion.[66]

"It is asserted by many that government is founded in property," Manning began, "But be that as it may . . . , the rich have great power and influence over the poor." In all governments, there were naturally two parties; "the great dividing line," he observed, "is between those that labor for a living and those who get one without laboring—or, as they are generally termed, the Few and the Many." At one point in the manuscript, Manning, once again borrowing directly from "Free Republican," specified that the Few were those whose property consisted chiefly of "rents, money at interest, salaries and fees—which are established on money which comes out of the Many." Elsewhere as well, Manning fell back on similar terminology, referring to the Few as "the salary and fee men." Yet his discussion in "Some Proposals" makes clear that he did not limit his definition of the Few simply to men of proprietary wealth. Not only rentiers and local money lenders but also merchants, speculators, and other men of mobile capital (along with lawyers, who facilitated their operations and took fees directly from the Many) contributed mightily to the distress of the laboring majority.[67]

It was eternally in the interest of this relatively small group, Manning argued, to have money scarce and prices low. Always, the Few looked to "alterations of money affairs," secured through the government, to maximize their advantages over the Many and increase their profits. Since the Revolution, moneyed men—especially speculators, lawyers, and merchants—had endeavored to consolidate their power. In the frenzy for profits, "if our stone walls had been money, they would have all been carried off" to pay for cheap, foreign manufactured goods. Hamilton's plan for the debt was but the final piece of a project long in the making.[68]

According to Manning, at the center of Hamilton's larger plan lay the desire to benefit the Few at the expense of the Many. Not *all* of the Few were to blame; at least some of those who lived without labor operated from "pure principles of virtue" and valued the cause of liberty more than their private interests. But such "pure principles" were no more widespread among the Few than among mankind generally. Hamilton's finance plan effectively mobilized the self-interest of the elite by first establishing a national bank, which would collect a large quantity of silver and gold—"the only sort of money that will pay either debts or taxes." Having removed this specie from circulation, the bank would then issue notes in large denominations, returnable so frequently that they would never reach the countryside. This currency would admirably supply the speculative markets of the Few with a sufficient medium of trade, but would deny that medium to country people involved in small-scale dealings. The resulting shortage of money would inevitably lead to a deflationary spiral, lowering the price of country produce, and ultimately the value of country property. Speculators—having already profited handsomely from Hamilton's war debt repayment scheme—would then step in, "purchase whole townships at a time," and establish a new aristocratic, moneyed order. The only way to head off this disaster, Manning claimed, would be to issue paper notes of small denominations directly in the hands of the Many, in the interior regions as well as along the seaboard—which is precisely what his substitute plan for repaying the original creditors would accomplish.

The economic analysis in "Some Proposals" was a *tour de force* for a self-educated farmer. It offered a brief but penetrating discussion of the class basis of American politics, one which stands up well beside similar efforts from such nationally known opposition writers as Thomas Jefferson and George Logan.[69] Manning was able to apply his own experience in trade to the larger problem of national fiscal policy without simply parroting the established wisdom. He provided both a plan to redeem the government's obligations to the original creditors and sound reasons why doing so was in the best interests of the country as a whole. Nor were his proposals impractical: paper money had circulated at or near par in many North American colonies before the Revolution, and in 1782, commissioners had been appointed in every state in order to validate all civilian claims against the national government. Moreover, several states (although not Massachusetts) had passed tender laws, authorized new paper money issues, and retired outstanding debt certificates at less than face value throughout the 1780s.[70]

In 1790, however, having come this far, Manning went no farther. At the beginning of "Some Proposals," he promised to sketch out "the most prudent and likely way" to get his plan adopted. Years later, in "The Key," Manning would imply that his thoughts on the subject were already maturing at this point. And in Part V of "Some Proposals," he offered the glimmer of a possibility, suggesting that the Many, aided by the more virtuous of the Few, would "bear down and destroy all the influences of those that oppose our liberties." But the manuscript abruptly broke off soon after, with nothing more on the subject. Apparently, Manning could not yet fully see how the Many might, by strictly constitutional means, check the ambitions of the Few. The bitter conflicts of the 1780s gave little guidance to constitutional democrats like himself about how the working majority of the country could protect its rights (and pocketbooks) from being diminished by the self-interested policies of the moneyed elites. Only over the next several years did Manning sort things out to his own satisfaction.

Politics, Religion, and Popular Organization

The remainder of George Washington's presidency heightened the fears of William Manning and his fellow democrats. Hamilton's funding program was adopted, as were his plans for a national bank and a national system of excise taxes. The French Revolution—initially hailed by most Americans as an extension of their own revolution—split the country badly after the execution of Louis XVI in January 1793. The ensuing European wars and their effects on American foreign policy became the focus of fractious domestic debates—especially after administration actions, culminating in Jay's Treaty, seemed to align the United States with royalist Britain and against republican France. While these controversies splintered the highest counsels of the national government, popular protests arose from Maine to Georgia. New organizations, known as Democratic Republican societies, appeared in both the larger seaboard cities and in rural towns, adamantly opposed to administration measures. Here and there, more violent outbursts erupted (notably the Pennsylvania Whiskey Rebellion in 1794, a protest against the excise tax on distilled spirits). President Washington responded by harshly criticizing the Democratic Republican groups as supposedly illegitimate, "self-created societies," and by ordering a huge show of military force to overawe the Pennsylvania rebels.[71]

Manning, increasingly alarmed at the drift of public policy, found little encouragement in the prevailing forms of political dissent. He was horrified by the events leading up to the Whiskey Rebellion, as if they were a reprise of the Massachusetts Regulation. Although he later placed most of the blame on the Federalist revenue policies and on Hamilton's eagerness to suppress the protest with lethal force, he could not condone the rebels' self-defeating resort to violence. More satisfactory were the Democratic Republican societies. Contrary to the Washington administration's charges that they were disorderly fomenters of faction, Manning thought that the societies' members were "men of republican principles and great abilities who did all in their power to enlighten the people to their true interests."

Unfortunately, the societies' best efforts were not good enough. Only one Democratic Republican club arose in what is now Massachusetts, the Constitutional Society of Boston. Manning was not a member, but he could easily follow the group's proceedings in the *Independent Chronicle*, which was friendly to the cause.[72] Both the Constitutional Society and its counterparts in other cities surely influenced Manning's thinking—for on specific issues, including his warm and enduring support of the French Revolution, Manning's opinions closely paralleled those of the organized dissidents. But Manning also thought that the societies relied too much on the established press at a time when Federalist newspapers outnumbered those sympathetic to the opposition. Lacking such a vehicle, the societies left themselves open to distortion by unfriendly editors, and thus hastened their own rapid demise after 1795. Living in Boston's hinterland, Manning felt even more keenly than he had in 1790 the need for an effective mode of instructing and organizing the friends of free government in all parts of the country. In his search for such an instrument, he seems to have found fresh inspiration not in secular politics but in religion—and in another set of challenges to the Massachusetts establishment that shook its foundations every bit as firmly as Shays' Rebellion had.

When William Manning's great-grandfather Samuel first settled in Billerica, orthodox Calvinism dominated New England's religious life. Despite continual challenges from dissidents—the spiritual heirs of Anne Hutchinson—the Puritan magistrates, in close cooperation with the established clergy, persisted in what they thought was a divinely inspired mission to build a Christian social order of visible saints on the North American mainland. Although subsequent generations pursued this repressive utopia with vastly diminished ardor, the power of the Standing Order remained intact and almost unassailable through the first half of the eighteenth century. Serious cracks did appear during the Great Awakening of 1736–1745, but the Congregational establishment successfully weathered the crisis. Most of the more than 260 New England Separatist congregations that sprang up during the revival ended up joining with the Baptists; the rest disappeared entirely over the next ten years or so. On the eve of the American Revolution, official Congregationalism was riven by doctrinal and ecclesiastical disputes (some of which directly affected Manning's political writings). Still, the Congregationalists cast by far the largest shadow across the region's religious landscape.[73]

The Revolution changed all that. As the war shifted southward in 1776, a religious revival swept across the Massachusetts hill country in the wake of the departing armies. Unlike earlier outbreaks of religious enthusiasm, the Separatists, Methodists, and other evangelical sects benefited with the Baptists from this "time of refreshing." In the 1780s, while leading figures in the so-called Old Light (and increasingly liberal) Congregational churches were complaining of immorality, infidelity, and a general falling away from religion, the evangelicals continued to enjoy a rapid increase in both congregations and membership. This impressive harvest of souls was only a prelude to even more significant and permanent gains by the dissenters in the 1790s.[74]

According to Billerica's longtime pastor, Henry Cumings, Manning's home town was never "rent and split asunder, into angry and virulent parties, by ecclesiastical disputes and parties." (The first dissenting church did not open its doors in Billerica until 1828.) But the absence of other denominational rivals did not mean that Cumings' church knew no divisions. In the mid-1790s, one of the pastor's admirers, Reverend William Bentley of Salem, noted in his diary that the original Billerica meeting house had fallen into disrepair, "a contrast to the usual attention of the parishes."[75] Such inattention normally signaled dissatisfaction on the part of the worshipers—or, even worse in the eyes of the evangelicals, complacency. In the absence of more thorough evidence, it is not fully clear why the Billerica congregation neglected to maintain its church properly. But we do know that Manning himself held views very different from those of his minister, and that when the meeting house was rebuilt in 1797 he did not purchase a pew.[76]

The differences between Manning and his pastor were theological, social, and political, and they grew primarily from the existing divisions *within* Congregationalism. Although he had been trained (after graduating from Harvard) by the Edwardsian Daniel Emerson, Cumings was widely acknowledged as one of the Standing Order's leading Arminian divines, who softened the established Calvinist doctrines on human depravity and limited atonement. He reportedly considered Jonathan Edwards' treatise *The Freedom of the Will* as the best possible argument for atheism, and firmly rejected the claim (championed by Edwards' disciples, the leading lights of the so-called New Divinity movement) that all the impulses of the self were necessarily sinful. Had God not implanted in human nature the religious impulse to do good, he insisted, there would be no reason to believe that anyone was capable of righteousness.[77]

Manning preferred Edwardsian orthodoxy—in particular, it seems, the tenets of the New Divinity men—to Cumings' liberalism. The description of human nature that he incorporated in "The Key of Liberty" easily could have owed its inspiration to any number of Protestant sects that flourished in Massachusetts amid the spiritual turbulence of the 1780s and 1790s. But it seems especially close, in view of its emphasis on selfishness, to the doctrines of a prominent New Divinity clergyman: "[Men] are sentenced by the just decrees of heaven to hard labor for a living in this world, and have so strongly implanted in them a desire of self-support, self-defence, self-love, self-conceit, and self aggrandizement that it engrosses all their care and attention—so that they can see nothing beyond self. For self (as once described by a divine) is like an object placed before the eye that hinders the sight of everything beyond."[78] Manning acknowledged that human beings could distinguish right from wrong, and act out of conscience. Yet, like the Edwardsians—and again, especially, the New Divinity men—he did not believe that this in any way mitigated the utterly sinful nature of humanity's selfish impulses.[79]

Cumings' and Manning's doctrinal differences had social overtones. Religious liberals like Cumings won a warm reception from wealthier and more commercially oriented congregations,

Portrait of Reverend Henry Cumings (1739–1823), n.d., artist unknown.
Cumings was Billerica's minister from 1763 until his death.

in part because their Arminianism placed much less stringent moral demands on those who would be saved than did the more orthodox Calvinism of the New Divinity men and others. Not only did they acknowledge the existence of an innate human tendency to do good as well as bad, but they made it the very basis of their theology. The existence of original sin in their eyes did not mean that humanity was totally depraved. A "religious affection, a propensity to worship," they believed, was as much a part of human nature as "the reasoning faculty." Cultivating this sensibility, this interest of the self, was justifiable not simply in instrumental terms—that is, because it had beneficial effects on the community—but also on its own terms, as a good in itself.[80]

Along with the evangelizing Methodists and Baptists, the New Divinity men were more likely to come from families of the lower and middling sort, and they drew their support chiefly from the less wealthy congregations of the hill country. Saintliness for these "farmer metaphysicians," as Cumings' friend Bentley called them, consisted of universal disinterested benevolence. The notion that following the impulses of the self could be morally justified, however beneficial the outcome, was completely unimaginable to them. Only that self-interest which was shared with others—a collective self-interest, in effect—was free from the taint of sin. It was not enough simply to lead an upright life and to respect the outward forms of piety. Self-satisfaction was no sign of salvation, just as the impulses of the self were no guide to goodness. Unless a person experienced a conversion—a "new birth," marked by a genuine change of heart—righteousness was impossible. Only the gift of God's free grace could make a sinner a saint.[81]

The political trajectories of Henry Cumings and William Manning in the aftermath of the Revolution further reflected their theological differences, in ways that switched around labels like "liberal" and "conservative." Manning became, if anything, a stauncher democrat than ever in the late 1780s and 1790s. Cumings, in keeping with his elitist Arminianism, turned politically more conservative, as did much of the New England Congregationalist clergy.[82] During the war, Cumings had railed against the corruption of power and compared the British to the Pharaohs;

after 1783, he stressed the need to defer to those in power, in accord with what he called the principle of "mutual subjugation."[83] He located the greatest threat to the republic's survival among those sinners who "under the baneful influence of levelling principles . . . cannot brook any civic distinctions and restraints, DESPISE GOVERNMENT and SPEAK EVIL OF DIGNITIES."[84] At first, Cumings identified these miscreants as the people who grumbled about taxation or war debts; later, he broadened his attack to include unnamed scoffing libertines, the opponents of Jay's Treaty, the friends of the French Revolution, and any who spoke ill of George Washington. By the early 1790s, he had become a stalwart defender of the Federalist regime; in 1796, he beseeched his congregation to dissociate themselves from those "discontented self-applauders" who were constantly carping about Federalist policies.[85]

Cumings may have had national targets in mind in his more vituperative sermons, possibly (after 1795) Thomas Jefferson himself. He may also have been singling out any number of his townsmen—including William Manning. In "The Key," Manning made no bones about his strong disapproval of Jay's Treaty, his admiration for the French Revolution and, in the 1798 draft, his disgust for the Federalist cult of Washington (with its "most fulsome and sickish praises and adulations"). More directly, Cumings sharply censured tavernkeepers and their customers, as men who preferred spirituous liquors to the spirit of the Gospel.[86] Manning returned the compliment. By 1797, he had pulled back from active membership in his old congregation; in the second draft of "The Key," he poured out his contempt for Federalist clergymen like Cumings who used their churches to elevate government officials as "infallible beings, or so perfect that we ought to submit to and praise them for all they do." Ministers, Manning warned, "ought to be watched and guarded against above all other orders especially when they preach politics."[87] If Manning's political views were more modulated than those of some other Massachusetts democrats, his break with Cumings' brand of Federalist piety was complete and irreconcilable by the late 1790s.

As this breach widened, Manning, inspired by tendencies both inside and outside Congregationalism, apparently discovered a new organizational structure, well suited to evangelizing ordinary farmers and mechanics about liberty and free government. Beginning in the mid-1790s, an early phase of what historians have called the Second Great Awakening broke across New England, bringing in its wake a series of institutional innovations, including the growth of home missions, Bible and tract societies, and religious periodicals—all of which would alter the face of American Protestantism.[88] Presbyterians, Congregationalists, Separatists, Free-Will Baptists, Methodists, and a host of smaller sects were caught up in the ferment. New Divinity ministers were especially prominent in the Massachusetts Missionary Society, founded in 1799, and their devotion to disinterested benevolence provided the movement with its militant zeal.[89]

Manning seems to have taken a special interest in the innovations of the Methodists, who began winning converts in Massachusetts in 1790. To be sure, there is nothing in Manning's writings to suggest that the Methodists affected his own devotions. Although both he and they believed in the power of conversion and a "new birth," the Methodists' doctrines on grace and salvation contained a strong element of Arminianism at odds with orthodox belief. Politically, however, the homespun egalitarianism of Methodism and the emotive Calvinism of the New Divinity men and others found common ground in opposition to liberal Congregationalism and its mercantile constituency.[90] Manning seems to have been particularly impressed by the Methodists' organizing principles (the "method" in Methodism), for in "The Key of Liberty" he would fill in the organizational gap of "Some Proposals" with the blueprint for a popular political society organized roughly along Methodist lines. In contrast to most secular political groups, such as the Democratic Republican clubs, the Methodists offered a framework for a regional, national, and even international organization. They also provided the vehicle for popular instruction. Members of Manning's society, like the Methodists, were to form "classes," the basic unit of local organization. The purpose of each class—again, this is reminiscent of the Methodists—was to study and help distribute the society's literature, including a monthly magazine and (Manning rather immodestly proposed) copies of "The Key of Liberty."

The parallels between these aspects of Manning's plans and the Methodists' organization do raise some questions about Manning's evolving intentions—for Methodism was never as egalitarian as its grassroots evangelizing structure may have suggested. Local groups repeatedly found themselves confronted by a Methodist hierarchy that could be vigilant about maintaining proper liturgical and ecclesiastical discipline. One of the manifest functions of the Methodist classes was to indoctrinate and reindoctrinate the members with materials provided by the church leadership.[91] To the extent that Manning learned any organizing lessons from the Methodists, he would have had to square them with his own, more thoroughgoing democratic professions. In this, the individual Democratic Republican societies, with their elaborate democratic rules and procedures, offered a surer guide, despite their lack of a solid national foundation.

Yet one wonders if Manning—a man who distrusted human nature—was not also quietly smitten with the idea of using his own classes as a means of indoctrination into the mysteries of what might be called Manningism. The pamphlet that wound up as "The Key of Liberty" would be Manningism's Bible (or, less arrogantly, its Wesleyan Bible commentary). Manning's monthly magazine would substitute for the Methodists' tracts. The classes would focus on teaching new recruits and shoring up the faithful, dispensing Manning's wisdom so that all members could better interpret an ever-changing political world. Manning did not lack the self-confidence necessary to hatch such a system; in the 1790s, he certainly grew convinced of the basic rightness and power of his ideas. It remained to be seen, however, how much his self-assurance and his skepticism about human nature would interfere with his planning—and whether his hopes for mobilizing the Many would turn into the design for a different kind of worshipful political sect.

Manning never mentioned the Methodists and their method directly. He had, however, plenty of opportunity to come into contact with them in the 1790s, as self-taught Methodist circuit riders crisscrossed the Middlesex region, preaching the gospel according to John Wesley and organizing classes for all those who wished to join the Methodist connection.[92] A syncretic intelligence, Manning could have easily accommodated his own orthodox propositions about human nature and government within the structure of mobilization that emerged from a different part of the theological forest. He then could move beyond diagnosing the country's ills and describe in concrete detail the kinds of initiatives he thought necessary to preserve and protect free government.

"The Key of Liberty" and Manning's Democratic Style

Manning wrote the first draft of "The Key of Liberty" (although he had yet to give it that title) in February 1797, a few months after the last fights about Jay's Treaty with Great Britain. Debate over the treaty—originally signed in 1794—had been ferocious, and Manning's draft treated it as an example of all that was foul in American politics. The treaty itself was bad enough, in its opponents' view, for it contained few of the British concessions originally envisioned, while surrendering important American maritime rights. Even worse, antitreaty partisans charged, the Washington administration had gained Congressional agreement through high-handed and unconstitutional means. During the prolonged furor, popular opposition reached new heights; even President Washington was not spared abuse. In July 1796, Thomas Paine unleashed a much-publicized attack on the president in the form of an open letter that accused him of hypocrisy and treachery.[93] Paine's tone was typical of the antiadministration upsurge. "The Key of Liberty" proved no exception.

Manning addressed his essay to "all farmers, mechanics, and laborers in America, and all others who are friends to liberty and free government." He intended to show it to the editors of the *Independent Chronicle*, with the hope that they would edit and print it.[94] Whether Manning actually sent them this first draft is unclear, but if he did, the editors turned it down. Over the following winter, Manning completed another, longer version (which Morison would help publish a century later), entitled

"The Key of Liberty." In April 1798, the manuscript arrived at the *Chronicle's* office in Boston. But by then the political climate had become increasingly hostile to writers with strong democratic convictions. The Democratic Republican societies, on the wane since 1795, had all but disappeared. The notorious XYZ affair was breaking, galvanizing anti-French resentment and bolstering the administration of John Adams, which had been elected two years earlier. In June and July, Congress would respond to antiadministration criticism with the Alien and Sedition Acts, and the editors of well-known opposition papers, including the *Independent Chronicle*, would feel the heat of repression.

Quite apart from the shifting political winds, Thomas Adams, the *Chronicle's* editor, may not have been instantly enthusiastic about Manning's acidulous essay—for one of Manning's proposals was to establish a new, independent monthly magazine, which Adams may well have seen as unwelcome competition. In any event, Adams declined to publish the manuscript, pleading ill health and lack of time to read it. As things stood, Adams had enough trouble on his hands. He would soon be arraigned for seditious libel under both the Sedition Acts and common law in connection with writings in the *Independent Chronicle*; his brother, Abijah, the newspaper's bookkeeper and later a coeditor, was indicted on similar charges by a Massachusetts court. Thomas, who genuinely was in poor health, died before his trial began, but Abijah was eventually convicted and would serve thirty days.[95]

Manning, undeterred, proceeded to revise yet again, producing a slightly shorter and much more cogent draft that toned down some of his more direct attacks (especially on the clergy) and explicated his sense of Christian duty. He was ready to deliver this revised "Key" in mid-February 1799, along with a letter bidding the *Chronicle's* editors to publish it and help ensure that "the Republican printers would not be personal sufferers by any prosecutions whatever."[96] Unfortunately, there is no evidence that Manning actually submitted the new draft; if he did, there is no record of the *Chronicle's* reasons for rejecting it, or that the editors even bothered to reply. Still, Manning refused to quit. He drafted letters to other partisan Republican printers. He compiled digests of "The Key." He brooded over alternate means of spreading the word.

Manning's tenacity is easy to understand: the essay amounted to a summa of years of reading and reflection about a wide range of issues. Along the way he had acquired some editorial skills of his own, despite his demurrals to the contrary. Each succeeding draft of "The Key" was a clear improvement over its predecessor; Manning's letters and apologias, intended for would-be supporters, displayed a growing sense of intellectual and stylistic authority. In the end, "The Key" not only represented a major investment of time and energy; it also surpassed, in scope and acuity, much of what appeared in the opposition press. As a literary artifact, it contained several layers of argumentation, each providing further clues about how Manning's mind worked and the context of his continuing self-education.

Even a cursory reading of the draft manuscripts shows that Manning was, as he claimed, a man of formal study. In passing, he referred effortlessly to the Massachusetts constitution of 1780, the federal Constitution, Washington's neutrality proclamation of 1793, and Jay's Treaty—documents he had obviously examined closely. Alongside his various biblical and theological references, he cited Lincoln's "Free Republican" essays and James Monroe's lengthy self-justification of his conduct as minister to France. He had also read various documents concerning France and the French Revolution, including an English translation of the envoy Joseph Fauchet's report to the French Directory on the state of Franco-American relations in 1797.[97] The program of self-education he recommended as "necessary to every freeman"— investigating everything from human nature to the latest legislative debates—was almost surely the one he himself followed as best he could.

None of this made Manning all that unusual, for plebeian autodidacticism was widespread in the new republic—even if it had not spread nearly as far as Manning hoped it would, or with the kinds of ideas he endorsed. The 1790s, in particular, witnessed something of a print revolution, which brought a proliferation of newspapers, periodicals, and inexpensive books to an ever-growing audience. Urban artisans joined libraries and reading groups, and read widely in the popular press. Country farmers read what newspapers they could find, and patronized book peddlers who brought them all sorts of titles, from legal texts and farmers' almanacs to pornography. The newspapers were especially rich sources of information, with their historical miscellanies and extended treatises.[98] Although Manning claimed he was not much of a reader of "ancient history," he had a good working knowledge of key developments in Holland and Great Britain from the sixteenth century onward, gleaned largely from the *Independent Chronicle.* He certainly subscribed to the weekly paper; judging from "The Key," he seems to have assembled a small archive of clippings that he referred to over and over again.[99] He also made use of the Billerica Social Library.[100] The extent and discipline of his reading were surely greater than the norm, but not so much greater for Manning to lack confidence that his intended readership of "Republicans, Farmers, Mechanics, and Laborers" could grasp his references and explications.

In absorbing all this learning, Manning did not passively trust everything he read, least of all the newspapers. When he found merit in a particular essay, he grappled with its arguments, accepting some points and rejecting others. Nine years after writing "Some Proposals," he remained deeply impressed by Lincoln's "Free Republican" essays—"the greatest collection of historical accounts" about ancient republics he had ever seen, he now acknowledged—even though he considered them contrary to free government and "no doubt written to destroy it." He particularly admired what he called Lincoln's "masterly manner" in using the struggles between rich and poor in the ancient world to illuminate the causes of political instability in the United States. But Manning's tone was tinged with irony. If he applauded Lincoln's history, he refused to accept his conclusion that the licentiousness of the Many destroyed free governments. Instead, he explicitly turned Lincoln's analysis upside down, insisting that history proved it was "the unreasonable dispositions and combinations of the Few, and the ignorance and carelessness of the Many" that caused free governments to fall.

Manning's reading in turn affected how he wrote "The Key." Although he never commanded the high-toned style preferred by newspaper editors of his day, he was clearly influenced by it. The essay's overall design fits the classical expository mode, opening with a broad statement of Manning's first principles about human nature and government before moving on to more specific historical observations about the fate of free government and concluding with a carefully outlined description of current problems and remedies for them. While he conformed to such conventions, however, Manning also transformed them, to accommodate his own voice. On its title page, for example, "The Key" contained the byline "A Laborer," with no hint of Manning's actual name. Superficially, Manning was following the form of such writers as John Dickinson ("A Farmer in Pennsylvania"), who adopted anonymous personae to lend their political writings a touch of romanticized rustic virtue.[101] But Manning's opening also subverted the conventional ploy—for he actually *was* a laborer as he defined the term, and his account of rural life was anything but romantic.

Newspapers and political pamphlets were not the only influence on Manning's rhetorical patterns. In some respects, "The Key" actually resembled a lengthy sermon or theological tract more than it did a political pamphlet. The tripartite structure of the traditional Protestant sermon—text, doctrine and reasons, application or improvement—is clearly visible in its organization. The argumentation in "The Key" amply displayed Manning's familiarity with Puritan sermonizing, the Bible, and the social thought of pietistic New England Congregationalism. His account of original sin, which apparently owed much to Edwardsian Calvinism, formed one of the linchpins of his politics. Elsewhere, Manning invoked the stories of Adam and Eve, Joseph, Hazael, and Haman from the Old Testament; he cited Solomon on education; his dire account of current affairs—"Gog and Magog are gathered together," he wrote, "to destroy the rights of man and banish liberty from the world"—borrowed liberally from popular millennial literature and the Book of Revelation.

Like his citations from secular texts, Manning's explicitly religious passages were never as simple as they might appear. He did not choose his biblical references at random. Many were exactly the same ones Cumings liked to rehearse in his Sunday pulpit;

Manning's reflections on them formed a sort of running commentary, an extension of his quarrel with the minister. Whereas Cumings blamed original sin solely for introducing hate into the world (and with it the need for orderly deference to one's superiors), Manning noted—with more scriptural warrant—that Adam's curse introduced man's eternal sentence to hard labor.[102] Whereas Cumings condemned lowly men of "levelling principles," Manning understood the Bible as saying that "the higher a person is raised in stations of honor, power and trust the greater are his temptations to do wrong."[103] Cumings construed the story of Haman as "a signal display of the wisdom and goodness of Providence," which occasionally used evil to produce good; Manning, however, viewed Haman as an exemplar of the depravity and pride of a man who "could boast of the highest preferments" on earth.[104] Cumings spoke of the need for "mutual subjugation"; Manning, of the need for "mutual assistance."[105]

Manning was not simply scoring debater's points, either against Cumings or against the larger body of liberal Congregationalist theology. Nor did he deploy biblical phrases in order to strike a popular rhetorical chord, or to fend off anticipated criticisms from the Federalist clergy. Repeatedly, "The Key" underscored how seriously Manning took his religion. His belief in man's blind devotion to self-interest and propensity to sin was a fundamental article of faith, which prompted his intense suspicion of both the Few and those among the Many who either lapsed into political apathy or counseled violent rebellion. Only if "graced by a Christian life and conduct agreeable to his own profession of faith," Manning argued, could any man expect to persuade others of his opinions; no Christian could refuse to obey "good and wholesome laws"; just as men were bound to respect their civic obligations, so they owed to their Maker a "reverence and a respect for the Sabbath and all holy ordinaries and institutions."

Manning's New Divinity leanings surely informed his devotion to constitutional order. Antinomian (as opposed to Arminian) critics of mainstream Calvinism had long questioned its tendency to place too much emphasis on the authority of the church and its laws, and not enough on the importance of individual faith. In doing so, antinomians often insisted on their right to disregard the accepted norms of the community, if those norms conflicted with what they thought was the clear word of God. The New Divinity clergy likewise denied that faithful adherence to the laws of the community or of the church played any part in making one a more fit candidate for sainthood. They were not, however, antinomians. If obeying the secular and spiritual authorities had nothing to do with salvation, it was nevertheless a duty imposed upon all true believers. Like traditional Calvinists, the New Divinity clergy insisted that there could be no salvation for anyone who flouted the law.[106] A parallel structure of feeling informed Manning's constitutional thinking. Every member of the community had an obligation to obey all laws "made by their representatives," he believed, "let them be ever so wrong or bad in their opinion."

For all its piety, "The Key" also confirmed that Manning was not solely or even primarily a religious thinker. His faith never crossed over into sectarianism or intolerance. As much as any backwoods dissenter, he insisted that "every person has a right to worship and serve his maker in the way his own conscience dictates." If Manning built his politics on Calvinist assumptions about human nature, his readings of contemporary political problems—and, even more important, his solutions for them— were always secular. And if his writing was beholden to the church, it also had the flavor of a very different, profane milieu— the tavern common room—and of yet another set of devices for holding his own in an argument.

The tavern, along with the church and the town meeting hall, was a hot spot of community life in the eighteenth-century New England countryside. The keeper himself was by law expected to be an orderly, honest, temperate person. Commonly, taverns were sites of official and semiofficial functions, from electioneering to militia training days. (In the 1760s and 1770s, while Manning was growing up, his father's tavern had been a site for several election day carousings and similar gatherings.)[107] Local taverns were also places where neighbors gathered to read newspapers, and to hear them read. Quite naturally, they served as informal debating halls and political lyceums—proving grounds for local political talent. "These public houses are in many places the Nursaries of our legislators," John Adams warned in 1761; in them, "an Artful Man who has neither sense nor sentiment may be gaining a little sway among the Rabble of a town." The political importance of the tavern grew during and after the Revolution, especially in the countryside, as traditions of deference fell away, and a newer, more rough-and-tumble democratic politics emerged. During the 1790s, Federalists complained bitterly of political "runners" and the "democratic literati" who "harangue[d] the mobs" gathered in local public houses.[108]

Nothing in the evidence suggests Manning used the contacts he had gained as a publican to advance his early career in town politics (although it is hard to believe he did not). But Manning obviously had a good ear for tavern talk, and he learned how to use it to advance his *ideas*. Manning's manuscripts, especially "The Key of Liberty," are full of the kinds of rural imagery and barbed quips familiar to tavern disputes—an earthy, epigrammatic style designed to deflate and confute the more pompous complexities of learned argumentation. "The poor man's shilling," he remarked in "The Key," "ought to be as much the care of government as the rich man's pound." Lawyers, for whom he showed a special contempt, were to Manning "a kind of mule order," holding neither judicial nor executive responsibilities; expecting them to curb the arbitrary rule of judges was, he thought, "like setting the cat to watch the cream pot." Although Manning admired learning, he had no use for it as an ornament—or instrument—of privilege: there was, he thought, about as much need for most schoolteachers to know how to read and write "all languages" as there was "for a farmer to have the mariner's art to hold the plow." Once challenged with the "true circumstances," uninformed, reflexive supporters of Jay's Treaty would shrink from their position and, "like lambs that are dumb after they are sheared, turn away and wish to hear no more about it." Manning may well have lifted some of these lines from farmers' almanacs, a genre he knew well. Some, like the reference to sheared lambs, had biblical origins.[109] But his more vulgar images plainly evoked the ambience as well as the verbal exchanges of the tavern. Federalists, Manning wrote, tried to frighten people into believing that without Jay's Treaty, the British would make war on the United States, and "rouse off a great gun 3,000 miles distant and blow all our brains out if we stepped out to piss."

The striking thing about these departures into tavern wit is not so much their bluntness as the ease with which Manning moved from a "low" to a "high" style—sometimes within the span of two sentences. In a discussion of "The Key," Richard Hofstadter once badly misrepresented Manning's views on education as indicative of an "anti-intellectualist populism" that contained "a dark and sullen skepticism of high culture."[110] On the contrary, although Manning plainly abhorred how the Federalist elite had arrogated learning to itself—possibly with Federalist Harvard at the top of his thoughts—his prose blended plebeian rhetoric and borrowings from learned tracts, always signaling his admiration for the latter. His respectful remarks about the historical mastery displayed by "Free Republican" (despite their very different conclusions) typified Manning's tone. His comments on a poor man's shilling followed a declaration, straight from John Locke, that the "end of government is the protection of life, liberty, and property." His remarks on the various forms of government were a second-hand imitation of (and challenge to) those contained in Montesquieu's *The Spirit of the Laws*.

In other instances, it is quite possible that some of Manning's quips and apothegms were, in fact, inspired by "high" sources, themselves couched in plainspoken phrases. His observation that lawyers were a "mule order" almost certainly built upon the polemical attack on the profession by the artisan-turned-politician Benjamin Austin, originally published in the *Independent Chronicle* in 1786 as a reply to "Free Republican." One of his lines about money—that it "will go where it will fetch the most as naturally as water runs downhill"—may have been a snatch of country wisdom; alternatively, he could have lifted it out of one of David Hume's essays. There is something immensely attractive about the porousness of this way of writing, with its overtones of Painite impudence and common sense, combined with a compatible and equally Painite respect for enlightened disputation. Naturally it attracted a man like Manning, who wrote at the time when the hierarchies of learned and low were out of joint—

a self-taught philosopher who, having been caught up by the Revolution, may never have heeded those hierarchies in the first place. It is a self-consciously *democratic* style.[111]

(How much Manning actually owed directly to Paine is an open question, but it is almost inconceivable that he was not well acquainted with Paine's ideas. If he did not read Paine's major writings from the Revolution, *Common Sense* and *The Crisis*, he would have been one of the few literate, politically minded Americans to have missed them, given their immense popularity. Some of the substantive remarks in "The Key"—on the necessity to obey bad laws, on the possibilities of worldwide equality and fraternity—have close parallels in *Rights of Man*, although they appear in other writers' works as well. Manning made repeated, ironic use of Edmund Burke's famous sneer at "the swinish multitude" in *Reflections on the Revolution in France*—the work against which Paine had directed *Rights of Man*. And several times, Manning conspicuously deployed the phrase "the Rights of Man," although he never cited the book, mentioned its author, or included any extended paraphrase from Paine's writings in his own work. Manning certainly would have objected to Paine's deist theology, especially as presented in the notorious *Age of Reason*, published only a short time before Manning started work on "The Key," which may account for Paine's absence. Even had he been able to put those differences aside, he might well have been wary about quoting Paine directly in the late 1790s, when Federalists and their clerical allies regularly maligned Paine in order to stigmatize all their opponents as impious blasphemers. But whether or not Manning drew directly on Paine, the ideas and rhetoric of "The Key" belonged to that larger body of popular democratic writing which Paine did so much to instigate and inspire.)[112]

Manning's persistent tone of respect for reason and orderly democratic procedures, mixed with demotic irreverence, showed up in other ways as well. In "The Key," as in "Some Proposals," he took care to qualify his attacks on the Few, lest they seem like caricatures. Refusing to share in the personalized animus of some plebeian critics of "high flyers," he went out of his way to stress that he did not believe that "any orders of men who live without labor are entirely needless or that they are all chargeable with blame."[113] Nor did he romanticize the Many as the peculiar possessors of some innate virtue or wisdom. A consistent, postlapsarian Calvinist, he believed all men were fallen—and that the more power they achieved, the more they would seek. He was a democrat not because he had an abiding faith in the virtue of the populace, but because he lacked an abiding faith in the virtue of the elite. Cognizant of the shortcomings of the ignorant and apathetic among the Many as well as of the potential tyranny of the Few, Manning always returned to the importance of a reasoned and orderly form of democratic challenge. "Learning" and "knowledge" were key words for him in the late 1790s, words to which he returned again and again; only by pursuing learning and knowledge—including the "knowledge that when laws are once constitutionally made they must be obeyed"—could the Many secure their rights and keep the Few from "putting darkness for light, and light for darkness, falsehood for truth, and truth for falsehood."[114]

In "The Key," the many strands of Manning's self-education pulled together as a comprehensive solution to the political dilemmas that had burdened him since the days of the Massachusetts Regulation. How, he had long wondered, could the well-being of the Many be secured constitutionally against the self-interested manipulations of the Few? Part of his answer was to inquire into how the moneyed minority bent monetary and commercial policy to their own ends and exploited the laboring majority—an inquiry that was well advanced by the time he wrote "Some Proposals." Beyond these important matters, numerous other questions remained. How did the Few consistently manage to benefit from the ignorance of the Many? Why, after the experience of the Massachusetts Regulation had events transpired that only enhanced the power of the nation's moneyed men? And how could a political movement be organized to end these abuses and secure free government once and for all? In pondering these issues, Manning began to generalize from his own experience—and to regard enlightenment and education as the bulwarks of popular liberty. Only if the Many had sufficient knowledge to act rationally in politics could they improve their rights. For freemen to be truly free, they had to win the freedom to think for themselves.

On their face, these were not particularly fiery propositions— but for Manning the ideal of universal knowledge had radical implications. The Few, he assumed, would not automatically relinquish their monopoly on knowledge; doing so would strip them of their most powerful weapon. The Many would have to fight hard to secure their mental independence; once victorious, they would have to institute democratic safeguards to ensure they would never lose what they had won. Their prospects looked unpromising over the winter of 1796–1797; they only worsened over the next few years, as the Federalist repression geared up and opposition editors fell on the defensive. In a last-ditch effort, Manning offered his collected political thoughts and a plan for action with democratic provisions and goals beyond anything he or any other American had yet envisioned.

"The Great Scuffle between the Few and the Many"

To turn from Manning's first efforts in "Some Proposals" to the drafts of "The Key" is to see how greatly he had expanded the scope and the force of his arguments during the 1790s. The narrow disquisitions about credit and paper money that had dominated "Some Proposals" gave way to much more wide-ranging propositions about politics and social life. The eternal struggle between the Few and the Many, portrayed in the earlier work as a fight over monetary policy, now unfolded as a more comprehensive struggle over labor, property, and free government itself. Although addressed primarily to Manning's fellow Americans, "The Key" took up the concerns of democrats the world over, including the French Revolution and the continuing war in Europe. By the time the manuscript concluded, Manning had utterly confounded what have since become standard categories for describing political thought in the early republic. He emerged as a partisan of the Many who was unalterably opposed to popular regulators; a sometime tavernkeeper concerned with "strict justice" in the marketplace who favored defaulting on a portion of the national debt; a small farmer who sought to forge a political alliance with artisans and laborers; a plebeian democrat who thought the creation and defense of free government required a better-educated populace and the support of at least a few leading men; a defender of individual rights and of the state governments who was also a nationalist (indeed, an internationalist) and a determined cosmopolitan.

After a brief preface and an autobiographical introduction, "The Key" set out Manning's views on human nature and the dangers that selfishness posed to free government. Manning then picked up and elaborated on his earlier discussion of the Few and the Many. He explicitly based his argument on a Lockean labor theory of property. "Labor is the sole parent of all property," he began; without labor, "the land yieldeth nothing"; every "necessary of life . . . is generally esteemed valuable according to what labor it costs." It followed logically that a man's property ought to stand in some direct proportion to the amount of labor he performed. No one could own property without laboring "unless he gets it by force or craft, fraud or fortune out of the earnings of others."[115]

Stated this way, these axioms contained little that was new or controversial. The notion that labor created all property—self-evident to working farmers and artisans—was almost a cliché in eighteenth-century America, repeated in folk sayings and learned treatises alike. (Manning once again lifted this passage, like others, from the "Free Republican" essays.) Consistent with the emphases of his main literary source, Manning was no leveler. He did worry about the evil effects that great disparities of wealth posed to free government; Americans were fortunate, he wrote, to be "on an equality as to property to what they are in the old countries." But he did not hold that the root of injustice was material inequality, or that the distinctions between the classes could be cured by equalizing property. He forthrightly stated that because people were born with a wide variety of capacities, there would always be a very unequal distribution of property, even under the best of governments. Nor did Manning condemn commercial markets—or their supporting cast of bankers, merchants, and professionals—as preternaturally evil. Elaborating on hints in "Some Proposals," he praised commerce as a facilitator of human happiness—"a great advantage to the Many . . . making vent of our produce and furnishing us with necessaries and conveniences from other countries." The problem was that the large majority of those who lived without labor were not content to abide by the limits of justice; gripped by the self-interest known to all men, they set about perverting useful commercial institutions into engines of oppression.

Banks and the whole system of government finance had provided Manning with telling examples of this tendency in "Some Proposals," and in "The Key" the monetary system remained an issue in "the great scuffle between the Few and Many." The incomes—and thus the interest—of the Few lay in having "money scarce and the prices of labor and produce as low as possible," while the incomes of the Many were dependent on money being cheap and plentiful. Banks ostensibly served to provide the currency and credit necessary to conduct honest trade. But with the emergence of Hamilton's system, banking and currency policy had quickly fallen under the control of men who arbitrarily manipulated their remittances and the money supply in order to enrich themselves and their friends—actions that also served to bring "the Many into distress." Since 1791 the appearance of state banks had somewhat alleviated the problem, by contesting the monopoly of Hamilton's Bank of the United States, by dealing honorably and impartially with the public, and by quickening the circulation of money among small dealers and tradesmen. Still, the Few retained a powerful hold on monetary policy and banking, which needed to be broken.

But that was not all. In addition to controlling the money supply, the Few also sought to monopolize the creation and diffusion of knowledge, and to discourage popular enlightenment. Forswearing all notions of justice, members of the various learned professions—doctors, merchants, clergymen, teachers, lawyers—combined to raise their fees beyond the abilities of poor men to pay. Betraying their trust, former officers in the revolutionary army formed what Manning thought was the most diabolical combination of all, the Society of the Cincinnati. Seduced by a resurgent social snobbery, the Few set themselves above the rest of the citizenry and then combined in politics to thwart free government. To that end, they used every available tool of subversion. They tried to keep the people ignorant. They undermined the liberty of the press. They favored obscurely written constitutions and laws, and, when necessary, quietly violated constitutional provisions that hindered their power. They indulged in elaborate governmental ceremonials and "kingly speeches" to impress and silence ordinary legislators and citizens. They encouraged a bellicose spirit in order to justify the raising of standing armies to overawe their own people. They provoked needless wars with the Indian tribes in the Northwest, wasting lives and treasure. When all that failed, they resorted to the time-honored techniques of electoral bribery and personal threats.

The conspiratorial overtones of these passages would seem to stigmatize Manning as a captive of what some historians have loosely called the "paranoid style" in American politics.[116] Most glaring of all were Manning's increasingly pointed attacks on the Society of the Cincinnati as a sinister, secret brotherhood, the principal coordinating force behind the various organizations of the Few. We now know these concerns to be grossly exaggerated. When first announced, however, many people were rightly worried about what the formation of a hereditary society of former army officers portended. In 1784 the Massachusetts legislature had passed a resolution condemning the society as an *imperium in imperio* whose regular meetings and correspondence among state societies could prove "destructive of the liberties of the State." (Subsequent efforts by Washington and others to eliminate the hereditary character of the society's membership, even though ultimately unsuccessful, helped deflect criticism of the Cincinnati but did not eradicate it.)[117] Although Manning and others overstated the central, directing role of the Cincinnati, their general fear that moneyed elites were organizing to protect their interests was hardly unfounded.

Moreover, Manning's fuller remarks about how the Few gained and kept power reveal a supple approach to politics, one superior to the standard, brittle republican themes about corrupt cabals. Some of his shrewdest observations concerned the psychological dimensions of power—and how, even in a formal democracy, the

Many could accept what he perceived as their undemocratic subordination. Peoples and nations trained to worship great men, Manning argued, did not easily shake the habit. Even when revolutions occurred, the rebels quickly fell under the influence of a few charismatic leaders, "who after they have obtained their object can never receive compensation and honors enough from the people for their services." As the people were always ready to believe the best about their heroes, they too readily accepted whatever lies or excuses their new rulers passed around. Free and democratic government, the prize once striven for, degenerated into yet another variety of passive servility.

Popular deference could become especially pronounced in times of general economic prosperity—as in the United States in the 1790s. Whatever his personal difficulties, Manning never doubted that at the moment he was writing, the laboring majority knew themselves to be living in "the best times for their interest that ever they enjoyed." In "The Key," as in "Some Proposals," Manning raised a note of moral disquiet, charging that ordinary citizens had been bewitched into buying unnecessary luxuries (especially British imports) which sapped their savings, numbed their souls, and dazzled their common sense. He then explored the wider political ramifications of this prosperity and of the complacency it had encouraged.

The reasons for the flush times were, he insisted, easy enough to discern: a freer circulation of money, owing to the state banks that had begun to offset the Bank of the United States; an artificial—and temporary—tightening of labor markets and a rise in prices caused by increased speculation and consumer buying; the advantages that had accrued to American trade from the French Revolution and the European wars, so long as free trade lasted. By this reckoning, the emergent Republican opposition deserved most of the credit for helping to foster improved conditions; indeed, Manning believed that Federalist actions like Jay's Treaty purposely undercut the sources of the Many's prosperity. Typically, however, the incumbent Federalists presented themselves as the sole founders of an economic boom, by "continually crying up the goodness of the times—that we were the most free and happy people on earth; and that all our happiness arose from the goodness of our government and the wisdom and policy of the measures pursued by its administration." A good portion of the Many, ill-informed and all too human, believed exactly what they heard.

Americans, in Manning's view, had no peculiar propensity to fall for such demagoguery. ("On the contrary," he insisted, "I believe we are the most knowing and the best acquainted with the true principles of liberty and a free government of any people on earth.") In the prosperous 1790s, however, with each passing year, Manning saw more and more of the populace growing deferential to the great men, forgetting the first principles of democracy and allowing themselves to be gulled into supporting the Few. Worse, he saw even more of the citizenry simply withdrawing from politics, mainly out of self-satisfied ignorance—a withdrawal signified by the poor turnouts in statewide and national elections. So long as a growing proportion of the Many opted out of politics, the Few could win elections without converting a great many people to their cause.

Manning refused to accept that there was anything inevitable about this state of affairs. His tough-minded realism about the limits of human nature, derived from his religious beliefs, gave him the most cause for hope. Individual selfish impulses afflicted the Many as well as the Few. Nevertheless, Manning remained confident that the collective self-interest of the Many could, in the end, conquer their individual selfishness, provided only that they form their own associations, as had the Few. The Many constituted a clear majority. Let them organize to provide themselves with enough knowledge to act in behalf of their interests, and free government would be secure. Together they could see to the adoption of essential political reforms, especially of the judiciary and the process of constitutional review. Over the long term, an expansion of public education at all levels would break forever the elite's monopoly on knowledge and the means of communication. The whole process might be seen as a secular, political revival—an analogue to the spiritual evangelizing of the Methodist connection, or to the missionary efforts of the New Divinity Calvinists under the spur of disinterested benevolence. Simply by coming together and achieving enlightenment, the Many could

discern where their true self-interest—and their political salvation—lay.

Manning did not make this proposal idly. The concluding portion of "The Key" offered a constitution for his hoped-for organization (which he named the Laboring Society), described its
purpose in detail, and anticipated various objections that might
be offered against it. A national membership organization, the
society would aim principally to provide the laboring majority
with ready access to all the knowledge necessary for a free man—
including everything from a general understanding of human
nature to the credentials and views of all officeholders and candidates. The Republican press had filled that purpose for Manning,
but its reputation had been nearly ruined by the Few, who used
"all the arts and rhetoric hell can invent to blackguard the
Republican printers and all they print."[118] He therefore proposed
that the Laboring Society publish a monthly magazine to provide
the Many with ample information about elections, legislative
debates, and constitutional rights, which members could study
and discuss in neighborhood classes presided over by a librarian.
The classes in turn might serve as a political rallying point. "If
there should come on such times as there were in Massachusetts
in 1786," he observed, "all the Many would gladly be at the
expense of obtaining such knowledge and the Society would
come together like a building well-framed and marked."[119]

In its final form, Manning's plan cleared up whatever confusion
may have existed in his own mind between democratic procedures and Methodist-style indoctrination. He remained confident in his own ideas, but explicitly acknowledged he might be
proved mistaken in some of them. Officeholding in the society
would proceed from the bottom up, with no established, self-
appointed hierarchy of himself or anyone else. "The Key" and
the monthly magazine were to serve as touchstones for political
discussion in the classes, not as semidivine writs. The librarians
would make sure that reading material was available; whatever
authority Manning's words achieved would derive from the
reflection and reasoned assent of the members. Manning might
well have envisioned the class meetings proceeding in the knock-
about spirit of that other seat of political inquiry and disputation

which he knew so well, namely the tavern. (Indeed, he might have assumed that many classes would actually assemble in local taverns.) Above all, Manning expected that the Many would come to see things his way, but on the basis of their own independent study and thought, in the light of their own personal and collective self-interest, and not by imposition.

Manning's ultimate goal, however, was not simply to help the Many enlighten themselves. He wished to create a vehicle that would help turn the Few and their friends out of office and replace them with reliable democratic republicans. By his count, fewer than half those eligible to vote participated in elections for federal representatives and electors. He intended the Laboring Society and its magazine to help change this calculation by providing the Many with what they needed to know in order to vote with confidence. In the second draft of "The Key" (1798), Manning also toyed with the idea that the Laboring Society, once properly organized, should publicize misdeeds by public officials and, if necessary, manage impeachments against them. Politicians, elected and nonelected, would once again feel their constituents' presence and "act as servants and not masters."[120]

It was a bold vision of an invigorated democracy—and, given the stakes, Manning was under no illusion that his proposals would win immediate adherence. The Few would certainly denounce it as dangerous, an objection he thought beneath answering. But more sympathetic readers might think the idea too expensive and impractical. For their benefit he observed that, compared to suppressing rebellions and other irregular forms of protest, his plan was eminently inexpensive, practical, and just. With the support of a few influential Republicans in the state legislatures, and with the costs shared by local classes, there was no reason (at least on paper) why the society and magazine could not succeed. The federal and state governments might even be persuaded to help the project with a subsidy.

In the end, the practical-minded Manning could scarcely contain his enthusiasm for the project, and (especially in the 1798 draft) he portrayed its potential benefits in nearly millennial terms. Let the Laboring Society be established on a strong and lasting foundation, he rhapsodized, and Congress would have reason to boast of Americans being the freest and most enlightened people on earth. By convincing the world of the United States' determination to be free, the very existence of the society would do more to prevent a war than any other scheme. Were free governments and an international Laboring Society organized "throughout the world," all national differences might be settled by "social correspondences and mutual concessions." Everyone could then look forward to a prosperous future with an expansive economy of commerce, agriculture, and manufacturing, all in accord with the self-evident truth that "the happiness of a person consisteth in eating and drinking and enjoying the good of his own labors."

To be sure, Manning was not always the keenest observer of international affairs. In the 1798 draft of "The Key," for example, he echoed the *Independent Chronicle* and other Democratic Republicans in celebrating the momentous French coup of 18 Fructidor, Year V (September 4, 1797), believing it had narrowly averted a royalist restoration. Yet far from putting the French republic "on a stronger foundation than ever," as Manning claimed, the events of 18 Fructidor only paved the way for the seizure of power by Napoleon Bonaparte two years later.[121] Still, if Manning's wishful thinking sometimes blocked his better judgment, his ideal of a harmonious world united by peaceful commerce and mutual correspondence was a variation on a standard theme, shared by writers as far-flung as James Madison and Immanuel Kant. (If anything, Madison's hopes for a *pax democratica* actually exceeded Manning's.)[122] Nor would it be the last time in American history that democratic stirrings abroad would generate dreams of a new and peaceful world order—and even, perhaps, of history's culmination.

Manning's proposed Laboring Society combined his many political concerns into a single project—including his democratic assumptions, his respect for learning, and his constitutionalist convictions. Its intended membership reached beyond the propertied to include "all the free male persons" aged twenty-one and over "who labor for a living in the United States," as well as "all persons of any denominations" who subscribed to the society's principles—making it in conception by far the most democratic political organization in the nation. Its institutional framework was similarly democratic, grafting the evangelism of the Methodists and the grassroots structure of the Democratic Republican clubs of the mid-1790s. At the same time, knowing all too well that Federalists would object to his group as yet another fractious, self-created society, Manning modeled his draft on the "Institution" of the Society of the Cincinnati he so despised—thereby heading off any Federalist criticisms that his plan was anything less than perfectly constitutional.[123] The society's members were expected to live up to the same standards of respect for the law that they would demand from their representatives. To underline the importance of this commitment, Manning appended a covenant to his proposed constitution to be signed by every prospective member, whereby they pledged, among other things, to support the constituted authorities in suppressing insurrections.

Daring as it was, the plan did have several glaring limitations. Considering that slavery and race were already becoming flashpoints of democratic controversy, Manning was remarkably reticent on the subjects. To be sure, his personal contact with slavery was fleeting, which may help account for his silence. (On the eve of the Revolution, no more than four of Billerica's 312 ratable households included one slave each; after 1780, the courts held that the Declaration of Rights of the new state constitution effectively abolished slavery in Massachusetts.) Manning's manuscripts betray no racialist animosities, or any hint of discomfort about either the small number of free blacks who lived in and around Billerica or the far greater numbers who lived in the seaboard cities and the South. (Manning no doubt knew the free black who resided in the household of his neighbor and trading partner David Levenstone in 1800; he may also have known—or known about—Tony Clark, a free black farmer and shoemaker from Dracut who, in 1779, at age nineteen, enlisted in Captain Solomon Pollard's Billerica company, Manning's old outfit.) Far from being an early proponent of what historians have called "*herrenvolk* democracy" (that is, a democracy of the master race), Manning opened the Laboring Society to *all* free laboring men, thereby including free blacks as well as propertyless whites. Nevertheless, Manning, a man attuned to national and international affairs, supported a Republican interest whose national leadership consisted mainly of slaveholders. Slaves had no place in his vision of the Many. Nor did women, slave or free, of any color. And in these respects, the ideas contained in "The Key of Liberty" would be outdistanced by other democratic proclamations over the next thirty years.[124]

Manning's plan also failed to take full advantage of various popular organizations in existence when he wrote "The Key of Liberty." He appears to have known nothing about the first local journeyman's unions organized in Philadelphia and New York in 1792 and 1794—groups that emerged from conflict between employers and wage earners that was as yet in its infancy. More inexplicably, he slighted the potential usefulness of a number of democratic organizations that had survived into the late 1790s— notably, urban mechanics' associations and pro-Republican benevolent bodies in the major cities and towns, like New York's Society of St. Tammany. Manning was clearly aware that these groups and others annually brought together thousands of antiadministration dissidents for festivities and demonstrations on the Fourth of July. (Hence his stipulation, in the Laboring Society constitution, that the local classes meet to elect officers on the Fourth.) Yet beyond this, he never made any attempt to link his own plan with these existing organizations.[125]

Still, with all its defects, "The Key of Liberty" amounted to nothing less than a blueprint for a New Model Party—a marked advance over what most other democrats had in mind at the time. Traditionally, in Anglo-American politics, parties were directed by the elite, from the top down. And in republican America, such parties were much feared as potential solvents of a shared sense of political commonwealth and virtue. Even the leading Jeffersonian oppositionists of the 1790s, while grudgingly accepting the label "party," modeled themselves on the Whigs of the 1760s and 1770s—patriotic notables, fighting tyranny, who would disband once the Federalist menace had ended.[126] Manning, however, thought of parties much more broadly, as he suggested in a section on parties in the 1798 draft of "The Key". In his view, they were not just temporary divisions within the political elite, but long-standing, inevitable divisions throughout the whole society. All party conflict, he thought, had the same roots: a "conceived difference of interests" between the Few and the Many, and the "unreasonable desires of the Few to tyrannize over and enslave the Many."

Given the inevitability of this clash, Manning did not shrink from organized conflict between these two great parties. He welcomed it—so long as the party of the Many, the Laboring Society, was established and able to participate in full. Lacking any clear sense of how politics might operate after the Federalists were defeated, Manning left little precise indication of how this conflict would unfold in future, or of the parties' long-term relations and organization. He certainly did not go as far as early nineteenth-century democrats, like Martin Van Buren, in constructing a more modern sort of party, with responsibilities for nominating candidates and disciplining voters. But his plan marked a significant democratization of the concept.[127] It offered Manning's answer to the question that had long troubled democratic theorists: How can a government remain for long both free and democratic? The free government's enemies were always "crying out that there is not virtue and knowledge among my brother laborers to support such a government," he later observed; that they are "easily deceived, bribed, flattered, or driven to act contrary to their true interests." But those who make such charges had not considered what would happen if the means of knowledge were made widely available, as the Laboring Society would do. Then, Manning was certain, "there would always be a large majority that would read, see, think and act for themselves and their own interest and would zealously support a free government so long as self interest governs men."[128] During the next few years, his faith would be at least partly vindicated.

Republican Printers and Itinerant Jacobins

Manning did not take rejection easily. Rebuffed by the *Independent Chronicle*, he tried to rework his ideas and find other ways to get his project off the ground. Ideally, he would have liked the

Massachusetts Republican leadership—and, even better, the national Jeffersonian leadership—to get wind of the plan, promote it, and vote the appropriate subsidies to distribute "The Key" and the monthly magazine all across the country. Short of that, Manning understood the uses that could be made of commercial markets to spread the word and to provide the Laboring Society with the funds necessary to complete its work. Some of his early ruminations along these lines show up in the drafts of "The Key" and in his correspondence with the *Chronicle*. Almost all of his writing after 1799 developed these plans, including the possibility of funding the society's expenses by copyrighting its monthly magazine and "The Key of Liberty."

Manning became so involved in these schemes that he appears, at one point, to have thought about turning them and the society into a means for his personal support. In his excitement over copyrights, Manning drew up some distribution plans that emphasized how much money could be made if those copyrights were handled properly. Other copyrighted pamphlets, he noted, were priced well above their printing costs, and he was confident that "The Key" would sell enough copies to earn a handsome return.[129] In another version, he said that he would be happy to grant the copyright to interested printers, who would themselves stand to make "a handsome sum," provided only that he too might have a proper share of the profits. Beneath this revised scheme of operation, Manning attached a *nota bene:* "many are the advantages of good learning."[130] Intended as an encouragement to potential printers and distributors, the remark might also be taken as a note to himself. Had Manning's master blueprint for redeeming the republic become mainly a means to ensure his own self-advancement—or to pay off his mounting debts? Was the pious foe of the Few a crass, self-promoting entrepreneur at heart?

No. Manning's observations on Hamilton's fiscal policy in "Some Proposals" had revealed a mind knowledgeable about money matters; that he should try to turn this knowledge to the advantage of his political projects is not surprising. Appealing to the baser self-interest of potential printers or to the tastes of potential subscribers in order to help ensure the success of his project in no way contradicted his social and economic critique: it only confirmed his realism. Manning thought hard about how to make the Laboring Society economically viable, but he also insisted that it exemplify the principles of strict economic justice. He wanted the profits from both the subscriptions and the endowment fund earmarked for the good of the society, but he also wanted those who worked honorably on its behalf (including himself) to be properly rewarded for their labors. If copyrights helped encourage printers to publish "The Key," then he was all for it. But if anybody was to make money off his work, then he asked for his rightful share. Through it all, his priority was to put "The Key of Liberty" and the magazine into the hands of as many people as possible at a cost affordable to all.

In any event, Manning quickly dropped these enticements in favor of a very different approach, expunging even the appearance of selfishness, his own or anyone else's, from the project. In a piece he called "A Proposed Plan for Carrying 'The Key of Liberty' into Circulation"—plainly, given internal references, written after the others—Manning proposed granting the copyright to a board of directors, who then would apply the profits to a fund for the benefit of the state's Laboring Society. As for his own earnings, he was willing to sign over the rights "without a cent reward."[131]

All of this planning, of course, proved fruitless. There is no evidence that Manning ever sent any of his blueprints to anybody; if he did, they made no impact. There is reason to suspect, however, that "The Key of Liberty" may have circulated outside Manning's immediate circle at the end of the 1790s, and that the failure of the *Chronicle* and other periodicals to publish it may not have been due to editorial inattention or distraction. On the contrary, Thomas Adams and the others may have been only too familiar with what Manning had to say.

Even as Manning was writing and attempting to publish "The Key of Liberty," another self-described "labouring man," David Brown, was traveling around Massachusetts denouncing Federalist policies, and perhaps circulating a petition that asked for a redress of the people's grievances. By his own account, Brown visited more than eighty towns in the commonwealth, carrying with him a sheaf of writings (reportedly his own) from which he read to all who would listen in the stores, taverns, and private homes he passed along the way. According to other witnesses, he was not the only "itinerant Jacobin" traveling around the countryside stirring up passions against the government.[132]

Brown's travels might have gone unnoticed except that the residents of Dedham's Clapboardtree Parish—locally notorious as a hotbed of sin and Jacobinism—erected a liberty pole soon after he passed through the area, to which they attached a placard denouncing Federalist policies and calling for the retirement of President Adams. Although he had not been present at the pole's erection, Brown was charged with sedition and a warrant was issued for his arrest. The authorities finally caught up with him three months later in Andover, from where he was bound over to the Salem jail to await trial.

A picture emerges from the comments elicited by Brown's arrest, and from the accounts of witnesses at his trial, of an extensive political subculture, centered on the taverns and plebeian meeting places, where men like Brown (and presumably Manning, too) propounded their views. According to a letter by a "gentleman from Andover," Brown (a "wandering apostle of sedition") specifically mentioned visiting Attleborough, Bridgewater, Concord, and Dracut, among other towns across the state. Witnesses at Brown's trial testified that they heard him reading from the manuscripts in his possession, as well as from such other notorious works as Tom Paine's *The Age of Reason*, and discussing them with his listeners. The same Andover gentleman also offered an abbreviated summary of the writings in Brown's possession. According to him, they represented "officers of the government, the Clergy and Lawyers" as "enemies of the people" who had already consumed a large portion of the people's property and who were endeavoring to engross the rest and reduce them to "abject slavery." Stockholders, bankers, merchants, and other people of property also met with condemnation. The main object of these manuscripts, the gentleman insisted, was to "alarm the Farmers, Mechanics and Labourers, with an apprehension that the preservation of liberty and property depends upon a thorough Revolution."[133]

Even through the hostile filter of a high Federalist's testimony—which automatically equated democratization with a bloody revolutionary upheaval—we can hear the echoes, if not the actual call, of "The Key of Liberty." Or do echoes of what even the *Independent Chronicle* called Brown's "malignant and perverse misrepresentations" appear in "The Key of Liberty"?[134] Either way, the similarities are suggestive—not only about what the *Chronicle*'s editors viewed as the limits of safe political opinion in 1798, but also about the context within which Manning wrote "The Key". There is no evidence that Manning and Brown ever crossed paths. But they clearly came from different corners of the same political opposition and shared many of the same criticisms of the existing order.

More disturbing to the Federalist leadership, however, was that in the stormy climate of the late 1790s, members of the opposition Democratic Republican elite were openly expressing analogous views. Drawing-room agitators like Thomas Jefferson also spoke of a country divided between "antirepublicans" and "true republicans"—the former consisting mostly of returned Tories, merchants, speculators, stockholders, and both officeholders and office seekers ("a numerous and noisy tribe"); the latter made up of landholders and "the great body of labourers, not being landholders, whether in husbanding or the arts."[135] And in 1798, Jefferson's friends were also hard at work preparing for the coming elections—elections they believed would decide the republic's destiny—by stirring up opposition to the government's measures. The possibility loomed that they might well succeed, by winning the allegiance of the discontented lower and middling sort—cutting across differences in region, wealth, and religious outlook, to make a common cause.

It was this alliance of high and low, of national and local interests, in league against Federalist policies, that most alarmed and enraged friends of the Adams administration in Massachusetts and around the country. "We have seen of late, indeed within a single year," Fisher Ames lamented in April 1799, "an almost total change in the tactics and management of the parties." The Republicans—or "Jacobins," as Ames preferred to call them—had begun to organize themselves. "Emissaries are sent to every class of men," Ames complained, "even to every individual man that can be gained. Every threshing-floor, every husking, every party at work on a house-frame or raising a building, the very funerals are infected with bawlers and whisperers against government."[136] Ames was far from paranoid—for, using precisely these means, Republicans in Massachusetts and (with far greater success) in other states built the mobilization that effected the so-called revolution of 1800 that finally brought Jefferson to the presidency. Six years later, the same approach enabled the Republicans to take power in Massachusetts as well.[137]

In some respects, "The Key of Liberty" can be read as a manifesto for just this sort of electoral revolution. Manning always expected that a few of the great men would have to take the lead in galvanizing the Many (yet another mark of his realism, reflecting his sense of political psychology). And the national Republican leadership sounded many of Manning's themes. In several states, including Massachusetts, the party organized itself along lines quite similar to those Manning had suggested. There were statewide committees, consisting of a small number of prominent Republicans, many of whom were members of the state legislatures; beneath them were the county committees, town committees and parish or precinct committees, responsible for rousing the party's members and arguing its case before the public. Nathaniel Ames, Fisher Ames's "Jacobin" brother and a member of the Norfolk County Committee, would later describe the purpose of this organization in terms that could have almost been lifted directly from "The Key": "To watch over the Republican interest both in State and National Governments, especially as to elections and appointments—convey intelligence—confute false rumors—confirm the wavering in right principles—prevent delusion of weak brethren—and fight the most formidable enemy of civilized men, political ignorance."[138]

Of course, the pro-Jefferson Democratic Republican party was hardly the brainchild of William Manning and his friends—although state and local party committeemen may well have learned a great deal from the plebeian political subculture. Manning's writings contained a more sweeping democratic diagnosis of the country's ills than mainstream Republicans were prepared to proclaim—including, it seems, the editors of the *Independent Chronicle*. Nor did the party, as constituted, fulfill the hopes that Manning had for his Laboring Society. Within the Democratic Republican organization, subordinate units were held strictly accountable to their superiors.[139] The party's leaders, nationally and statewide, were not about to surrender their control to itinerant Jacobins like David Brown or country democrats like William Manning. Nor did Jefferson and his associates have any intention of expanding the power of the party's rank-and-file members over such potentially explosive functions as impeachments, as Manning had suggested in the 1798 draft of "The Key." Indeed, shortly after his election, Jefferson reverted to older eighteenth-century political assumptions and denied the need for further party development, now that the allegedly dangerous Federalist faction surrounding John Adams had lost control of the national government.[140]

Still, with all their differences, popular and elite opposition politics unmistakably converged at the end of the 1790s, especially around the need for an all-out popular movement to check the power of the moneyed interests. If, in the end, Jefferson's political vision held sway rather than Manning's, the national leadership of the emerging Democratic Republican party nevertheless embraced many of the plebeian democrats' key concerns. In return, the slaveholders, merchants, bankers, and lawyers at the head of the party won nearly unchallenged control of the federal government for the next generation. Dependent upon the energies and loyalties of ordinary men, they maintained this control only so long as they consistently represented the interests of the Many against the Few. The leadership's failure to meet this test in the 1820s helped give birth to the Jacksonian movement. And the party's failure in the 1840s to confront the growing threat that slavery posed to free government shattered the old allegiances, paving the way for secession and civil war.

All that, however, lay in the future. Jefferson's victory in the election of 1800 calmed widespread popular fears that the Federalists were on the verge of an irreversible triumph. It also helped move the terms of American politics in a decisively more democratic direction. Together, planters and plebeians had reduced to tatters old Federalist notions of deference, and had opened up the machinery of government as never before to continual, legitimate, and peaceful appeals from below. If this was not exactly what William Manning had in mind, we may easily imagine him reasonably pleased at the outcome.

Final Years

Unfortunately, one cannot say much about Manning after 1799 without resorting to excessive speculation. A few basic facts are clear. In 1803, he fell ill and had to rely on one of his sons to care for his land and livestock. Eleven years later, he died.[141] What was on his mind all this time?

The surviving scraps of Manning's draft correspondence prove beyond question that, despite his illness, Manning kept writing for several years after 1800.[142] Two of his fragmentary notes mention the Republicans' "complete victory" in the most recent Massachusetts elections—allusions that Manning could not have written before 1806. A longer piece speaks of a pamphlet about "Selvage's trial," which can only refer to an account of the murder trial in Boston of the lawyer Thomas O. Selfridge—first published in 1807.[143] From this we may hazard a small, safe conclusion: if Manning was emboldened by Jefferson's victory, he was not satisfied that it alone assured the well-being of the Many or of free government. His responses to Jefferson's specific policies (or those of the Massachusetts Republicans) are unknown. At some point, he did prepare a drastically shortened version of "The Key," eliminating all references to the Federalists' past abuses, but including no fresh complaints about the Jeffersonians—as if signaling his basic contentment with Jefferson's direction.[144] But he also remained certain that further democratic reform—*his* plan for reform—was still necessary.

Manning's undaunted attachment to "The Key of Liberty" is admirable. But as he continued his search for the means to implement his plan, he seems not to have noticed that the urgency he felt was no longer so widely shared. He did make an effort to keep in touch with changing political realities, shifting the focus of his appeal from the Republican printers to the state's Republican party leaders. His overall assessment of the Few and the Many certainly continued to be relevant after 1801, not least in Massachusetts, which remained a Federalist stronghold. Still, Manning appears to have been unmindful of just how thoroughly American politics had moved onto new terrain, and how his countrymen after 1801 may have been at least temporarily relieved of the sense of impending political disaster that animated "The Key." An abler talent might have thoroughly rewritten the pamphlet, recasting the eternal struggle between the Few and the Many to take account of the new political conditions. But part of Manning's soul remained stuck in 1799. We can imagine him an old sick man, poring over his manuscripts, doing his best to salvage something from his labors, hoping that somebody, somewhere, would finally listen.

The record is much clearer, sadly enough, about Manning's personal and family affairs after 1799. Observance of a proper family order, Manning had insisted in "The Key," was one of the prime social duties that we should not neglect; otherwise, "we cannot be happy here nor hereafter." These duties included an obligation to be "a kind husband and wife, a kind parent, a kind master, a kind brother and sister, a dutiful child and servant." The aged, he wrote, deserved respect; children—girls as well as boys—deserved the guarantee of a basic education. Moreover— and here he may have reflected on the prolonged dispute over his own father's will—it was important "to be always willing to forgive injuries and settle differences in the shortest and cheapest manner," an injunction which held for dealings with kin as well as with strangers.[145]

There is no way of knowing how well Manning practiced what he preached. He did aid his eldest son (who had earned a goodly sum completing contract work on the Middlesex Canal) by selling him, in 1802, a small woodlot, and then five years later deeding over half the farm to him.[146] But Manning's benevolence did not extend to his second son, Jephtha, upon whom he depended the most heavily during his declining years. Between 1798 and 1803, while Manning worked on "The Key" and speculated about how best to establish his Laboring Society, Jephtha (who also worked on the canal) provided him with more than $500. And after 1803, when Manning was too sick to work the farm any longer, Jephtha assumed primary responsibility for his care, feeding him "along with his nurses and other company."[147] Finally, in 1812, with no other alternative in sight, Jephtha sued his father for $1,500 in connection with the unpaid accounts.[148] The enfeebled elder Manning did not show up in court, and his son was awarded 107 acres of the family estate plus a half interest in the house and barn.[149]

William, Jr., and Jephtha thus assumed joint control of the whole property—effectively depriving the rest of the family of an inheritance. In such situations, which occurred regularly in settled agricultural communities like Billerica, younger brothers were expected to find other work, and sisters were expected to marry. Manning's third son, Theophilus, did his part, hiring on with the Middlesex Canal Company, first as a common laborer, then as an overseer, and finally, after the canal's completion, as the captain of a packet boat line, shuttling freight and passengers along the new waterway. Theophilus' prospects seemed assured when he married the daughter of a prosperous local saw-and-grist mill operator; after his bride died young, he married her sister, raised a family, and established himself as a Billerica landowner. One of Manning's seven daughters also married and moved away. But William and Jephtha and the remaining sisters never left home, never married, and left no direct heirs. At this distance it is impossible to say whether they hung on out of caution or out of courage.[150]

Manning died in 1814. Lacking any cash, like most small holders, he also left no will. To help settle the estate's bills and cover Manning's burial expenses, the family auctioned off what it could of his personal estate. The required probate inventory gave at best a sketchy account of what Manning had acquired over his lifetime. (Most likely, he had bequeathed to his wife and children whatever valuable items his estate contained before his death.) Prospective purchasers would have found themselves inspecting the remnants of an unexceptional life: Manning's clothing, furniture, and bedding (as in many small estates, the costliest items of all), some basic farm tools and implements, some farm produce, a gun, a sword, and five powder horns. Only one small notation on the inventory, easy enough to miss, told anything about the dead man's overriding purpose in life. Among Manning's belongings was "a lot" of books, titles unnoted, that belonged back at the Billerica Social Library.[151]

Thereafter, William Manning's remaining traces fell into obscurity. William, Jr., obtained sole rights to the farm when Jephtha died in 1834; upon William's death in 1852, his last surviving siblings, Jerusha and Lucinda, bought the property from their cousins and other kin, paying each of the relatives ten dollars. Bit by bit, the place became battered and worn. Jerusha died in 1857; a few years later, Lucinda, now past seventy, abandoned the house and moved to Chelmsford after being harassed by "tramps, gipsies and other molesters," who camped upon the grounds and drove away her cattle. She died in 1880, after arranging in her will for the property to be managed by an educational trust, with the profits going to the Baptist Church of North Billerica. Lacking the resources to maintain the grounds, the trust had trouble finding tenants and the house fell further into disrepair.[152]

At the end of the nineteenth century, a group of backpacking college students scandalized local opinion by nearly setting fire to the dilapidated Manning farmhouse. The ensuing publicity prompted one of William Manning's descendants to form the Manning Family Association, Inc., and raise money to restore the property.[153] Thanks to the association, the house still stands today on its original site, serving some of its old functions, although authenticity has partly given way to practicality: in its latest incarnation, the carefully maintained tavern houses a Szechuan Chinese restaurant. Apart from the manuscript essays and a gravestone epitaph on a nearby hillside, it is all that remains to memorialize William Manning and the world he lived in.[154]

Conclusion

In 1807, a manufacturer named Francis Faulkner arrived in Billerica and (after securing secondary water rights from the Mid-

Photograph of the Manning manse, c. 1890.

dlesex Canal Company) built New England's second woolen goods mill. Faulkner flourished—but his mill was only the harbinger for even greater enterprises elsewhere in the Middlesex countryside. In 1813, the year before William Manning died, a group of merchant capitalists in Waltham, eighteen miles away, established the Boston Manufacturing Company, hoping to collect under one management—and as nearly as possible under one roof—all the stages in the manufacture of cotton cloth, from processing the raw material to weaving the final fabric. The experiment proved successful. Ten years later, another group built even larger establishments along the Merrimack River on land adjoining Billerica, and from then on, their new city of Lowell was the dominant economic force in the area. Capitalist manufacturing, not the household-based farming economy that Manning knew, proved the wave of the future—and with it eventually came new forms of conflict between propertied owners and propertyless wage earners, conflict quite unlike anything Manning had known. Rural Massachusetts society did not utterly collapse, even in Middlesex County. It was simply more difficult to notice amid the industrializing clatter of the nineteenth century.[155]

Which brings us back to where we started, with Henry David Thoreau. The eccentric Thoreau actually did look beyond the everyday busyness of his Middlesex neighbors, whom he held in such ironic contempt. Only when he left Concord to glide downriver, past "ancient Billerica . . . now in its dotage," did he find something of an older political sensibility in the fields and faces of the farmers who remained, a sensibility he attached to the adventures and sacrifices of the Revolution.[156] Yet Thoreau had no knowledge of the political writings that had come out of that milieu. How could he? Most of it lay unpublished, or gathering dust in the files of some dead newspaper, or in the indictment records of some long-ago sedition trial. By then, the prevailing memory of the democratic impulses of 1775 was getting reduced in the heroic national mythology to the momentary struggle of the "embattled farmers" at Lexington and Concord celebrated by his neighbor Emerson. The subsequent political lives and writings of the Revolutionary foot soldiers, and the agitation some of

them helped foment after the Revolution, were already beginning to be forgotten.[157]

Yet if Manning's writings and those of others like him were
largely lost to Thoreau's generation and to the generations that
followed, they need not be lost to our own. As Manning's essays
indicate, the American Revolution fostered democratic ideas that
were at once a departure from the hierarchical, deferential
assumptions of traditional English Country party republicanism
and intensely suspicious of the emergent capitalist order. These
ideas did not peter out after 1800. Manning's way of thinking, if
not his actual words, lived for decades amid the prolonged transformation of the United States into a modern industrial nation.
Although the Laboring Society never got off the ground, many
of the basic thoughts behind it—the egalitarian interpretation of
labor as the source of all property, the critique of the moneyed
Few and their political corruptions, the hopes for an America in
which class power and privilege were neutralized by wholly constitutional means—reappeared in various political movements,
inside and outside the major parties, over the coming century.
One strand of this thinking turns up in the self-justifications of
successful nineteenth-century entrepreneurs—including such
magnates as Andrew Carnegie—who portrayed themselves as
honorable producers, pitted against the financial interests.[158] But
the main thrust of the small producers' democracy would stimulate very different kinds of men and movements, from the Anti-
Masonic and Jacksonian insurgencies and early labor movements
of the 1820s and 1830s to the Populist uprising and the permanent national trade unions of the 1880s and 1890s. Some of these
movements drew inspiration from a dense transatlantic network
of radical thinkers and political organizations; some, from a continuing plebeian intellectual tradition stretching back to Paine,
which scholars have only just begun to reconstruct.[159] Manning
failed to inform and shape that many-sided tradition—but his literary remains shed light on its early direction.

Manning's writings also underscore the remarkable political
achievements of the Democratic Republicans and their supporters in the 1790s. The Revolution had secured the right of ordinary citizens to participate in the affairs of state, but it had not

settled what their role should be. A wide range of possibilities had opened in the 1770s and 1780s, from irregular, self-appointed, popular committees of safety to established town meetings and provincial legislatures. At the close of the war, when the most popular and militant of these possibilities ceased to exist, the mass of the citizenry found its role in politics severely curtailed. Men with small property holdings could, of course, vote in most elections; and many more men were expected to play an important constitutional role in ratifying the new systems of government. But for the most part the making of decisions—the actual stuff of politics—was left to others. Ordinary men might petition their representatives; they might even protest. But they had no recognized, legitimate way to ensure that their voices would be heard, either in support of or in opposition to government policies.

The limitations of this form of popular politics became all too apparent to Manning during the Massachusetts Regulation. All the petitions, popular conventions, and protests organized to oppose the policies of Governor Bowdoin and the creditor elite got nowhere. Yet the outstanding outcome of this failure was that it goaded ordinary people like William Manning to search for, and ultimately discover, new kinds of political organization. Manning took from this the additional lesson that some permanent machinery was necessary to sustain and inform that organization—and he was not alone. Out of this continuing process of political invention would eventually emerge the mass democratic parties of the nineteenth century, one of America's most distinctive contributions to modern politics.

This contribution, in turn, reminds us of things about our political history that many Americans have been too apt to forget. Amid the momentous, continuing revolutions in what was the Communist world, we have been witnesses both to the resilience of the democratic idea and to the fact that it must be fought for, won, and continually reinvigorated in each generation if it is to survive. Thanks to the work of many historians, we now know much more than we once did about the American struggles of blacks, women, and others to secure the democratic rights denied them at the nation's founding. But we have yet to acknowledge adequately how the democracy established by the Revolution remained hotly contested at the end of the eighteenth century and the opening of the nineteenth. The Revolutionary expansion of popular political participation to include men of the lower and middling sort like William Manning, and legal protections for their rights to organized dissent, continued to be an issue for many years. As ever, democratization proceeded less from the self-protective sagacity of political elites than from the purposeful thinking and agitation of quite ordinary people. This popular, postrevolutionary ferment was not a crude, demi-intellectual upsurge. On the contrary, it was often animated—as with William Manning—by a far-reaching democratic vision that made its mark along with that of the nation's political leadership. Indeed, the two grew together.

Finally, Manning's observations speak to some uncomfortable truths about America's main political traditions from the 1790s to the present. Over the centuries, of course, numerous revolutions in American life—most dramatically the destruction of slavery—have vastly enlarged the meaning and potential of democracy in the United States. Social and political changes that Manning did not anticipate have torn away some of the most flagrantly despotic features of the early republic—including some that Manning himself took for granted. The terms of debate about politics and society have also shifted, as popular movements have learned to use the government as a means to ward off the injuries and injustices of unchecked capitalist growth. (Today, it is a top-down conservative coalition that scorns government as the foe of "we, the people"—even as that coalition's policies widen the inequalities that divide the rich from the rest of us.) Yet throughout our history, Americans have faced a challenge of deciding how best to achieve the common good. Is that good best served by maximizing the profits and opportunities of moneyed wealth? Or is it best served by directly maximizing the income and security of ordinary people? These questions and the challenge persist.

William Manning was of another age, as was his mapping of American society and politics; he himself outlived the immediate pertinence of some of his most ferocious anti-Federalist polemics. But who can say, even with all that has happened, that the

United States has fully grappled with the dilemmas of powerlessness, apathy, and corruption that Manning detected? Who can say that we have come to terms with the political inequalities and "the great scuffle" that divides the latter-day Few and the latter-day Many? Who can say that William Manning's expansive democratic principles have been fully realized anywhere in the world?

The Documents

NOTE
ON THE TEXTS
AND EDITORIAL METHODS

◆

Only one copy of "Some Proposals for Making Restitution to the Original Creditors of Government" exists—the unfinished version that Manning's family saved and deposited at the Harvard College Library. Any notes, earlier drafts, and later versions have been lost or discarded. If Manning ever submitted the manuscript to a member of the Massachusetts legislature (as he plainly intended to do), no copy has found its way into the relevant archives. A transcription of the surviving manuscript, complete with cross-outs and misspellings, was published by Ruth Bogin as "'Measures So Glareingly Unjust': A Response to Hamilton's Funding Plan by William Manning," *William and Mary Quarterly*, third series, 46 (1989), 315–331. For our own edition, we have modernized and corrected the text.

There are four surviving manuscript versions of "The Key of Liberty," with no indication that Manning wrote any others. The earliest of the four is dated March 3, 1797. In his 1799 draft, Manning recalled that he first wrote "The Key" in February 1797; this oldest surviving manuscript is almost certainly what he was referring to as that first draft, although it may be a slightly polished, transcribed version. The most obvious differences between the 1797 version and later ones are that it lacks a title and (at least as currently preserved in Harvard's Houghton Library) that it begins rather than ends with the Laboring Society constitution. In most other respects, the 1797 draft resembles the later ones, although it lacks Manning's subsequent remarks on the funding system, the Federalist cult of Washington, and various other matters.

There is no evidence that Manning actually submitted this version of "The Key" for publication, and some indication that he did not. A letter from the author to Thomas Adams and Isaac Larkin, then the editors of the *Independent Chronicle*, appears on page one of the 1797 draft, asking them "to publish the following in numbers as you can spare room." In a subsequent letter to Adams, however, Manning rehearsed their private dealings but made no mention of any contact taking place as early as 1797.

The second version of "The Key" is dated February 20, 1798, and is the one published in 1922 with an introduction by Samuel Eliot Morison. In his later letter to Adams, Manning confirmed that he had sent this draft to the *Independent Chronicle* in April 1798 and that Adams had politely turned it aside. This is the longest of the extant versions of "The Key."

Manning completed the third surviving version no later than mid-February 1799. In a letter to Adams apparently dated February 15, 1799, Manning spoke of this version as a revised and shortened draft of the one he had sent in the previous April. (Unfortunately, there is no evidence to confirm that Manning actually sent this draft to the *Chronicle*.) That the revised text in question is this third surviving draft, however, is clear from other material written by Manning around the same time.

Longer than the 1797 manuscript but condensed from the 1798 version that Morison eventually presented, the 1799 text of "The Key" is more cogent and accessible than either of the previous drafts. We have therefore chosen to publish it in preference to Morison's text. But the timing and nature of the changes suggest that Manning was concerned with more than just style when he made his editorial decisions. The last of the Alien and Sedition Acts had been passed in July 1798, and there are reasons to think that he made some of the changes with an eye on the government crackdown. For example, the 1799 draft is the only one that includes Manning's remarks about the duties of a Christian and of a benevolent husband, which he may well have added in order to deflect potential attacks on his work as impious—a common theme of the New England Federalists and their clergymen allies. The later draft also left out some of the most controversial material from 1798, including Manning's elaborations of his complaints against specific orders of the Few and his criticisms of former president George Washington. Because of the intrinsic interest of this excluded material, we have reprinted much of it in the section below entitled "Other Writings."

The fourth, drastically shortened version of "The Key" is the most curious of them all. It is impossible to date with precision. Most likely, though, Manning composed it after 1799. Its discussion of how the proposed monthly magazine might best be distributed and of how to attract "a good Republican printer in each state" places it among Manning's musings about how he might finally launch his project. Manning's severe cuts—which excised all his specific complaints about Federalist policies—might be explained by his desire to make his essay punchier and more attractive to a prospective printer. But there is also another explanation—namely, that after Jefferson's inauguration in 1801, a long rehearsal of Federalist abuses in the national government would have looked out of date.

William Manning often expressed his hope that some "learned Republican" would draft over and correct "The Key of Liberty." Within certain limits, we have honored his request, and extended it to cover all the works included here. Our aim has been to provide modern readers with clear and accessible texts.

Manning's syntax and style contained many idiosyncrasies which, when reproduced in print, block easy comprehension. He habitually used ampersands in place of the word "and"—a strain to the eyes of all but the most hardened of scholars. He also repeatedly began sentences with ampersands, or with the word *but*, in ways that grow monotonous and, at times, confusing. We decided to change silently all his ampersands into *and*s, as well as to remove the initial *and*s and *but*s except where their retention seemed justified by his rhetorical thrust.

Manning's capitalization and punctuation were inconsistent.

He was oblivious to paragraphing; at times he went on for pages with no break. (We have broken up these passages as we saw fit.) In some places, Manning ended his sentences with dashes, in others with small diagonal marks which look like periods. He capitalized some words and phrases, only to write them in lowercase elsewhere in the manuscripts. Worse, his handwriting did not always make it clear whether some letters were capitals or not. Rather than belabor readers with incessant editorial intrusions and explications, we have simply revised the inconsistencies in accordance with modern American usage. We have done the same with his spelling.

Here and there, Manning's word order, elliptical phrasing, and use of pronouns leave his meaning obscure, at least at first reading. His grammar was flawed: subjects and verbs sometimes disagree. He also occasionally repeated the same word twice in a row. In cases of unclear phrasing, we have silently edited his text in the interest of improved comprehension; never, however, have we deliberately altered the original meaning. Whenever Manning's meaning remained uncertain to us, we have retained the original wording and supplied a footnote, explaining different possible interpretations. Where the lapses are glaring, we have corrected Manning's grammar (to accord with modern American usage) and eliminated all word repetitions. We have also eliminated all the passages which Manning himself crossed out.

Manning occasionally deployed archaic English ("doth" for "does," "sayeth" for "says") when he wanted to evoke either a legal or a Biblical tone. We have left these intact. On the other hand, we corrected other now-archaic usages (e.g., "listen" for "hear," "learn" for "teach") where the original seemed confusing.

Some readers may regret our decisions. The changes dilute the manuscripts of some of their flavor, although not entirely. We recognize, too, that they render our edition unsuitable for certain kinds of scholarly research, for which only a faithful, word-for-word, solecism-for-solecism copy will suffice—or, short of that, a modern text heavy with editorial apparatus, flagging and explaining each and every change. But various factors eased our minds in editing as we did. All readers interested in an absolutely faithful copy of "Some Proposals" may consult Ruth Bogin's edition.

Likewise, Samuel Eliot Morison's corrected edition of the 1798 draft of "The Key" appears in *William and Mary Quarterly*, third series, 13 (1956), 202–254. Morison's is a fairly accurate transcription (although he made some silent emendations of his own, especially with Manning's paragraph structure). For those scholars who wish to have a more accurate copy of that version of "The Key," we have prepared a list of the Morison edition's transcription errors and silent revisions of wording and placed it on deposit at Houghton Library. Finally, for those interested in reconstructing a closer approximation of Manning's original text of the 1799 "Key," we have also compiled a list of all our additions, deletions, and substitutions (not including punctuation) and have deposited it at Houghton.

As for the annotation, we have not attempted to elucidate every obscure reference in the manuscripts. To have done so would have made for an overlong manuscript of our own. We have tried, simply, to provide the information necessary for all interested readers to understand what was on Manning's mind.

The original 1922 edition of *The Key of Libberty*, published in Billerica and introduced by Samuel Eliot Morison, received two long and favorable reviews in the radical press: "The Key of Libberty," *The Freeman* 7 (May 2, 1923), 173–174; and James O'Neal, "An Early Labor Philosopher," *The Call Magazine* (New York), June 10, June 17, and June 24, 1923. On the strength of O'Neal's remarks, Manning rated one line both in Max Nettlau, *Der Vorfrühling der Anarchie* (Berlin, 1925), 106; and in Rudolph Rocker, *Pioneers of American Freedom: Origin of Liberal and Radical Thought in America* (New York, 1949), 51. An analysis of Manning's syntax, orthography, and voice appeared in Henry Alexander, "A Sidelight on Eighteenth-Century American English," *Queen's Quarterly* 31 (1923), 173–181.

The first serious flurry of academic interest in Manning occurred after the outbreak of World War II. Merle Curti, Willard Thorpe, and Carlos Baker included an excerpt from "The Key" in their well-known documentary collection *American Issues: The Social Record* (1941; 4th ed. Chicago, 1960), 186–194. Eugene Perry Link cited Manning's work several times in his fine study *Democratic Republican Societies, 1790–1800* (New York,

1942), 49, 91, 96, 158, 175; and Curti included a brief discussion of "The Key" in *The Growth of American Thought* (1943; 2nd ed. New York, 1951), 141–142. An excerpt also appeared in a collection of popular early American political writings, edited by Irving Mark and Eugene Schwaab, *The Faith of Our Fathers: An Anthology Expressing the Aspirations of the American Common Man, 1760–1860* (New York, 1952), 358–361.

In 1956, Lawrence Towner reprinted "The Key," together with Morison's introduction, as "William Manning's 'Key of Libberty,' " in *William and Mary Quarterly*, third series, 13 (1956), 202–254, thereby making the entire text much more easily available to scholars. Richard Hofstadter included an extended but misleading discussion of Manning's views on education and the learned professions in his *Anti-Intellectualism in American Life* (New York, 1963), 151–153. Carl Bridenbaugh cited Manning in passing in *The Spirit of '76: The Growth of American Patriotism before Independence* (New York, 1975), 149. More recently, references to Manning and his writings have turned up in Richard Bushman, "Massachusetts Farmers and the Revolution," in Richard M. Jellison, ed., *Freedom, Society, and Conscience: The American Revolution in Virginia, Massachusetts, and New York* (New York, 1976); Barbara Karsky, "Le Paysan américain et la terre à la fin du XVIIIe siècle," *Annales: E.S.C.* 38 (1983), 1374, 1385, 1388; Michael Kammen, *A Machine That Would Go of Itself: The Constitution in American Culture* (New York, 1987), xxiii; Ruth Bogin, "Petitioning and the New Moral Economy of Post-Revolutionary America," *William and Mary Quarterly*, third series, 46 (1989), 315–331; Nathan O. Hatch, *The Democratization of American Christianity* (New Haven, 1989), 26–27, 128; Gordon S. Wood, *The Radicalism of the American Revolution* (New York, 1992), 276–277; and Christopher Tomlins, *Law, Labor, and Ideology in the Early American Republic* (Cambridge, forthcoming 1993).

SOME PROPOSALS FOR MAKING RESTITUTION TO THE ORIGINAL CREDITORS OF GOVERNMENT

1790

◆

The first Continental Congress assumed control of the revolutionary war effort in 1775 without having the means to pay for it, and had to rely on a series of ad hoc measures to keep its armies in the field. These measures included issuing millions of dollars worth of unfunded currency notes; giving the army permission simply to requisition or impress needed supplies along its line of march; borrowing from investors and suppliers, both foreign and domestic, in return for loan certificates or government bonds; and, finally, asking the states to levy taxes and contribute the sums raised to the cause. The burden of the first and last of these measures fell fairly equitably on the whole citizenry, in rough proportion to any one individual's ability to pay. But the government's proposals to repay the remainder of the outstanding debt raised a bitter controversy.

The bulk of the outstanding debt had been originally issued to small holders in amounts of $500 or less. Over the course of the war, however, most of the certificates fell into the hands of a relatively small number of moneyed men, who purchased them at a considerable discount. In 1790, Alexander Hamilton, the newly appointed secretary of the Treasury, proposed repaying the outstanding debt at its face value—thereby ensuring an enormous windfall profit to the speculators who had purchased the certificates. Manning took strong exception to Hamilton's plan, and his outrage prompted him to write "Some Proposals."

Some Proposals
For Making Restitution to the Original Creditors of Government
and
To Help the Continent to a Medium of Trade
Submitted to the Consideration of
The Member of the State Legislature of Massachusetts,
February the 6th, 1790

◆

Some proposals for Makeing Restitution to the Original Credi=tors of Gobernment & to helpe the Continant to a Mediam of trade — Submited to the Consideration of the Member of the State Legislator of Massachusets February the 6th 1790 —

Honoured Sir by Reading the Many altercations, proposals & Disputes in the publick papers about funding & the Manner of paying the Continantal & State Debt, I have bin Led to a Serious Consideration of the afare & although I am not an Original Creditor nor anyway Interested in the Desition of it More than as a Member of the Society, yet I Cannot but Vue with Abhorance all the argu=ments that have as yet bin offered in favour of paying the hole Sume to the present holders, formely Believing that if it Shold be done it would eventually prove the Destruction of our Dear bought Libertyes &, of all the State Governments & these Gloom=

=My apprehentions are heightned when I See by the proposals of the Secretary of treasury to Congress how fast they approch to a Kong Desition & No alhenticated plan or Sittion is offered in oppostion thereto. Being thus purswaded although I have Nither Larning nor ability for the purpose yet to Clear My Selfe from the Guilt Contenting or parsively Submiting to Measures So Glaringly unjust I have Composed & beg that you would Seriously & thoroughly Examine the following arguments & plan which are in oppostion to D Measure & Mak Such use of them as you think best —

In order to give My Sentiments fully & plainly I have Divided them into Six General heads or parts in the following Order In the 1st I have Indeavoured to Shew in Short terms the unjustness of paying the hole Sume to the present holders —

First page of William Manning's manuscript "Some proposals for Makeing Restitution to the Original Creditors of Government & to helpe the Continant to a Mediam of trade," 1790.

Honored Sir:

By reading the many altercations, proposals, and disputes in the public papers about funding and the manner of paying the continental and state debts, I have been led to a serious consideration of the affair. And although I am not an original creditor nor anyway interested in the decision of it more than as a member of the society, yet I cannot but view with abhorrence all the arguments that have as yet been offered in favor of paying the whole sum of the debt to its present holders—firmly believing that if it should be done, it would eventually prove the destruction of our dear-bought liberties and of all the state governments.

These gloomy apprehensions are heightened when I see by the proposals of the secretary of Treasury to Congress how fast they approach to a wrong decision, and how no authenticated plan or system is offered in opposition thereto.[1] Being thus persuaded, although I have neither learning nor abilities for the purpose, yet to clear myself from the guilt of consenting or passively submitting to measures so glaringly unjust, I have composed, and beg that you would seriously and thoroughly examine, the following arguments and plan—which are in opposition to said measures—and make such use of them as you think best.

In order to give my sentiments fully and plainly, I have divided them into six general heads, or parts, in the following order:

In the first, I have endeavored to show in short terms the unjustness of paying the whole sum to the present holders.

In the second, I have proposed a plan to make restitution to the original creditors and to help the continent to a medium of trade.

In the third, in order to remove the prejudices that are against paper money, I have first given a short description of the nature of money and justice; and then raised and answered sundry objections that will be the most likely to be made against it.

In the fourth, I have shown why hard money is scarce in America and that we have no reason to expect a medium of silver and gold at present.

In the fifth, I have shown how it is that a few men of great influence are interested unconstitutionally to oppose such a plan as this, and then considered separately sundry plans that have been made instead thereof.

In the sixth, I have enumerated sundry advantages we might receive from such a plan and the disadvantages' for want thereof, and then shown which I think would be the most prudent and likely way to get it adopted.

Part I

◆

*WHICH IS TO SHOW THE UNJUSTNESS OF PAYING
THE WHOLE SUM TO THE PRESENT HOLDERS*

Many and loud are the arguments in favor of this measure, and I have no doubt they are greatly interested.

The principal ones are: that the governments' promise was to such-a-one or to the bearer; that the governments did receive the full value of what they promised to pay; that it has been the custom of nations to fulfill such promises to the bearer, let them depreciate as much as they will; and that we must do so, too, or there will be no trust put in us in the future.[2]

To which I would answer: the government did both receive and promise to pay the full value of said securities. And if the original creditors had promised to wait ten years for their pay, and then had instead sold their securities for one shilling on the pound, in that case the government would in justice have been obliged to pay the full sum to the bearer, and the original creditor would not have had any reason to complain of being taxed to redeem them—for they did as they pleased with their property.

But will anybody dare to say that this was the case? Did the poor soldiers—when they had the promise of the government to be paid once in three months and had waited two or three years for their pay, and were then discharged and sent home to their needy families with nothing but certificates stating that there was so much due to them from a government that had broken its promises so many times already and had neither funds established nor time set for the payment thereof—I say, did these poor soldiers act voluntarily in selling their certificates under par? Surely, no.

Or did the other public creditors—who lent their money or did other services for the government; and waited the time they had agreed to; and then were obliged to have their securities scaled down (by which many of them lost in their original value); and then agreed to wait another term; and afterwards waited until the same government (by compelling them to pay their private debts and taxes in hard money) obliged them to sell their public securities for what they would fetch, when they could get neither interest nor principal from the government—I say again, did these act voluntarily? Surely, no.

In all these cases, the original creditors of the government acted more like persons beset with robbers and prudently delivered up their purses rather than their lives. Shall the government now go on—under a pretense of fulfilling its obligations—and tax those sufferers to pay the full sum to those who never gave one-quarter of the value for them? The heavens forbid our committing such a horrid deed as this. Every honest man must shudder at the thought of it.

We might go on to pay the present holders a thousand times over, and then a great part of the sum would be still due the original creditors. Let other nations do as they will. No person in his senses would trust such a government when in distress a second time. The only way to maintain public or private credit is to do justice to the original creditors and make restitution and compensation to those who helped us in time of need as soon as we are able.

But the great question is, how shall restitution be made and justice be done in this case, when neither Congress nor the states have either money or credit to do it with. Which brings me to the second part.

Part II

◆

A PLAN TO MAKE RESTITUTION TO THE ORIGINAL CREDITORS
AND HELP THE CONTINENT TO A MEDIUM OF TRADE.

1. Let Congress pass an act that all the government's domestic securities shall be redeemed only at eight shillings on the pound, and that it shall make a restitution to all the original creditors of said debt (excepting the commutation pay to the officers of the army) of twelve shillings on the pound—to be paid in paper money as hereafter described. Also, let all the states pass similar acts on their debts.

2. Then let Congress make a bank of paper money at least sufficient to pay all the old Continental Army a second time their twelve shillings on the pound and pay them or their heirs immediately. And let there be a sinking fund on said money of 5 percent which will redeem it all in twenty years. Also let it be receivable and a lawful tender in all past and future contracts, debts and taxes—excepting such part of the impost as Congress shall judge necessary to pay the foreign debt with; such future contracts as shall be made with full understanding between the parties for hard money; and also such private foreign debts as by the treaties of peace were to be paid in sterling money.

3. In order to keep up the value of the money, let there be taxes of all kinds, equally assessed and vigorously collected, so that all the public creditors, both continental and state, may be paid as fast as they want it. And if the money should depreciate so as not to do justice to the creditors, let it be detained in the Treasury until it will fetch its just value.

4. In order to do justice to those who have suffered losses by the depreciation of the public securities down from the original creditor to the present holder—also to include those persons that may suffer by sharpers taking advantage of their ignorance of the turn of the times and purchasing their property on trust expecting to pay less than full value—let there be a scale of depreciation fixed as near as possible in each state. And let it be strongly rec-

ommended to all persons concerned therein that they settle with their antagonists on reasonable terms if possible; or take their disputes to indifferent persons to judge for them, whose judgment shall be final.

For those who can't settle in this way, let there be juries chosen or drafted in each county to sit as a court of inquiry and hear all complaints against persons for refusing to settle such demands. If, on hearing such complaints and evidences, two-thirds of said jury are of the opinion that restitution ought to be made, let them give the complainant a certificate specifying the cause, as represented to them, and recommend a settlement to the person complained of. And let the complainer pay the jury's cost.

If the person complained of refuses to settle for the space of three months after this, then let the complainer prosecute at a court of law, as in other cases, allowing a trial by jury. But let there be a time fixed on after which no complaint or action of this kind shall be brought, excepting on special occasions.

Although the last proposal will be attended with considerable trouble and difficulty, and justice will not be attained exactly, yet the fault will not lie in government but in individuals and it will soon be over. The great difficulty will be to remove the prejudices of the people against paper money. Which brings me to the third part.

Part III

In order to remove the prejudices that are against paper money, I shall first give a short description of money and justice; and then I shall raise and answer sundry objections that will be the most likely to be made against it.

1. Money is not property when considered in itself, but only a representative thereof and is simply this: a thing of lighter carriage than property which a man may carry in his pocket and use to purchase anything he wants therewith, whether for necessity, convenience, or comfort. It matters not what is made use of for a medium, provided it will pass currently. For instance, if a dollar or a piece of paper or a chip or a cob pass currently all over a

nation for two bushels of corn or any other property to the value of the said corn—whether it does so by consent or by law, it makes no difference—it is a representative of so much property.

2. Strict and plain justice between debtor and creditor is that the former pay unto the latter the full value of what he received with interest therefor, and no more; viz., if I sell unto a man sixty bushels of corn (or a yoke of oxen or any other kind of property to the value of said corn) for nine pounds or thirty dollars and trust him a year, then when he pays me he ought to give me so much as will purchase said property again with interest, and no more—provided said property is just as plenty [i.e., costs the same] as when the debt was contracted.[3]

Thus I have in short terms given my ideas of money and justice. I shall next proceed to raise and answer sundry objections which are likely to be made to the plan.

Objection 1: But saith the creditors both public and private that paper money will depreciate and I shall lose a great part of my property.

Answer: First, the creditors should consider that by far the greatest part of the debts now due were contracted in paper money times. Although they have been reduced down by the scale of depreciation enacted by the Continental Congress to the value of silver at that time, yet it is evident that hard money will fetch more than double now to what it would then or for several years after paper money died.

Also, more than half the remainder of the debt now due was contracted before the war. During the depreciation of paper money, it was excused from taxes by law and a creditor has paid none on it in but few instances ever since.

Also, the public creditors have received payments and forbearance money of the government, as have many of the private creditors, while the debtors—who are a vast deal more numerous than the creditors—have been taxed and have paid, in many instances, for the property they owed far more than it will now fetch (which is all the creditors ought to have been paid).

Also, the creditor in paper money times would take neither principal nor interest, but immediately after silver money came again debtors were called on for five or six years' interest. And taxes were still continuing high and the prices of land, labor, and produce were falling fast—which brought debtors into a most distressed situation and has proved the ruin of thousands who, if they could have had justice done them, would be living well now. Also, when these debts were contracted any kind of property would fetch cash with little or no trouble, but now there are but few articles that will fetch it and it costs debtors almost as much as they are worth to turn them into cash—and in many instances I have known it to cost more—by which distresses they are obliged to spend what little time they can get for the purpose in laboring on the best of their lands in order to get the most present profit, by which their farms are impoverished and almost ruined. Besides all this they have suffered from hard-hearted usurers; from being compelled to give unlawful fees to the judicial and executive powers; and from being obliged to spend a vast deal of time and money in settling their affairs and quieting their creditors, which would have been needless had there been a sufficiency of money.

All these things considered, the debtors in general now pay as much as three pounds for every one pound they owe—so that the creditors could have no reason to complain if the paper money should depreciate to that degree, but would receive their just due. (I do not mention this supposing that it will ever depreciate so much—for if they will only attend to the following description of our circumstances and see the great difference there is between what they were then and what they now are, then they must suppose that it will be entirely our own fault if the money does depreciate much.)

Second, when the war began and the governments first made paper money, it was laid out immediately for supplies for the army, chiefly in and near the seaports, and business of all kinds (except preparing for war) was struck dead—so that the money did not circulate back into the countryside very quickly.

Also, the people were not acquainted with but one mode of taxation and collection.[4] Consequently, the government could not tax the people equally sufficient to keep the money good; and if they had attempted it, the people would have been discouraged and, by the influence of the Tories, gone back and joined the enemy—so that we had no other way to do but keep making paper money.

Also, not only Congress but each state kept making paper money according to their necessities, and on different plans, until it was said there were nearly fifty sorts in circulation at one time.

Besides all this, there were vast quantities of counterfeit money flung into circulation by our enemies, both from within and without. Also, our ignorance of the nature of money, the weakness of our governments, and the inequality of the prices of things throughout the continent gave great advantage to hawkers and speculators, who cheated the honest farmer and laborer out of a great part of their property.

Under all these disadvantages in the infancy of our governments, when we were involved in a war with one of the most powerful nations in Europe—I say under all these circumstances and disadvantages—it is a matter of wonder and one of the greatest proofs of the virtues of America that the paper money kept good for so long as it did.

Third, we have scarcely any of these disadvantages to encounter now in this plan. By the money being paid to the old Continental Army, it will be circulated all over the continent at once. Our governments are all established, and have but little else to do but regulate our money and pay our debts. Also, in the place of fourteen, there is but one government to regulate it.[5] Instead of fifty sorts of money, there will be but one (except hard money) to puzzle the people with. Also we are used to almost every mode of taxation and collection. And as to its being counterfeited—by its being in the Treasury so often and by its quick circulation, the money will be more easily detected and kept from being counterfeited than both hard money and the vast quantity of orders and public securities that are now in circulation.

Under all these advantages, it must be the fault of government if the money should depreciate.

Objection 2: But the people will not like the proposed money nor understand it, because it is not to be redeemed with hard money.

Answer: Money is generally (and rightly) called the blood of the community, and whenever it is kept out of circulation the people are injured by it. Consequently, it is as just to tax it as any other property. And by this plan it will certainly all be redeemed in twenty years, and those that keep it by them will pay the tax and we shall be at no cost for assessing or collecting it.

As to people not understanding how to deal in money, it can't be too hard to learn as many other things they have been subjected to—such as the scale of depreciation, and the numerous kinds of orders and money we have been perplexed with in years back. The manner of dealing in it will be plainly this: in paying debts that are now due, the depreciation of 5 percent must be cast from the date of the money to the time it is paid; and in contracts that are made after the money, they must be cast from the contract until the payment. The real value of all money in trading is what it will fetch the possessor—so that it is nothing more than to know how to cast interest, and 5 or 11 percent is as easy to cast as 6.

Objection 3: But perhaps some will say it is a new, unprecedented thing and will be a disgrace to our national character.

Answer: That it is not newer than our circumstances are. We have chosen and established a new kind of government, and if this plan will enable us to do justice among ourselves and pay what we owe to other nations, it would be no matter what they thought of it.

But that is supposing it were entirely new, which is not the case. If I am rightly informed, Holland or some other parts of the states thereof, after their war was over and in similar circumstances with us, ran out three rank of such kind of money before they got hard money enough for a medium, and they were not in half so good circumstances to regulate it as we are now.

Objection 4: But how will Congress pay our foreign debt if we have a paper medium?

Answer: Let Congress lay an impost on foreigners and on such articles as can bear it best, sufficient to pay the interest at least on the foreign debt. Also let Congress purchase from among ourselves shipping and such articles as will circulate or sell best in the nations where Congress owes, and then send those articles there, and sell them for what they will fetch, and pay it so.[6]

Objection 5: But, saith the salary and fee men, what shall we do if the money should depreciate?

Answer: Such men as we must have, if their salaries fall, it is the business of government to make additions thereto.

Objection 6: But saith the merchants that are indebted to foreigners by the treaty of peace with Great Britain: we are obliged to pay our foreign debts in sterling money, and how shall we pay them if we have a paper medium?

Answer: That if said debts must be paid in money, we can spare it the better for having paper. And if they can be paid in anything, the paper money is as good for the merchants as it is for anybody. It would be infinitely better for the continent to have them all turn bankrupts than to have them trade and send off the money as they have done for many years back—which I shall show under the next general part.

Objection 7: But paper money will either cause silver and gold to be hoarded up or sent out of the country; and as we must have hard money some time or other, we had as good reason to worry about it now as ever.

Answer: That if this is true, the same may be said of bank money orders, certificates, or any other kind of credit or barter, all of which are used instead of money. It is evident that almost all of our business is done in this way, and has been so almost ever since the country was first settled. Many of the states have always had paper money and kept it good, equal to silver and gold. But the plain truth is that if Congress and our merchants were all out of debt to foreigners, if labor, manufactures and produce were as cheap here as in the old countries, and if we exported more in value than we imported, then the balance of trade would be in our favor and money would grow plenty.

But this is not the case, for, by the misconduct of our merchants or the want of a due regulation to our trade, they have not only run themselves vastly into debt to foreigners but also sent almost all the money out of the country (which I shall show under the next part). Paper money cannot cause the exportation of what is already gone, nor cause anybody to hoard up that which they cannot get.

Also, the largeness of our domestic debt, which is computed by the secretary of the Treasury at 70 million dollars, was contracted when money was excessive or plenty, and it demands plenty of money and quick circulation to repay it with.[7] By this plan Congress would have time to regulate trade and give encouragement to the importation of hard money to supply the place of the paper as that dies away.

In short, I think it is the quickest way, if not the only way, to get a medium of hard money and believe that many others will think so too if they will only consider thoroughly what I shall offer under the next part.

Part IV

◆

WHICH IS TO SHOW WHY HARD MONEY IS SCARCE IN THIS COUNTRY AND THAT WE HAVE NO REASON TO EXPECT A MEDIUM OF IT AT PRESENT.

In order to do this I shall here insert sundry things that have been published to the world as truth and reason—with such contradictions as I have heard of—respecting the balance of trade and debts of our merchants.[8]

By accounts laid before the British Parliament in the year 1765, it was asserted that from the returns of the Customs House books, the balance of trade between the then North American colonies for nine years back (viz., from 1756 to 1764, inclusive) stood as follows: exported from Great Britain to America, £18,338,199; imported from America, £7,713,506; balance against America, £10,624,693, or £1,800,000 yearly. The merchants then owed above £5,000,000 to Britain.

By another account laid before Parliament in 1774, America had imported from Great Britain in the years 1771, 1772, and 1773 £10,500,000 in value of merchandise, or £3,500,000 annually; and that the American merchants owed the British merchants at least 6 millions of money, all of which lay on interest during the war, which made it nearly 9 millions.

It has also been said that by the extravagant importations since the war, American merchants have (instead of paying their debts) gotten into debt near 6 millions more. This, if it is true, is not to be wondered at when we consider further what extravagances we have run into since the war in importations and consumption of foreign articles. At the close of the war there was a large quantity of hard money among us, and by reason of the large sums of paper money that had lately died away, the prices of everything were exceedingly high. Our governments being young and our trade without regulation, foreigners from all parts of Europe came hither with their manufactures and produce, where they could sell and get cash for their goods at more than double what they could get anywhere else, and they could carry the money away.

Also, our own merchants could make double by carrying money for goods compared to what they could get by carrying our produce and lumber. Consequently they carried but a little else. Scarcely a ship went for several years but what carried large sums. In one, according to the accounts in London, was carried upwards of £200,000 sterling. From the great profits the merchants made at first by trading in this way, and since they were not considering how soon the money would leave them, they got trusted for goods and brought them here until finally they were obliged to sell them for much less than their sterling cost.

Not because they did not make fools of enough of the people to purchase the goods so long as they were able—for almost the whole continent was clothed from head to foot in foreign manufactures, and most of the clothes were of the poorest kind, that were scarcely worth owning. And not only clothes: the merchants brought every kind of article for use ready made, even horseshoes and toothpicks, and also very humanely—to suit our circumstances as we were then acting—they brought a number of coffins, ready made.

In one year which was 1784, there was imported upwards of 8 million pounds worth.[9] If these things are true which have been published as facts—and from our own knowledge they appear provable—we have no reason to wonder why money is scarce in America. For if our stone walls had been money they would have all been carried off soon, because money as naturally goes where it will fetch the most as water runs down hill.[10] So that not only is it the case that this enormous debt of the merchants (which is near fifteen millions sterling), and our foreign national debt (which is twelve million dollars) must be paid before hard money will come and stay on the continent; but we must also labor and manufacture things as cheap here as they do in other countries—which will not only dishearten people but prove the ruin of the country. For according to calculations of those who pretend to be judges, it takes nearly three times the labor in this new and uncultivated country to bring produce to maturity compared to what it doth in old countries, where they have been under cultivation for two or three thousand years.

Consequently the price of labor has always been higher in this country by near three for one and is no damage to us either—provided we would live within ourselves and let foreign trade and manufactures alone. It is from this cause chiefly that our merchants have been continually getting into debt ever since they traded in foreign manufactures, and they will continue so to do until we have a medium that will not pass off of the continent.

Thus, I think it is plainly evident that the immense debt that the Congress and our merchants have contracted with foreigners, our improvidence in sending the money out of the country, and also the necessity of the price of labor holding higher here than in other countries, render it not only unlikely but next akin to impossible that we should have a medium of hard money at present—which brings me to the fifth part.

Part V

◆

*WHICH IS TO SHOW HOW A FEW MEN OF GREAT INFLUENCE
ARE INTERESTED TO OPPOSE SUCH A PLAN AS THIS
UNCONSTITUTIONALLY AND THEN CONSIDER SUNDRY
PLANS THAT ARE OFFERED INSTEAD THEREOF.*

First, it is asserted by many that government is founded in property. But be that as it may. The following are not only allowed but provable truths: that the rich have great power and influence over the poor; that self in the best of men is too much like an object that is placed before the eye, which hinders the sight of anything beyond; and that touch a man's interest (or his ideas thereof) and we may be sure to have him in opposition with his full strength; also, that in all governments there are naturally two distinct, contending parties and that the great dividing line is between those that labor for a living and those who get one without laboring—or, as they are generally termed, the Few and the Many; and, further, that there is nothing which excites jealousy between these Few and Many more than the alterations of money affairs.

The reasons for it are obviously these; viz., as the interests and property of the Few consist chiefly in rents, money at interest, salaries, and fees—which are established on money and which come out of the Many—they are interested in having money scarce and the prices of things as low as possible. For instance, if they could reduce the prices by one half, it would in its operation be just the same to them as though their salaries were doubled.

And these are not all the advantages the Few receive from the scarcity of money (especially the lawyers and the judicial and executive powers of government), for it brings the Many into wants and necessities and obliges them to come to them for justice, mercy, and forbearance—so that it not only doubles the value of their fees but adds double and treble to their employments.

So that although it is not only implied but fully expressed in almost all the constitutions on the continent that all men are born free and equal and have an equal right to defend their lives, liberties, and properties; and that government was instituted for the common good, not for the profit, honor, or private interest of any one man, family, or class of men; and that the desires and interests of the majority of the great body of the people ought to control in all matters of government; and also that a great part of these Few are under oath to support these constitutions; yet it being so contrary to their private interests, it cannot be expected that the Few will be forward for this plan.[11] But on the contrary that from these Few, together with those who have gotten their public securities for a trifle, there will be a formidable body of powerful men who will combine in opposition thereto and will make every shift, turn, and proposal to hinder it from taking place.

Here, before I proceed any further, I would observe that I would not have it thought by what I have said that I think all those who can get a living without work are thus hostile to the rights of mankind. But on the contrary I verily believe that there always was and always will be some of all professions who from pure principles of virtue are strong advocates for the rights of mankind, and who will not only forgo their private interest but risk their lives and characters in the cause of liberty. Also that from the general knowledge of these rights in America among the laborers, and by the largeness of their numbers caused by the necessity of so much labor being done here, I believe that we shall soon unite so strongly with those of great abilities as to bear down and destroy all the influences of those that oppose our liberties and to establish them so as to be the most happy people that ever lived on earth.

But to return: those of the Few who will oppose this plan are as sensible of the need of a medium of trade as anybody or persons whatsoever. Now they have got a government established at such a distance from the influence of the common people that they think their interests and influence will always have the greatest sway,[12] they begin to tell us of the need of a large quantity of circulating property in this country; they tell us that some of their best judges say that the whole of the national debt put into circulation would not be too much; also they tell us of the great importance of attending to the interests of the farmers and common laborers, and of the great disadvantages and frauds we have been subjected to in years back for want of a medium of trade by orders and certificates, etc. (See "The Observer" in almost all his ten first numbers, and proposals of the secretary of the Treasury to Congress.)[13]

But let us attend to what they propose for a remedy—which is (1) bank money, and (2) funding the public securities and paying the interest punctually to the present holders so that they may pass currently as gold and silver at their nominal value—and see whether it will be for our benefit or not.

First, as to the banks, they are of the most pernicious consequences to the common people—for in order to establish them, they first collect a large quantity of silver and gold together (which is the only sort of money that will pay either debts or taxes) and have it lie entirely dead and out of circulation; then, they make their bills so large and returnable so often that they are of no service in small trades and cannot circulate into the country. By this the merchants are furnished with a medium that answers their end, while the country people have none. And so those who established the banks (and the merchants served by them) have it in their power to reduce the prices of labor, manufactures, and produce to what level they please.

Second, the same may be said of the public securities: that they are so large that they will not answer in small trades and are no tender in discharge of either debts or taxes; also that they are chiefly owned in the seaports—so that the country can have no advantage of their circulation, but must be driven about like slaves to pay the interest of them in hard money, which is mostly sent out of the country or shut up in the banks by the merchants.

By these distresses, the prices of land, labor, and produce will be continually falling until these sharpers will be able with their securities to purchase whole townships at a time and bring us into lordships. In these circumstances, with the state governments being not desired by the great ones and with the common people not able to support them, they must soon fall and come to nothing.

These are the two principal plans that are pursued by those Few who would be glad to enslave the country—which if they can obtain will answer their ends to all intents. But there are sundry other plans which many are in favor of who either think we have money enough for a medium, or who despair of ever having any.[14]

One is not to establish any funds for the redemption of the public securities but grant a tax for that purpose to be paid in orders and certificates—so that the people may purchase them under par from the creditors. But this would operate very unjustly. Many of the public creditors who have the greatest and most just demand for their pay will be obliged to sell their securities at the lowest level, while those that are more able will keep them till the last and get the full value of those that are least able to pay. Also this plan will give liberty to hawkers and sharpers to continue their taking advantage of the honest parts of the community, by making them give double what the creditors sell for.

Another plan is to reduce the public securities down and fund them at their present going value. But this would be an evident and bare-faced breach of faith in government, which would destroy all their credit in future.

Another is to redeem them at one-half their nominal value and to make a restitution of the other half to the original creditors. But this would be attended with as much difficulty as my plan would be, and we should have no relief as to a medium of trade. The public in general would pay, and the public creditors in general would receive—as I have already shown—nearly three for one. Also, the private debtors could have no relief in this way, but would be obliged to pay their debts in hard money—which would be three times their value, as above recited.

These private debtors are vastly more numerous than the creditors, and (as the case in general is now circumstanced) have not only as good a right to justice as the creditors but ought to have the preeminence. The late war was principally carried on by the middling sort of people who, from the scarcity of money and the goodness of private credit before the war, were greatly in debt to the great men; and these great men were principally against the war. Many of them turned Tories and joined the enemy. A great part of those who stayed behind were so fearful of our being overcome that they did not advance their property so freely as those who were less able. Also those who were friendly to the cause took in their debts in paper money when it was depreciated, so that they lost a great part thereof. The remainder they lent to government, by which it has met with another reduction, until in many instances they have become debtors only by being friendly to the cause.

All these things considered which are facts, I think if the measures of government must favor one side or the other, the debtors ought to have it.

Thus having shown how some are interested to oppose the plan, and having considered what is proposed instead thereof, I shall proceed to the last part.

[The manuscript breaks off here.]

THE KEY
OF LIBERTY
[1799]

◆

Manning started writing "The Key of Liberty" in response to the prolonged public controversy over Jay's Treaty. Signed in 1794, the treaty settled a number of outstanding issues between Great Britain and the United States on terms many Americans thought humiliating. Antitreaty forces organized furiously to block its implementation, even after the U.S. Senate voted its formal approval in June 1795. Seizing upon a constitutional ambiguity, the treaty's opponents in the House of Representatives threatened to withhold the funds necessary to carry out the treaty's terms. The Federalists counterattacked by having local organizers flood the House with protreaty petitions, while proadministration papers warned of an impending war with Britain unless the treaty was carried into effect. Under the onslaught, House Republicans who had any political weakness whatsoever faced heavy public and private pressure. The tie-breaking vote in favor of the treaty was cast by a member of the Democratic Republican opposition, Frederick Muhlenberg of Pennsylvania, chairman of the Committee of the Whole. Early in the controversy, he had received a warning from the Federalist father of his prospective daughter-in-law that "if you do not give us your vote, your son shall not have my Polly"; after the vote, he was stabbed by his brother-in-law, a Republican hothead.

"The Key of Liberty" announced Manning's unswerving loyalty to the antitreaty cause. It also proclaimed his disgust at the Federalists' tactics in the latter stages of the battle—an object lesson, he thought, in how the Few would stop at nothing to overwhelm the Many and obstruct free government.

THE KEY OF LIBERTY

Showing the Causes Why a Free Government Has Always Failed
and a Remedy against It.
Addressed to the
Republicans, Farmers, Mechanics, and Laborers in America
by a Laborer
[1799]

◆

The Key of Libberty

Shewing the Causes, why a free Government has always failed. & a Reamidy against it. Adresed to the Republicans. Farmers. Mecanicks & Labourers in America by a Labourer

The Content

The Preface

To the Reader

The following adress was written In February 1797 Just after the Brittish Treaty was adopted. & though it has bin Sence Drafted over & Some what altered—yet as party Spirit has bin high it May be Looked upon as two Ridged in Some parter of it. & as the author is not Mastter of the

The Contents

THE PREFACE

To the Reader:

The following address was written in February 1797, just after the British treaty was adopted. Though it has been since drafted over and somewhat altered, yet as party spirit has been high, it may be looked upon as too rigid in some parts of it. And as the author is not master of the arts of spelling, grammar, and composition, it may be disagreeable on that account. Also, many may not discern, or may totally deny, the different interests between the Few and Many as described in it.

Yet your candid attention and thorough perusal are requested to the remedy proposed—for if the doctrine is not true, I think there is no better method to convince the people of it than by getting them thoroughly possessed of the knowledge described below. The proposed means of obtaining it is simple and easy. It is only a cheaper and more sure way than by common newspapers, which have of late become so numerous, lengthy, and contradictory that farmers and laborers cannot be at the expense of the time and money they cost.

Here, in order to convey my ideas more clearly, I will give a further description of the proposed monthly magazine.

It is meant by it to convey as nearly all the knowledge described below as possible. But a magazine containing forty or fifty pages of a common pamphlet size would be full large enough for the perusal of a common laborer. In order to lay a good foundation for obtaining said knowledge, it is proposed to have the first numbers contain both the state and federal constitutions, complete with all their amendments and some of the principles on which they were founded. Also, a congressional register from the first Congress in 1789 to this time, with the names of the members of each Congress and the numbers of votes they were chosen by; and the yeas and nays on some of the most important matters they have decided upon, together with the substance of the most important speeches made on both sides. Also, a state register in nearly the same manner, with many other things relating to what is passed, etc. If many of the first numbers were fitted with such things, it would show how negligent we have been in elections, and how to remedy it in future. It would also be a strong inducement to those that take the magazine to wrap them together in yearly volumes and preserve them safe to the latest generations.

Some may suppose that the organization proposed, and the duties of the presidents described below and in Article III of the Constitution, to be both needless and dangerous—especially some of the orders of the Few, who have long enjoyed those privileges themselves and wished to exclude others from them. But the duties of the officers of the proposed organization are equally the right and privilege of every person, and there is no more danger of opposition to government from such a society than there is from the Cincinnati, the Freemasons, or any other order of the Few.[1] On the contrary, it is presumed that if such a society had been formed twelve years ago, it would have prevented all the insurrections that have happened since the Revolution; and that it is the most sure, if not the only, way to prevent them in future. Without such an organization, magazines and newspapers cannot be read with confidence, nor the necessary knowledge obtained in elections. For what is everybody's business is nobody's and never done. But with an organization and by the presidents' doing their duty, all may be easily and cheaply obtained and more than half the cost of the magazine saved, especially to those that live at a distance from post roads.

It may be said with truth that there always was and always will be a great many that never will see for themselves, and others that will be easily bribed to act contrary to their own interests. But if such means of knowledge as the proposed monthly magazine were established and carried to their doors with such trifling expense, it is further presumed that there always would be a large majority that would read, see, think, and act in elections for their true interests, and would zealously support a free government so long as self-interest governs men.

To conclude, whatever may be your opinions on this address or of the principles and sentiments of the writer, be assured that it was drafted with the most sincere desires to support a free government on the principles we have established it, and to promote the unity, peace, and happiness of mankind. Also from a consciousness of duty by the

Author

INTRODUCTION

To all the Republicans, Farmers, Mechanics, and Laborers in America. Your candid attention is requested to the sentiments of a Laborer.

Learning and knowledge is essential to the preservation of liberty; and unless we have more of it among us, we cannot support our liberties long.

Millions and millions of lives have been lost and oceans of blood have been spilled in revolutions to establish free governments. But melancholy to relate, the history of all ages proves that they have been but of short duration in comparison with arbitrary ones. It is but about twenty years since our revolution in America, when we established governments so free and rational that they commanded not only the wonder and admiration of America but almost all over Europe. Yet we now see a majority of our leading men not only sickening at republican principles but also using their strongest influence to bring us under an arbitrary government. And this too at a time when they are under the greatest struggles to establish free government similar to our own almost all over Europe. At such an important crisis as this, I conceive it to be not only the right but the duty of everyone to search diligently for the causes of this change, and, if possible, to find out a remedy for so great an evil. Under this conviction, I undertake to give you my sentiments on them.

I am not a man of learning, for I never had the advantage of six months schooling in my life. I am no traveler, for I never was fifty miles from where I was born. I am no great reader, for though I have a small landed interest, I always followed labor for a living.

But I always thought it my duty to search into and see for myself in all matters that concerned me as a member of society. And when the revolution began in America I was in the prime of life, and highly taken up with the ideas of liberty and a free government. I was in the Concord fight and saw almost the first blood shed in the cause. I thought then and still think that it is a good cause, which we ought to fight for and maintain. I have also been a constant reader of public newspapers and have closely attended to men and measures ever since—through the war, through the operation of paper money, framing constitutions, and making and construing laws. Seeing what little selfish and contracted ideas of interest would twist and turn the best picked men and bodies of men, I have often almost despaired of ever supporting a free government. But firmly believing it to be the best sort, and the only one approved of by heaven, it has been my unwearied study to find out the real cause of the ruin of republics and a remedy.

I have for many years been satisfied in my own mind what the causes are and what would prove a remedy, provided it was carried into effect. But I had no thoughts of publishing my sentiments until the adoption of the British treaty in the manner it was done. Then, seeing the unwearied pains and the unjustifiable measures taken by a large number of all orders of men who get a living without labor in the adoption of said treaty, and in elections, contrary to the interests of the laborer, I came to a resolution to improve on my constitutional right and state to you my sentiments.

In doing which I must study brevity and but just touch on many things on which volumes might be written. But I hope I shall do it so as to be understood. As I have no room for compliments and shall often make observations on sundry orders of men and their conduct, I beg leave once and for all to observe that I am far from thinking that any order of men who live without labor are entirely needless, or that they are all chargeable with blame. On the contrary, I firmly believe that there is a large number in all orders who are true friends to liberty and that it is from them and their superior ability that it has always received its principle support. But I also believe that a majority of them are actuated by different principles.

Also, as I am not furnished with documents and other information as men of learning are, I may represent some things different from what they really are. So I desire that they may be taken only as my opinion and be believed and practiced upon no further than they appear evident and for the good of society.

A GENERAL DESCRIPTION OF
THE CAUSES THAT RUIN REPUBLICS

The causes that I shall endeavor to make appear are a conceived difference of interest between those that labor for a living and those that get a living without bodily labor.

This is no new doctrine if I may judge from the many scraps of history I have seen of ancient republics. The best information I ever had on this subject, and the greatest collection of historical accounts, was by a writer who wrote ten long numbers in the *Chronicle* in December 1785 and January 1786 styling himself a "Free Republican."[2] In his four first numbers he recites a long and bloody history about feuds and animosities, contentions and bloodsheds that happened in the ancient republics of Athens, Greece, and Rome, and many other nations between the Few and the Many, the patricians and plebians, rich and poor, debtor and creditor, etc. In his fifth number, he draws the dividing line between the Few and Many as they apply to us in America. Among the Few he reckons the merchant and physician; the lawyer and divine; all in the literary walks of life; the judicial and executive officers; and all the rich who could live on their income without bodily labor—so that the whole contention lies between those that labor for a living and those that do not. Then he tries to prove that unless the Few have weight and influence in the government according to their riches and high station in life, the government cannot be free; and he proposes great alterations in the constitution in order better to accommodate the interests of the Few, even to deprive the people of the liberty of voting for governor and senators.

These sentiments—being urged in such a masterly manner just before the adoption of the federal constitution—have been so closely followed by the administration ever since (although they are directly contrary to the principles of liberty and were no doubt written to destroy it). Yet if they were republished at this time, they might be of great service to the people and convince the author that his great searches and labors were not lost—any more than the doings of Joseph's brethren were when they sold him into Egypt.[3] And if republished, they would help to prove the necessity of the remedy I shall prescribe.

I have often looked over his ten numbers and searched other histories to satisfy myself as to the truth of his assertions. But I am very far from thinking as he doth that the destruction of free governments arises from the licentiousness of the Many or their representatives. On the contrary, I shall endeavor to prove that their destruction always arises from the unreasonable dispositions and combinations of the Few, and the ignorance and carelessness of the Many.

Which I shall attempt in the following manner:

1. Give a description of mankind in order to show the necessity of government;

2. Describe a free government;

3. Show how the Few and Many differ in their ideas of interests;

4. Show how and by what means the Few destroy free government;

5. Make some illustrating remarks on the operation of these causes in our governments, and then point out a remedy.

1. A DESCRIPTION OF MANKIND AND THE NECESSITY OF GOVERNMENT

To search into and know ourselves is of the greatest importance, and the want of self-knowledge is the cause of the greatest evils suffered in society. If we knew what alterations might be made in our minds and conduct by alterations in our education, circumstances, and conditions in this life, we should be vastly less censorious of others for their conduct, and more cautious of trusting them when there is no need of it.

Men are born and grow up in this world with a vast variety of capacities, strengths, and abilities both of body and mind, and have strongly implanted in them numerous passions and lusts continually urging them to acts of fraud, violence, and injustice towards each other. Although they have implanted in them a sense of right and wrong (so that if they would always follow the dictates of their consciences and do as they would be done by, they would need no other law or government), yet as they are sentenced by the just decrees of heaven to hard labor for a living in this world, and have so strongly implanted in them a desire of self-support, self-defense, self-love, self-conceit, and self-aggrandizement that it engrosses all their care and attention—so that they can see nothing beyond self. For self (as once described by a divine) is like an object placed before the eye that hinders the sight of every thing beyond.[4]

This selfishness may be discerned in every person, let their conditions in life be what they will; and it operates so powerfully as to disqualify them from judging right in their own cause. There is no station in this life that a man can be raised to that clears him from this selfishness. On the contrary, it is a solemn truth that the higher a person is raised in stations of honor, power, and trust the greater are his temptations to do wrong and gratify those selfish principles. Give a man honor and he wants more. Give him power and he wants more. Give him money and he wants more. In short, he is never easy: but the more he has the more he wants.

The most comprehensive description of man I ever saw was by a writer in the following words, viz.: Man is a being made up of self-love, seeking his own happiness to the misery of all around him, who would damn a world to save himself from temporal or other punishment. And he who denies this to be his real character is either ignorant of himself, or more than a man. Many persons, were they to hear such a description of themselves, would cry out as Hazael did: "What, is thy servant a dog?" etc.[5] But if they should once get into the circumstances he was in, and have the power and temptations he had, they would prove themselves to be just such a dog as he did. Haman is another striking evidence of the depravity and pride of the human heart. For though he could boast of the highest preferments in the greatest kingdom on earth, yet the poor devil exclaimed: All these things avail me nothing so long as Mordecai refused to bow the knee.[6]

From these natural dispositions of mankind arise not only the advantages but the absolute necessity of civil government. Without it, mankind would be continually at war on their own species, stealing and robbing, fighting with, and killing one another. This all nations on earth have been convinced of and have established it in some form or other; and their sole aim in doing it is their safety and happiness. But for want of wisdom or some plan to curb the ambition and govern those to whom they gave power, they have often been brought to suffer as much under their government as they would without any; and it still remains uncertain whether such a plan can be found out or not.

2. A DESCRIPTION OF A FREE GOVERNMENT

There are many sorts of government, or rather names by which governments have been distinguished—such as despotic, monarchical, and aristocratical. In these the power to govern is in the hands of one or a Few to govern as they please. Consequently they are masters and not servants, so that the government is not free.

There are also sundry names by which free governments are described, such as democratical, republican, elective, and free governments, all of which I take to mean nearly the same thing, or that all those nations who ever adopted them aimed at nearly the same thing; viz., to be governed by known laws in which the whole nation had a voice in making by a full and fair representation, and in which all the officers in every department are (or ought to be) servants and not masters.[7]

The sole business of government is to keep the peace and secure the protection, safety, and happiness of individuals in this life. No government can be free where the rights and liberties of conscience are abridged. Every person has a right to worship and serve his maker in the way his own conscience dictates, and to Him only is accountable for his religious sentiments and conduct in this life. However anxious and concerned a true Christian may be for the future happiness of others, and however confident he may be that his own opinion is right, he cannot enforce it on others in any better way than by timely and friendly arguments, counsels, and admonitions—graced by a Christian life and conduct agreeable to his own profession of faith. And as there can be no religion without morality, so no Christian can refuse obedience to good and wholesome laws made for his protection and happiness in this world.

That government is the most free that causes the greatest sum or degree of individual happiness in this world with the least national expense. The happiness of a person consisteth in eating and drinking and enjoying the good of his own labors, and feeling that his life and liberties (both civil and religious) and his property are all safe and secure; and not in the abundance he possesseth, nor in expensive and national grandeur, which have a tendency to make other men miserable.

Economy in expenditures ought to be the first principle of a free government. The people ought to support just so many without labor as is necessary for the public good and no more, and ought to pay them so much salary and fees as would command sufficient abilities and no more. All taxes for the support of government ought to be laid equally according to the property each one has and the advantage he receives from government, and collected in the easiest and least expensive manner. The sole end of government is the protection of the life, liberty, and property of individuals.[8] The poor man's shilling ought to be as much the care of government as the rich man's pound and no more. Every person ought to have justice done to him freely and promptly, without delay.

These are the principles and objects for which all governments are or ought to be supported. But plain, simple, and just as they appear to be, yet from pride and selfishness of man such have been the contentions and wars about them as has laid a great part of the world in blood and ashes, and near seven-eighths of the people now existing receive little or no advantages from them.

Great pains have been taken and the wisdom of many nations and states has been put to the rack to delineate the rights of the people and powers of government, and to form constitutions so that the blessings of government might be enjoyed without being oppressed by them; and it is thought that it has been much improved upon since the American Revolution. The constitution of Massachusetts, although it doth not materially differ from the others, yet it is allowed to be as complete a model for a free government as any on the continent, so I shall describe one principally by reference to it.[9]

In the Massachusetts Bill of Rights, it declares all men to be born free and equal as to their rights in and under the government, as in Article I; and that all power lays in the people and all the officers of government are their servants and accountable to them as in Article V; and no man, corporation, or body of men, however high by birth, riches, or honors, have any right by them any more than the poorest man in the government, as in Articles VI and VII; and that the people have the sole right to reform, alter, and totally change their constitution or administration of government as they please, as in Article VII; and the people have a right to meet and deliberate on all matters of government at such times, places, and bodies as they please, provided they do it in a peaceable manner, as in Article XIX; and the people have a right to know and convey to each other their sentiments and circumstances through the medium of the press, as in Article XVI.

A free government is a government of laws made by the free consent of a majority of the whole people. But as it is impossible for a whole nation to meet and deliberate, so all their laws must be made by men chosen for that purpose; and the duty of all those men is to act and do in making laws just as all the people would, provided they were all together and equally knew what was for their own interests.

In making laws there cannot be too many pains taken to make them plain to be understood, and not too numerous. For this end (as all bodies of men are liable to the same rashness and mistakes as individuals are), so the legislature is divided into two branches, the Senate and House of Representatives, not that they have separate interests or objects to act from, as some pretend, but that they may guard against each other's rashness and mistakes, and see that the laws are made plain and not needlessly.

As a further guard against unnecessary laws, the executive is given a partial negative on the passing of them, and the opinion of the judges may be called on in difficult matters. (Not that the judicial or executive powers ought to have any voice in deciding whether a law is good or bad.) But they ought to have a voice about whether it can be carried into execution or not, without interfering with other laws and needlessly multiplying them. For there is nothing more essential in a free government than to keep the legislative, judicial, and executive powers entirely separate, as in Article XXX—not only separate departments, but entirely different sets of men (for reasons which I shall hereafter give).

The business and duty of the judicial power is to hear and examine all complaints and breaches of the laws, and pass sentence; not on the law—whether it is good or not—but whether it is broken or not, and in every respect according to law.

The business and duty of the executive power is to execute all the laws according to the orders and precepts he receives from the other powers of government (without any reference to their being right or wrong in his opinion, for that would be legislating and judging, too).

There is one exception to the above described duties of the judicial and executive officers; viz., if there should ever be a legislature so corrupt as to make any law contrary to the Constitution and declared rights of the people, it cannot be binding on any person, much less on the judicial and executive officers, who are all under a solemn oath to support the Constitution. But on the contrary, should any judicial or executive officer or member of a jury attempt to put such a law into execution, or explain any law contrary to the Constitution—it being the supreme law of the land—he ought to be immediately removed from office and made incapable of ever holding any other office under the government again.

Here I would observe that I have often wondered that free governments have not erected separate courts with judges elected by the people or appointed by the legislature for certain terms on purpose to guard against invasions on the Constitution, and for the impeachment, trial, and removal of all officers for either inability or misconduct; and to have their trial in the vicinity where they belong. Nor can I see why all appointments to office might not be made by the same court. It appears absurd to me to load the executive with so much business as the appointment of all officers, when he has so much other business of importance to attend to. And to detain a legislature to impeach and try an officer of government, and oblige witnesses to attend and travel (perhaps) scores or hundreds of miles when the whole issue of the cause is only the loss of an office which thousands of men as good as he stand ready to fill his place. It is true that such a court would add another branch to government. But it would not add anything to their business, and it would so simplify and make plain the business and duty of the other branches as finally to make a great saving. It would dry up many streams, if not the whole fountain of corruption that destroys all governments.[10]

In order to support a free government, there are many duties incumbent on every member of the community, especially on those that labor for a living. They must inform themselves about the nature of mankind, the necessity of government, and about their own rights and liberties as established in their constitutions; that all laws made by their representatives must be obeyed, let them be ever so wrong or bad in their opinion; and that there is no remedy for grievances but by petitioning and using their rights in elections.

The same reverence and respect (in a great measure) ought to be paid to the laws and constitution in a free government as is paid to monarchs and great men in arbitrary ones. But at the same time it is not only the right but the duty of everyone to speak their minds freely on all laws and measures of government, and all men in office; and to point out the disadvantages they feel or fear from them. There is also a duty to listen to what others say, as well as what they feel or think themselves (for a majority must govern), and to attend closely and constantly on all elections, using their privileges in them and taking the greatest pains to find out the true characters and abilities of those for whom they vote. Let no private interest, connection, or relation induce them to vote for those that are not true friends to a free government. Also, it is the duty of all to see that their children are well taught to read and write, and that all the above principles are initiated into them in their youths. It is from a neglect of these duties that free governments are destroyed.

I would not be understood as thinking that these political duties are all that are necessary in this life. For there are many religious and social duties which, if neglected, ensure that we cannot be happy here or hereafter, such as:

The duties and worship we owe to our maker, and reverence and respect for the Sabbath and all holy ordinances and institutions.

To cultivate a respect and love for all mankind, and never refuse friendship and good neighborhood to any on account of their sentiments about futurity, let them be ever so contrary to our own, provided they obey the laws and regulations of society in this world.

To cultivate habits of industry, prudence, neatness, and moderation in living and dress.

To be faithful and punctual in our dealings.

To have respect for the aged and for strangers.

To be a kind husband and wife, a kind parent, a kind master, a kind brother and sister, a dutiful child and servant.

To be kind to the poor, to the sick, and those that are unfortunate.

To be always willing to forgive injuries and settle difference in the shortest and cheapest manner.

In short, to obey the injunction of our Savior: "In all cases, whatsoever ye would that men should do to you, do ye even so to them."[11]

All these religious and social duties are an immediate and heartfelt reward to the doer, and if people would only consult their own happiness in putting them into practice they would greatly lessen the expense if not entirely do away with the necessity of government.

Having thus described a free government, I shall proceed.

3. TO SHOW HOW THE FEW AND MANY DIFFER IN THEIR IDEAS OF INTEREST

"In the sweat of thy face shalt thou get thy bread until thou return to the ground" is the irreversible sentence of heaven on man for his rebellion.[12] And there is scarcely anything more terrible to human nature than to be sentenced to hard labor during life—especially if one is not brought up to it in youth. Yet it is absolutely necessary that a large majority of the world should labor or we could not subsist. For labor is the sole parent of all property. The land yieldeth nothing without it, and there is no food, clothing, shelter, vessel, or any necessary of life but what costs labor and is generally estimated valuable according to what labor it costs. Therefore no person can possess property without laboring, unless he gets it by force or craft, fraud or fortune, out of the earnings of others.[13]

But from the great varieties of capacities, strength, and abilities of men, there always was and always will be a very unequal distribution of property in the world. Many are so rich that they can live without labor. So, also, can the merchant, physician, lawyer, and divine, the philosopher and schoolmaster, the judicial and executive officers, and many others who can get a living honestly and for the benefit of the community without bodily labors. And as all these professions require a considerable time and expense of property to qualify themselves for them; and as no person after thus qualifying himself and making a pick on a profession by which he means to live can desire to have it dishonorable or unproductive—so they all naturally unite to make these professions as honorable and lucrative as possible.

Also, as ease and rest from labor are reckoned among the greatest pleasures of life, pursued by all with greatest avidity and, when once attained, create a sense of superiority; and as pride and ostentation are natural to the human heart: these orders of men generally associate together and look down with too much contempt on those that labor. On the other hand, the laborer is conscious that it is labor that supports the whole, and that the more there are that live without labor—and the higher they live or the greater their salaries and fees are—so much the harder must he work, or the shorter must he live. This makes both parties look on each other with a jealous and envious eye.

Before I proceed to show how the Few and Many differ in money matters, I will give a short description of what money is. Money is not property of itself, but only the representative of property. Silver and gold are not so valuable as iron and steel for real use, but receive all of their value from the use that is made of them as a medium of trade. Money is simply this: a thing of lighter carriage than property that has an established value set upon it either by law or general consent. For instance, if a dollar, or a piece of paper, or a chip would pass through a nation or the world for a bushel of corn or any other property to the value of said corn, then it would be the representative of so much property. Also, money is a thing that will go where it will fetch the most as naturally as water runs downhill. For the possessor will give it where it will fetch the most. When there is an addition to the quantity of money, or an extraordinary use of barter and credit in commerce, the prices of property will rise. On the other hand, if credit is ruined and the medium of exchange made scarcer, the prices of all kinds of property will fall in proportion.

Here lies the great scuffle between the Few and the Many.

As the interests of the Few—and their incomes—lie chiefly in money at interest, rents, salaries, and fees that are fixed on the nominal value of money, they are interested to have the money scarce and the prices of labor and produce as low as possible. For instance, if the price of labor and produce should fall one-half, it would be just the same to them as if their rents, fees, and salaries were doubled—all of which increase they get of the Many. Besides, the fall of the price of labor and produce, and the scarcity of money, always bring the Many into distress and compel them into a state of dependence on the Few for favors and assistances in a thousand ways.

On the other hand, if the Many could raise the price of labor and produce, and have money circulate freely, they would pay their debts and enjoy the good of their labors without being dependent on the Few for assistance. Also, when prices are high, a prudent and industrious person may presciently lay up something against a time of need. But the person that doth not work and lives high when the prices are up will soon spend all his property.

The greatest danger is from the judicial and executive departments of governments, especially from lawyers. These officers, all depending upon their fees and salaries for a living, are always interested in having money scarce and the people in distress. The scarcer the money, the lower the price of labor and produce; the greater the distress of the Many, the better for them.[14] It not only doubles the nominal value of their fees and salaries but doubles and triples their business, and the people are obliged to come to them cap in hand and beg for mercy, patience, and forbearance. This gratifies both their pride and covetousness. But when money is plenty and circulates freely, they have little or nothing to do.

This is the great reason why judicial and executive officers ought to be kept entirely from the legislative body. And unless there can be wisdom enough in the people to keep the three departments of government entirely separate from each other, a free government cannot be supported. For in all these disputes of jarring interests, it is the business and duty of the legislature to determine what is right and what is wrong. And it is the duty of all in the nation to regulate their conduct according to the laws the legislators make. To such laws the Many would be ever willing to submit—provided that the three departments were kept separate, and that they were fully and fairly represented in the legislature; and the Many would be always willing and zealous to support that government.

But the Few cannot bear to be on a level with their fellow creatures, or submit to the determination of a legislature where (as they say) the swinish multitude are fairly represented.[15] They sicken at the idea, and are ever hankering and striving after monarchy or aristocracy, where the people have nothing to do in matters of government but to support the Few in luxury and idleness. For these and many other reasons, a large majority of those that live without labor are ever opposed to a free government. And though the whole of them do not amount to one-eighth part of the people, and not one-half of them are needed in their professions, yet by their arts, combinations, and schemes they have always made out to destroy free government sooner or later.

Which I shall endeavor to make appear by pointing out—

4. THE MEANS BY WHICH THE FEW DESTROY FREE GOVERNMENT

The sole foundation on which the Few build all their schemes to destroy free government is the ignorance and superstition of, or the want of knowledge among, the Many. Solomon said, "Train up a child in the way he should go, and when he is old he will not depart from it."[16] And it is as true that if a child is trained up in the way he should not go, when he is old, he will keep to it. It is the universal custom and practice of monarchical and arbitrary governments to train up their subjects as much in ignorance as they can as to matters of government and policy, and to teach them to reverence and worship great men in office and to take for truth whatever they say without examining or trying to see for themselves. And they often make an engine of religion, mixing it with their politics to drive their subjects by the terrors of the other world to submit to their tyrannical measures in this one.

A people or nation being thus trained up from their youths to habits, customs, and manners directly contrary to those necessary in a free government, they are not easily changed. Consequently, whenever revolutions are brought about and free governments established, it is done by the influence of a few leading men, who after they have obtained their object can never receive compensation and honors enough from the people for their services. And the people—being brought up from their youths to reverence and respect such men—go on in the old way, neglecting to see for themselves. Being very fond of being flattered, they readily hear those whom they know have done them great services.

These are the principal grounds on which the Few work to destroy free governments. But there always are many among the orders of the Few who are true friends of liberty; and many of the laborers who understand their true interests, who warmly oppose the measures of the Few—so that it requires the utmost precautions and cunning of them to attain their ends. Finding their schemes and views of interest borne down by the Many, to gain the power they cannot constitutionally obtain, the Few endeavor to get it by cunning and corruption.

Conscious at the same time that with usurpation, when once begun, the safety of the usurper consists only in grasping the whole. To effect this, no cost nor pain must be spared. The Few first unite all their orders in societies and conventions, and establish secret correspondences so that they may act in concert with each other. In all measures they then seek to deceive the people and promote their own schemes, aiming principally at the enlargement of their numbers, fees, and salaries, which oppresses and destroys the rights and liberties of the Many.

As learning and knowledge among the Many is the only sup-

port of liberty, so no pain is spared by the Few to suppress it—
though they seldom attempt it in an open and direct way. Instead
of promoting cheap schools and woman schools for children to
read and write while they are so young as to be spared from
labor, they are continually crying up the great advantages of
costly colleges, national academies, and grammar schools.[17]
Although many of these may be necessary in a free government,
yet as they are generally improved, they greatly promote the
views and interests of the Few by bringing up a numerous and
needless set of youth to live without labor; and they make numerous places for them with high salaries and fees (when the learning
necessary for the Many to have might be better promoted with
half the costs).

Also, in colleges and academies, the Few are extremely careful
to keep out all friends to liberty from being presidents, tutors,
or instructors of the youths in them—so that instead of their
being taught the true principles of a free government and to reverence the laws and constitutions and the sacred rights of the
people, they teach them to reverence and worship great men in
office, to support the honor and dignity of their own professions,
and to teach and preach these things to all the swinish multitude.[18] By this way, they add greatly to their numbers and
employment.

As a knowledge of the laws, of the characters, abilities, and
doings of all men in office, and a knowledge of each other's
sentiments and circumstances, so that they might unite in
elections, is absolutely necessary to the support of liberty; and
as this knowledge cannot be obtained but by the liberty of
speech, and of the press, and of associations, and by correspondence with each other: so no pains nor arts are spared by
the Few to frighten and drive or flatter and deceive the people
out of the use and improvement of these all-important rights
and privileges. Whenever they can obtain this, the day is
theirs. When a people become so negligent and careless as not
to improve these privileges, or so cowardly as to give them up,
they are just fit for slaves.

Another very important object to the support of liberty is the
formation and construction of laws (as I have said before). No

care, pains, or precautions ought to be spared to make them as few, plain, comprehensive, and easy to be understood as possible. But instead of this the Few spare no pains nor arts to have them as numerous, intricate, and hard to be understood as possible—so that no person can understand what is law or what not but by applying to a lawyer, or some judicial or executive officer. In this way, also, they add vastly to their numbers and employments.

It also adds vastly to the power and influence of the judicial and executive officers. Here I would observe my opinion that free governments are commonly destroyed by the combinations of the judicial and executive powers in favor of the interests of the Few. They do it by explaining and constructing away the true sense and meaning of the constitutions and laws, and so raise themselves above the legislative power and take the whole administration into their own hands and manage it according to their own wills and the interests of the Few.

The Free Republican in No. 9 saith that in many of the ancient republics, the judicial power became the mere instrument of tyranny and oppression, and he proposes lawyers as a necessary order in a free government to curb the arbitrary will of the judges. But I thought that would be like setting the cat to watch the cream pot. For though they are neither judicial nor executive officers but a kind of mule order engendered by and many times overawing both, yet from their professions and interest lawyers are the most dangerous to liberty and the least to be trusted of any profession whatever.[19]

The greatest curb to the arbitrary will of judges that ever was invented is the trial by juries. But numerous ways have been invented to pick and pack, overawe and mislead them—so that unless the people get knowledge enough to keep the three powers entirely separate from each other, there will always remain great danger of losing our liberties from this quarter.

Another thing by which the Few often distress and injure the Many and make business for their party is by artfully managing money or the medium of trade. Instead of trying to keep it at an even value and in free circulation, and instead of trying to keep public and private credit good, with a free trade to all parts of the world—which it is the business and duty of government to do—

they are interested in doing directly the reverse, and have it in their power to do it in numerous ways.

Another great means by which the Few destroy free governments is by raising standing armies and making needless wars. Although it is absolutely necessary for every nation to be in constant readiness to defend itself against foreign invasion or domestic insurrections, yet the best and only safe defense of a free government is by a well-regulated and disciplined militia. Every able-bodied male ought to be trained up to the use of arms and arts of war from his youth, and be constantly equipped for the defense of his liberties and his country—as well as to have a knowledge of what his rights and liberties are—and to have it all done in the cheapest and easiest manner possible.[20]

But this mode of defense doth not suit the views and schemes of the Few. They wish for a standing army of slaves to execute their arbitrary measures. For this end they use all the means in their power to prejudice the people against supporting a militia. By making it as costly as possible, by introducing costly uniforms and large and pompous musters and shows, and by raising all the disputes between officers and soldiers they can, they try to pave the way for a standing army. Also, they will catch hold of every little misunderstanding or uneasiness, either in their own nation or with foreign nations, to raise an insurrection or foreign war only for a pretext to raise and keep a standing army.

So apt is mankind to be wrought up into a passion by false reports and slight offenses that it is an easy matter for artful and cunning men to set peaceable neighbors and families at variance with each other where there are no grounds for it on either side. In the same manner, towns, states, and nations may be (and often have been) set at war against each other, and thousands and millions have been slain on both sides equally thinking that they were fighting in a good cause when the whole matter in dispute would have made little or no uneasiness between honest neighbors.

Nor do I dispute but that it has been often agreed upon by rulers of nations to make war on each other only that they might have a pretext to raise and keep up a standing army to deprive their own subjects of their own rights and liberties. This is a great object with the Few. When attained, it adds so much to their numbers and strength that they have but little more to fear, and the Many have but little reason to expect that they can maintain their liberties long.

There is one more object of the last importance for the Few to carry their points in without which they cannot obtain the foregoing points. That is elections. Here lies the grand scuffle between the two parties. If the Many know their own strength, rights, and minds equal to the Few, they never need to fear any danger from them. For the numbers interested with the Many are near twelve to one of the Few, and every man elected into office remains a man still and is moved by the same principles and passions as other men are—so that the fear of offending his constituents, the honor of the office, the love of the reward, and to be worshipped into the bargain, carries ten thousand charms with it, and he will ever be faithful to that side that was the cause of his election.

Consequently, the Few have to muster all their craft and force in elections. They will all unite in extolling the greatness, goodness, and abilities of their candidate and in running down and blackening the characters and abilities of the candidates on the other side.

Also, they will appear to the electors in a variety of ways. Some they will flatter by promising favors—such as being customers to them; or helping them out of debt or other difficulties; or helping them to a good bargain; or treating them; or trusting them; or lending them money; or even giving them a little if they will vote for such and such a man. Others they will threaten: If you don't vote for such and such a man—or if you do, etc.—you shall pay me what you owe me or I will sue you; or I will turn you out of my house, or off of my farm. I won't be your customer any longer. I will wager a guinea that you dare not vote for such a man, and if you do you shall have a bloody nose for it.

Or they will hire somebody to communicate these things to them.

Also, they will hinder votes from being counted or returned right. And often they will themselves—or hire others to—put in two or three votes apiece.

All these things have been practiced, and may be again. More on elections below.

ILLUSTRATING REMARKS

In the foregoing descriptions, I have but just touched on the principal causes and means by which free governments have been destroyed. I shall now proceed, fifthly, to make some illustrating remarks on the operation of these causes in our governments since the American Revolution.

When the American Revolution began, there was a remarkable union throughout the continent, considering our different customs, habits, and laws, and the scattered situation we lived in. Of all the different constitutions that were then formed, nearly all agree in the essential principles and means of establishing and preserving liberty and a free government. But in all of them it may be seen that there were some in the conventions that formed them who had an idea of these jarring interests between the Few and Many. And long before the war was over, the operation of these causes was plain to be seen in almost every deliberate body of men, and has been gradually increasing ever since.

REMARKS ON THE COMBINATIONS OF THE FEW

Towards the close of the late war, the officers of the Continental Army were considerably borne upon by not being paid according to contract, and many of them thought they were not notified enough in the adoption of the state constitutions. At the close of the war they formed themselves into a society by the name of Cincinnati. This institution caused great alarm and many pointed publications in newspapers, considering it as a dangerous body. This uneasiness caused them at their first general meeting to make great alterations in their constitution, which they published together with a very plausible letter endeavoring in it to make the world believe that they never would nor could prove any harm.[21]

But from that time, there was a continual noise and writing from one end of the continent to the other against the badness of the public credit and the weakness of the federal government. When the Shays affair happened in Massachusetts, it was headed by one of this order, and many of the rest of them were put under pay to suppress it. Immediately after that a convention was called to mend the federal government when a hard trial was made chiefly by this order to establish a monarchy, expecting that their president would be made king.[22] But though they failed in that, yet by their arts and schemes they have wriggled themselves into almost all the offices of profit and honor in the federal government. From this order also originated the funding system by which those that labor for a living will have millions and millions of dollars to pay—for which the public never received, and the possessor never gave, one single farthing. Also from this order originated the Indian war which has cost us thousands of lives and six million dollars without the least advantage to us.[23] From this order also originated the British treaty and our disturbances with France.

When I charge these things to the Cincinnati, I do not mean that they did them alone, but as planners and leaders in them. For to them also may be charged the organization of almost all the other orders of the Few, who follow after and support them in their measures.

The order of speculators, stock jobbers, and land jobbers are made up principally of Cincinnati. By the funding system they have risen like a black cloud over the continent, and have gained wealth like the nabobs of the East. They have got the principal command of the funds, and not only swindle individuals out of their property, but greatly agitate our public councils and shook the state of Georgia almost to its foundation.[24]

The merchants have organized themselves and have their Chambers of Commerce and correspondences from one end of the continent to the other.[25]

The doctors have established medical societies and have both their state and county meetings.[26]

The ministers of the Congregational order—and all others for aught I know—have formed themselves into societies. Many of them are incorporated and have their state and county meetings, and many of them have turned preachers of politics instead of divinity.[27]

The judicial and executive powers are by their professions and business often together and perfectly know each other's sentiments and interests.

The lawyers have long since established their bar meetings, and from their arts—and the ignorance of the people in trusting them to legislate—they have become the most influential and powerful of any order among us. And our laws have become so numerous and intricate that it is impossible for a common man to know what is law and what not.[28]

And all literary men and teachers at our seminaries of learning are united and have close connections with the other orders.

Here I might show at large how each of these orders unite to make their own professions as profitable and honorable as possible; how many of them have multiplied in numbers four-fold since the American Revolution—and that it costs the poor man four times as much to employ them now as it did then; how all these orders unite in supporting all the great national schemes and plans of the Cincinnati; and how they have explained away the true sense and meaning of our constitutions and laws. I might also prove the extensive uses of their combinations by pointing out many little arts and names that have flown from one end of the continent to the other to frighten and flatter the Many into their measures—such as Federalist, Jacobin, Cockade, etc.[29]

I might easily show, too, that these combinations of the Few are not confined to America or to Europe. For since the American and French revolutions, the Few are alarmed and combining all over the world. Gog and Magog are gathered together to destroy the rights of man and banish liberty from the world.[30] And unless there are similar exertions among the Many in favor of liberty, I fear it will yet fall a prey to their superior arts and cunning.

But to particularly describe these things would be too lengthy for this address. Therefore, I shall only make a few remarks on some of the most important decisions of the federal government and on elections, before I point out the remedy.

REMARKS ON THE FUNDING SYSTEM

The funding system was established by the first Congress, in which the people were not fully represented; but notwithstanding, it was very ably opposed by a large number of the members. And after a warm debate which lasted several months, it was adopted by a majority of only one: forty against forty-one. By raking up all the state debts and the old Continental money from its tombs, the system mounted the whole debt to near eighty million dollars—when, according to the opinion of the members that opposed it, there was but little more than twenty millions justly due. We have already paid near forty million dollars interest on this debt, the one-half of which would have paid the whole debt.

Consequently, what we have already paid and what we have now to pay comes to near one hundred million dollars—that the public never received nor the possessor never gave one single farthing for—the pernicious consequences of which we and our posterity shall feel for ages. For supposing that there are two million male persons on the continent and it was equally divided among them, it would come to fifty dollars apiece. And according to the way taxes are commonly laid in Massachusetts, it will come to more than two hundred dollars apiece for common or middling farmers to pay.

All this is not one-half the damage of the funding system. For this is the sole pretext for all imposts, excises, stamp acts, and land taxes that are laid upon us—while the real intent and meaning of the Few by them is to make places for numerous sets of officers with high salaries and fees, and to make long sessions and a great deal of business for Congress and the federal government. It is always the art of the Few so to manage these measures as to take the whole of the revenues (let it be more or less) to pay the interest and support government. And it has been declared as a fact that Washington's eight-year administration, while we were in the greatest prosperity, ran us more than eight million dollars further into debt.[31] If it had not been for the creation of this unreasonable and unjust debt, a moderate impost duty collected in the seaports would have been abundantly sufficient for the support and every purpose of the federal government.

REMARKS ON THE ADOPTION
OF THE BRITISH TREATY

As this treaty, together with the powers assumed by the president and Senate to make it, and the conduct of the Few were so extraordinary at the adoption of it, all of which being so dangerous to liberty, I shall be more lengthy in my remarks upon it.

The Federal Constitution by a fair construction is a good one principally. But I have often wondered that a convention of such wise men should spend four months in making such an inexplicit thing. For (as one said of it) it appears too much like a fiddle with but few strings, but so fixed as that the ruling majority may play any tune they please upon it. The treaty-making power is as well guarded as any part, but as it has been exercised it destroys the whole end the people had in view when making it. For the sole end the people had was to establish a government for national purposes only, and they were determined to have it a representative one. To that end they declared that they would not be represented with less than one from every thirty or forty thousand, and gave no power to make laws but in such a body of men.

The letter of the Constitution as it respects treaties stands thus:

In Part 1, Section 1, it saith all legislative powers herein granted shall be vested in a Congress of the United States, which shall consist of a Senate and a House of Representatives; and it declares that all powers and sovereignties not expressly given to Congress are reserved to the states or the people; and all the express powers given to Congress are enumerated in Part 1, Section 8.[32]

In Part 2, Section 2, there is a solitary clause that saith the president shall have the power by and with the advice and consent of the Senate to make treaties. But the section saith nothing about what kind of treaties. And as there are many sorts, some of which are laws unto themselves and some of which need laws and appropriations to carry them into execution, these it cannot mean without flatly contradicting the Constitution, as above.[33]

Treaties of peace and treaties with insurgents and rebels, that need no law to enforce or carry into execution, the president may make with advice, etc., but not without—for this clause was meant as a check and not as an enlargement of his powers. The true and only meaning of the Constitution and the people that accepted of it was that all treaties and dealing with foreign nations should be done by the superior authority of the federal government—which is the legislative power—and negotiated through the president in the same manner as the president corresponds with foreign ministers through his secretary.

Much has been said about treaties being the supreme law of the land. If that is granted and if we also grant the power in the president and Senate to make treaties, then we may dismiss the House of Representatives and all the State governments and save the expense of them, for they can make no laws but what can be annotated by treaties and by the explanations which the judicial power can put upon them.

But I cannot see a word of it in the Constitution. In Part 6, there is a clause that plainly declares that the Federal Constitution, the federal laws, and all treaties shall be supreme to the state laws and constitutions.[34] But it saith nothing about which of the three is supreme—excepting that it appears reasonable to take them as they stand; viz., first the Constitution, secondly the laws, and thirdly treaties. By such a construction, the judges are bound by solemn oath not to give judgment against either of the former in favor of a treaty. If he doth, he perjures himself.

I would not be understood as thinking that treaties are less binding than other laws when they are constitutionally made. For it is the duty of the federal legislature to see that the Constitution, laws, and treaties do not clash with each other. And as their objects of legislation are few, they are highly to blame if there is any contradiction in them. Consequently, the business of the judicial and executive powers will be plain.

This I take to be a fair construction of the Constitution. I am the more confirmed in it by the great pains that were taken by the Few to force a different one upon it at the time the treaty was adopted—which I will describe as it appeared to me.

When the monster first came into view, it was reprobated from one end of the continent to the other. Scarcely anyone dared to open their mouths in favor of it. But as it was an instrument that but few people could comprehend, the petitions against it were chiefly from the seaport towns. And though they were almost unanimous, and couched in humble terms, yet the president signed the treaty and proclaimed it the supreme law of the land.

Hence arose a great question whether it was binding, and how we could get rid of it. Great dependence was put on the state legislature for a remedy. But as it had been very prosperous times with the Many for several years, and as the Few had been borne upon by the high prices of labor and produce, and as prosperity is a time of inattention and necessity the mother of invention, so the Few by close attention in elections had got a large majority in the state legislatures of lawyers and other fee officers who were favorable to their interests. So that at their first meeting after the treaty was published, to our great surprise, the question of undiminished confidence in the president was put and carried in almost all the states.

Then all our hopes lay in the federal House of Representatives. When they met the same question was put, but met with a check. And when the question of the treaty came forward, there was a large number of the most powerful representatives who advocated it with all their powers, thundering out treason and rebellion against all those who dare say anything against it, declaring that it was constitutionally made. But to the immortal honor of the other side, after near twenty days warm debate, they declared to the contrary by nearly two to one, if I mistake not (sixty-seven against thirty-eight).[35]

Here the matter must have died for want of supplies, had it not been for the most treasonable arts and doings of the Few. Finding their characters if not their lives in danger, they racked their inventions to compel the House to grant said supplies for the treaty. To effect this, circular letters were sent from the center to every part of the continent with a printed petition and memorial ready for signing. They were attended with a collection of the most horrid and frightful falsehoods that ever were invented by the devil in order to frighten the people to petition the House to grant said supplies, representing that the House was unconstitutionally withholding them and trying to usurp all the powers of Congress to themselves; and that unless the treaty took place Britain would certainly make war with us and that their power over us and vengeance upon us would be such that they would rouse off a great gun three thousand miles distant and blow all our brains out if we stepped out to piss.[36]

They also represented the certainty of a civil war in such a light that we could almost hear the small arms crackle: that the House of Representatives was led entirely by one Gallatin, who was a vagrant foreigner and had no interest in this country, and was trying to overthrow the government, and had been the sole cause of the Pittsburgh insurrection, which had cost the government more than twelve hundred thousand dollars; that the only choice we had was to follow this odious Gallatin or the virtuous and wise and glorious Washington, who had led us by the hand for twenty years and had been the cause of all the blessings and prosperity we had received for eight years back; and that now was the only time to choose which of these characters we would follow.[37] And if any person attempted to contradict them in these cursed lies, their eyes would sparkle, their chins quaver, and they would call them Jacobins, Shaysites, disorganizers, and enemies to all government.

I do not pretend to say that such representations were everywhere so. But they appeared so to me where I was, and I thought if the swinish multitude had behaved in such a manner they would soon have had the adulterous Hamilton after them with fifteen thousand men.[38] And though he could find nobody but men peaceably following their honest callings, yet he would have boasted of the expense of twelve hundred thousand dollars and laid the whole blame to Gabriel or some person as innocent as he (as he did the Pittsburgh insurrection to Mr. Gallatin).[39]

Sad to relate, for want of the means of knowledge among the people, they were so frightened with these lies that they hastened to see which could get his name to the petition first. I told many of them afterwards what they signed for. Some would say they signed for the treaty; some for the good of the country; some to keep from war; some for Washington; and some to stand by the Constitution. And when I asked them the true circumstances of the affair, some would—like lambs that are dumb after they are sheared—turn away and wish to hear no more about it. Others would most heartily curse their deceivers. But to return: these petitions, thronging in from every quarter on the House, gave great courage to the minority and equally depressed the majority—so that after a long struggle a bare majority was obtained in favor of the supplies.

Thus, by the combinations and arts of the Few, with the order of Cincinnati at their head, a seal was put upon the worst instrument that ever was signed in America. I shall not attempt here to point out its full consequences, although I firmly believe it to be the sole cause of our differences with France—and where they will end, God only knows. I should not have been so lengthy on the adoption of this treaty had it not been one of the first acts of violence by the Few to sever the ignorant people from their true representatives and so destroy legislative authority by mounting the executive and judicial powers above it.

There are many other things that I might mention to prove this difference of interests between the Few and Many and the determination of the Few to destroy our liberties—such as the Excise Act, Stamp Act, land tax, the alien and sedition bills; also, their zeal and preparations for war and for a standing army.[40] All of these things are needlessly and evidently calculated to increase the numbers and salaries and fees of the Few. But I shall only make one remark on them, and that with pleasure; viz., that all these odious acts and measures have been adopted with but a very small majority, and have been opposed by the minority with as great abilities and firmness as ever graced any bodies of men. And this, too, from mere principles of virtue and regard for the rights and liberties of their constituents even when these principles were not supported by the constituents themselves—as will plainly appear by the following

REMARKS ON OUR ELECTIONS

I have often wondered that under the present means of knowledge and in opposition to the numerous arts of flattery, deception, threatening, and falsehoods practiced by the Few in elections, that the Many get so fully represented as they do, and that there are so many representatives that expose themselves to the abuse of the Few by supporting our cause when we support them so poorly. All the hopes I have of a remedy are by a reformation in this important object. Therefore I shall be more particular in my remarks on them.

In order to be short and comprehensive and more plainly to show the necessity of the remedy I shall propose, I will make the following statements as my opinion, founded on the best calculations I can make, believing they are not far from the truth.

1. That although it is the duty of every representative and elected officer to act for the true interests of a majority of his constituents and agreeable to the Constitution, yet the nature of mankind is such that the love of honor and reward and the fear of losing his office will generally make him favor the interests of those that have the greatest influence in his election or appointment.

2. As to the real numbers of the Few and Many, I suppose by the qualifications required of persons to entitle them to vote for representatives in the different constitutions throughout the continent that there is about one-sixth part of the census as it is now taken that have a right to vote, or that there are nearly six thousand voters in every district for a federal representative (excepting in those states where they have many slaves).

3. That not more than one-eighth part of those voters live without labor, take the seaports and country together.

4. That one-third part of those that live without labor are true republicans and friends to the rights and liberties of the Many.

Consequently, the Many are in numbers eleven to one of the Few.

5. That in our most contested elections of late, when the greatest pains have been taken on both sides to collect votes, though some towns and districts have voted more full than others, yet on average not one-quarter part of the voters have been brought to act on either side.

Consequently, our elections have been carried in favor of the interests of the Few. There have been many representatives to Congress chosen from districts with less than five hundred votes, and it has been publicly said that things have been so managed in the federal state of Connecticut that there has not usually been more than sixteen hundred votes put in for a representative in the whole state where they have more than forty thousand voters.[41]

Now, if the above statements are true (which I take them to be), the question is how so few among us can govern and carry their points in elections contrary to the true interests of so many? To which question I answer that the two main reasons are those which have proved the destruction of many republics, which I have before described. The first is the want of knowledge among the Many and their readiness to hear and follow the schemes of great men without examining and seeing for themselves as described above. The second is the complete organization and joint exertions of the Few in the arts of threatening, flattery, and falsehoods as above, to which the reader may turn.

But in addition to those, there are particular circumstances we have been in since the French Revolution that have given great advantage to the arts and schemes of the Few. One is the free circulation of money and the high prices of labor and produce. Such times (as I have before shown) are greatly in favor of the interests of the Many if rightly improved, and operate in the same proportion to the disadvantage of the Few, while they last. But as a time of prosperity is a time of inattention and necessity is the mother of invention, so while the Many have been eating and drinking and running into costly fashions and manners of living and blessing themselves that tomorrow shall be as this day and much more abundant, the Few have been closely attending to all elections from the highest office in the federal government down to the lowest town officers, and have obtained a large majority in all the legislative powers made up of lawyers, justices, and other fee officers—which (as I have before shown) are the most dangerous sets of men to be trusted with legislative power of any in the world. Also, they have closely attended to the appointment of all officers in the judicial and executive departments in order to keep all from being in office that are opposed to their interests and schemes. It is said with great sanctity that these officers are appointed by the governors and presidents. I would ask how the presidents and governors come by a knowledge of the characters they appoint, for they cannot have a personal knowledge of one to a thousand of them. And the Many pay no attention to these things. Consequently, they are all appointed by the recommendations, arts, and schemes of the Few.

Also, if anyone has happened to get elected or appointed into office that has been friendly to the interests of the Many, or any other persons that have shown any degree of abilities in favor of the Many and in opposition to their measures, then immediately all the arts of the Few are set to work to ruin them both in character and estate. Also, as public newspapers are almost the only source of obtaining the necessary knowledge in elections, every art has been used to ruin the character of the republican printers and hinder the publication of anything that is for the interests of the Many.

Another art has been practiced with great effect not only to hinder persons from using their influence in elections but to stop the mouths of the elected—that is the monarchial custom of opening every session of the legislative bodies with a kingly speech by the presidents and governors, and echoing them back in humble terms unbecoming to representatives of a free and sovereign people.[42] For as I have before shown, the executive power is the last and lowest department in a free government, and though it is their duty to state facts and point out dangers and disadvantages, yet they have no right in the least degree to dictate measures to the legislative power.

While the Few have been closely pursuing all these measures to deceive and influence the Many, they have been continually crying up the goodness of the times—that we were the most free and happy people on earth; and that all our happiness arose from the goodness of our government and the wisdom and policy of the measures pursued by its administration. By this measure they deceived thousands of honest men among the Many and made instruments of them to abuse the characters and turn out some of the best of our representatives. For all those who labored for a living felt them to be—and knew them to be—the best times for their interest that ever they enjoyed.

But the goodness of the times arose not from the measures of government but principally from the three following things:

1. The free circulation of money arose partly from the state banks which were erected to oppose the partiality of the Continental banks, which were used principally to aid the funding and speculating measures of the Few.[43]

2. The high prices of labor and produce arose in a great measure from such a vast numbers leaving off work and attempting to live by speculation, trading, and other callings as there has of late been done; and from the costly fashions and high manner of living introduced by them. If all those would go to work that are not needed by the public in other ways and would live as cheap as they did fifty years ago, it would soon make a difference in the price of labor and produce.

3. But the greatest cause of all was the revolution in France, and the wars in Europe. This made a vast demand for all kinds of produce for exportation; and both the contending powers in Europe—wishing to get our influence and trade on their side—gave extraordinary prices for what we had to spare (and France paid us cash for what they had).

That was the main reason for money being plenty and the price of labor and produce high. This, too, was the reason why the Few were so offended at France and made the British treaty, choosing rather to have connections with Britain—where they have a balance against us annually of more than five million dollars. This they know will keep money scarce, the price of labor and produce low, and keep the Many under their control.[44]

Thus, by the combinations, arts, and schemes of the Few, the advantage they have taken of the times, and the ignorance and inattention of the Many, although the Few do not exceed one-twelfth part of the people in numbers, yet they have carried their points in most of our elections and in the appointments of all the judicial and executive officers; and in many other ways they have almost destroyed the principles of our liberties and undermined the foundations of a free government. Unless there is a better means of knowledge among the Many, we cannot support our liberties long.

In the foregoing remarks I have often mentioned the ignorance and want of knowledge among the Many. But I would not be understood as thinking that we are more ignorant than other people and nations are. On the contrary, I believe we are the most knowing and the best acquainted with the true principles of liberty and a free government of any people on earth. Our fathers fled here for the sake of liberty, and we have been brought up in the enjoyment of it from our youths. We are on an equality as to property to what they are in the old countries, and we are as free from superstitions and bigotry as any nation. Also, many have been the attacks of tyrants upon us to deprive us of our liberties. But we have always risen superior to them, and I firmly believe we shall again. At the same time, as we are more seriously and dangerously attacked now than ever we were before, I think we cannot be saved without more knowledge still.

The greatest and only means by which the Few carry their plans into execution is by their associations and correspondences or complete organization, by which they know each other's minds so as to dart their plans like flashes of lightning from one end of the continent to the other. The Many have just as good a right to associate for the obtaining of knowledge as the Few. And if the Many were one-quarter part so well organized as the order of Cincinnati and the other orders of the Few are, they would always carry their points in elections—being in numbers so vastly superior. Although the elections to the federal government are seldom and more out of the knowledge of the Many, yet as that government was erected for national purposes only, if strict attention were paid to elections to the state governments, town officers, and jurymen, the federal government would never attempt to enslave the people. If the Many knew their own interest as well as the Few do theirs and acted upon the same principles as they do, the people would never admit a Tory to be so much as a hog constable in town.[45]

As to the arts and measures that have been practiced by the Few to ruin individuals in character and estate who are opposed to their measures, it would be vastly more in the power of the Many—and more just for them—to ruin the characters of the Few who are opposed to liberty. And this they might do by withholding employment from those who were so opposed and giving it to those who were friendly to liberty. For what is the profession of a merchant, lawyer, physician, or divine good for if nobody would employ them?

All these things might be carried into effect by the Many with a trifling expense laid out in knowledge and attention to their true interests.

Having thus described the causes that destroy free governments and the circumstances we are brought into by them, I will now point out—

THE REMEDY AGAINST THEM

The remedy against these great evils that I shall point out is a constitutional, cheap, easy, and sure method of conveying necessary knowledge among the Many. To do this I will: first, describe the knowledge necessary for every free man to have; and, second, point out the method of obtaining it; and then offer some remarks in vindication of the plan.

First, the knowledge necessary for every free man to have is:

1. a knowledge of mankind and the little different interests that influence all orders of men;

2. a knowledge of the principles of a free government and the constitution he lives under;

3. a knowledge of all the laws that immediately concern his conduct and interest so as to govern his life according to them;

4. a knowledge that when laws are once constitutionally made they must be obeyed—let them be never so wrong in his mind—and that there is no remedy for grievances but by petitioning the authority that made them and using his rights and influence in elections;

5. a knowledge of the true principles, character, and abilities of all those he votes for into any kind of office;

6. a knowledge of the existing sentiments, wishes, and circumstances of all those of his interests in the town, county, district, state, and nation to which he belongs—so that he may unite with them in elections and petitioning for redress of grievances;

7. also a knowledge of the most interesting debates and decisions in the legislatures and the conduct of all the officers of government in every department. Every freeman ought to have all this knowledge independent of any orders of men or individuals who may be interested to mislead or deceive them.

Second, a description of the means by which it may be obtained.

As this knowledge cannot be obtained without the expense of a continued series of the publications that can be read with confidence as to their truth; and as newspaper knowledge is ruined by the arts of the Few; and as the order of Cincinnati have performed such wonders by their associations, I propose a Society of the Many or of Laborers to be formed as nearly after the order of the Cincinnati as the largeness of their numbers and circumstances will admit. The society is to be composed of all the republicans and laborers in the United States who are willing to be at the expense of obtaining the above described knowledge. In order to be clearly understood about how such a society may be formed, I have drafted a constitution for it—modeled as nearly after the constitution of the Cincinnati as the numbers and circumstances of the Laboring Society will admit—and placed it at the close of this address, ready for signing, to which the reader is referred.

REMARKS IN VINDICATION OF THE PLAN

As all new things make a great stir at first, so it may be expected that this will have many objections raised against it. The orders of the Few may denounce it as dangerous to government. But it is perfectly constitutional and only what all the orders of the Few have practiced upon the Many (as I have before shown).

The opposition of the Few to the plan arises from selfish principles and from their enmity to free government; therefore, I will not say much to this objection. But the trouble and expense of it may be a more serious objection in the minds of some. Therefore I request your attention to the following statements and calculations.

As to such a magazine, it is not like three or four newspapers in a week that are good for nothing except when they are fresh from the press. Magazines will answer the same purpose if they are had any time in the month.[46] Consequently, one will answer for a whole neighborhood, and a librarian would be well paid for his trouble by having them handy.

As to the town, country, and state presidents and other officers, if they should do their duty without any pay but the honor of it, they would receive as much as militia officers and many town officers do for their services. And if they are well paid, it cannot be much to an individual.

As to the cost of the magazine, I have no doubt but that a good republican printer would deliver one in every town in the state for a dollar a year large enough for a laborer to peruse—provided it should become general and supposing six neighbors should join together, it would be but one shilling apiece, for which they would have such valuable reading for themselves and their families for a whole year.

As to spending three or four hours on the Fourth of July to choose officers, it is no more than thousands do now.[47] And if there should not be more than one-quarter of the society to attend the meeting, the officers might be chosen and the organization kept up just as well as if they all met.

As to establishing funds, suppose a class or an individual puts in seventeen dollars. The interest of that would pay for a magazine forever without the trouble of annual or quarterly payments. And if the State of Massachusetts should grant a fund for the whole state, it would not cost more than the Shays affair did, which never would have happened if such a society had been formed then. And suppose Congress should grant funds for the whole continent, it would not cost more than the Pittsburgh insurrection did, which would never have happened if there had been such a society. For these insurrections happened entirely for want of knowledge among the people. To what better purpose could individuals make donations than to such a society as this? If General Washington should grant twenty thousand dollars towards it (as it is said he offered towards a national academy), it would in my opinion be to a better purpose and make thousands think better of him than they did for his signing the British treaty.[48]

Some may suppose it would be very difficult to form such a society. But only let a printer be agreed with to advertise such a magazine and thousands would take them if they had nothing in view but amusement. They would soon find that it would be vastly the cheapest way to organize themselves as proposed to get them, and the society would come together like a building well framed and marked. Also, by thus being organized to superintend the magazine and newspapers they take, the editors thereof would be furnished with the means of conveying the above described knowledge and would be induced to do it as completely as possible from the principles of self-interest. Consequently, they would be read with confidence as to their truth, let the contradictions of the Few be what they will.

Some may yet think this will be a slow way to bring about a reformation in our present circumstances. But if I am not vastly out of my calculation about the numbers of the Few and Many, only let us pay as close attention to all elections as the Few have done and we will purge the state legislatures from fee officers. Let us also keep a full representation there and attend closely to the choice of jurymen and the jury boxes. In short, vote no man into any office without the best satisfaction you can get that he is a true friend to liberty and a free government. Study the constitutions and your rights and liberties established in them. But above all keep from insurrections, riots, and rebellions and never oppose any of the constituted authorities by force. For this always gives advantage to the Few—and the Many always have the cost to pay. If good men are persecuted, fined, or imprisoned wrongfully, bear it patiently. Make a common cause of bearing such fines and make those being persecuted as comfortable as possible. Listen to grievances from every part and unite in remonstrating and petitioning for redress, knowing that there is no other way than that and in using our rights in elections to get relief. If we keep firm and united in this way, we shall soon see an alteration in every department of government. The Few will all feel as if they are acting in the presence of their constituents and will act as servants and not masters.

If such a society were formed, all hurtful customs and fashions might be reformed, and many impositions of sundry orders of men guarded against. Also agriculture, manufactures, economy, and industry might be promoted—for it is for the want of such means of information that a great part of the studies and improvements of learned men and societies established for those purposes are entirely lost.

Such a society, well established, would convince the world that America can and will be free, and that Americans know how to support their liberties as well as to gain them. It could also become a model for all other republics to pattern after.

And I have often thought that in some such way, similar societies might be organized throughout the world as well as governments; and by social correspondences and mutual concessions to each other, all differences might be settled so as to banish war from the earth.

For it is from the pride and ambition of rulers and the ignorance of the people that wars arise. No nation as a nation ever gets anything by going to war with another—for whatever their conquests may be, the plunder goes to a few individuals and always increases the miseries of more than it helps. All the advantage of national dealings is in commerce and the exchange of the produce of one country for another. And whenever they go to war with each other, these advantages are lost—so that if the individuals composing nations knew what was for their true interests and happiness, as they might do by such societies, more than seven-eighths of them would be willing to pay, or lose the whole in dispute, rather than go to war.

Having thus far pointed out the causes and the remedy, I will now give some further reasons why I think this plan will answer the purpose. Although I am no great reader, yet from what I have read and heard, all the republics both ancient and modern, they have all been troubled and rent with these contentions between the Few and Many. And though numerous have been the schemes and plans that have been tried by the Many to support their rights and liberties, yet from the superior arts of the Few they have sooner or later been overpowered and government dwindled into vile aristocracy or monarchy.

The most effectual plan of the Many was the establishing of the Roman tribunes. Some writers say that these enabled them to support their liberties over five hundred years. Others say that these tribunes soon mounted into power, became the ready associates of those they were to guard against, and betrayed the interests of the Many. But the plan I have proposed (if well established) will enable every man to be his own tribune, and will continually grow stronger and stronger so long as self-interest governs mankind.[49]

What most establishes me in the opinion that this plan will answer comes from my own observations of the operation of these causes in our own government, especially the causes, conduct, and final issue of the insurrection that happened in Massachusetts in 1785 and 1786. As I lived near the scene of action and received frowns from both sides for being opposed to their measures, it drew my closest attention and observation. And though I have been too lengthy already, yet I must here give a short history of it.

ON THE SHAYS AFFAIR IN MASSACHUSETTS

At the close of the British war, although our paper money had died away and left the people greatly in debt by it, and a great public debt was on us by the war, yet there was a large quantity of hard money among us sufficient for a medium. But for want of the proper regulation of trade and with the prices of labor and produce being higher here than in other countries, our merchants shipped the hard money off, load after load, by the hundred thousand dollars together to Britain for trifling gewgaws and things that were of no service to us, until there was but little left. Taxes were extremely high. Some counties were two or three years behind. And with the prices of labor and produce falling very fast, creditors began calling for old debts and saying that they would not take payment in paper money. Those who had money demanded forty or fifty percent for it. And fee officers demanded three or four times so much fees as the law allowed them, and were so crowded with business that sometimes it was hard to get any done. Property was selling almost every day by execution for less than half its value. The jails were crowded with debtors. And with the people being ignorant that all their help lay in being fully and fairly represented in the legislature, many towns neglected to send representatives in order to save the cost—so that the Few only were represented at court [that is, the Massachusetts state legislature, known as the General Court], with an aristocratic Bowdoin as governor at their head.[50]

Under all these circumstances, the people were driven to the greatest extremity. Many counties took to conventions, remonstrances, and petitions to a court where they were not half represented. But not being heard, and in some instances charged with seditious meetings and intentions, under all these circumstances, some counties were so foolish as to stop the courts of justice by force of arms. This shook the government to its foundation. For instead of fatherly counsels and admonitions, the dog of war was let loose upon them, and they were declared in a state of insurrection and rebellion.

In these circumstances, the Few were all alive for the support of the government, and all those who would not be continually crying, "Government, Government," or who dared to say a word against their measures, were called Shaysites and rebels and threatened with prosecutions, etc. But with a large majority of the people thinking that there was blame on both sides, or viewing one side as knaves and the other as fools, it was with great difficulty and delay before a sufficient number could be raised and sent to suppress those who had closed the courts.

But the suppression was done with the loss of but few lives. This put the people in the most zealous searches after a remedy for their grievances. Thousands and thousands of miles were ridden to consult each other on the affair, and they happily effected it in a few months only by using their privileges as electors. Bowdoin was turned out from being governor and Hancock was almost unanimously elected in his place.[51] Many of the old representatives shared the same fate, and a full representation was sent from every part of the state, which soon found out means to redress the grievances of the people, though they were attended with the most difficult circumstances, so that everything appeared like the clear and pleasant sunshine after a most tremendous storm.

This is a striking demonstration of the advantages of a free elective government and shows how a people may run themselves into the greatest difficulties by inattention in elections, and how they can retrieve their circumstances by attending to them again. This Shays affair never would have happened if there had then been such a society as I now propose. Many people then would have sacrificed half their interest to have been possessed of such means of knowledge.

This affair, too, is a striking demonstration of the madness and folly of rising up against a government of our own choice when we have constitutional means of redress in our own hands. For although it was supposed by many that if Hancock had been governor at that time—even after the courts were stopped—that the whole affair might have been settled with less than a thousand dollars cost; yet it was so managed that it cost the state (in time and money) near a million dollars, and it almost entirely ruined hundreds of honest, well-meaning men that only needed the means of knowledge I have described.

Thus, my friends, I have freely given you my opinion of the causes that destroy free governments and of a remedy against them, not in the language and style of the learned (for I am not able), but in as plain a manner as I am capable. And I have done it from a conviction that it was my duty, and for the happiness of mankind. If I have misrepresented anything or used any unbecoming language, it is for the want of knowledge and learning. For I am a true friend to all orders of men and individuals who are friends to true liberty and the rights of man. The remedy I have described is not a costly one, for confident I am that each penny laid out in it would soon save pounds in other needless expenses. Therefore, unless you see more difficulty in applying it or less need of it than I do, you will immediately put it on foot and never give over until such a society is established on such a lasting foundation that the gates of hell will not prevail against it—which may the Almighty grant is the sincere desire of a

Laborer

CONSTITUTION OF
THE LABORING SOCIETY

INTRODUCTION

1. Whereas it hath pleased the Supreme Governor of the universe for the fall of man to pass the irreversible sentence on him that in the sweat of thy face shalt thou eat thy bread, therefore it is undoubtedly the duty of every person who is blessed with the faculties of a sound body and mind to apply himself industriously to some honest calling for the benefit of himself and society.

2. Although there are many callings which men may live honestly by without labor, yet as labor is the sole parent of all property by which all are supported, therefore the calling ought to be honorable and the laborer respected.

3. And whereas not only the constitution of our government allows of association and the liberty of the press, but all orders of men who live without labor have improved thereon, therefore we whose names are hereunto subscribed, in order to establish as cheap, easy, and sure conveyance of knowledge and learning for a laborer to have as possible; and to promote similarity of sentiments and manners, industry and economy, agriculture and manufactures, etc., do hereby constitute ourselves into a society of friends by the name of the Laboring Society.

ARTICLE I

Section 1. The persons who constitute this society are all the free male persons in the United States who are twenty-one years of age, who labor for a living, and are willing to join and submit to the regulations of it.

Section 2. Also there are admitted into it all persons of any other denominations, provided they subscribe to its funds and submit to the regulations of the society.

ARTICLE II

The society shall be divided into meetings like the order of the Cincinnati; viz., class, town, county, state, and continental meetings.[52]

Class Meetings

Section 1. The class meetings may be formed by a greater or lesser number just as their situation, circumstances, or inclinations suit. A single person may be a class if he will be at the expense thereof; or twenty may join and have them a librarian to use the magazine by turns or meet together and hear it read.

Town Meetings

Section 2. The town meetings are to include all the classes belonging to each town unless they are too large; and in that case they may divide as they find necessary. They shall meet annually on the Fourth of July at four o'clock in the afternoon and choose them a president, vice-president, clerk, and treasurer or collector.

County Meetings

Section 3. The county meetings shall be formed by the presidents of the town meetings, when they can attend, and when they cannot, the vice-presidents may attend in their stead. They shall meet annually on the first Tuesday in September and choose officers as the town meetings did.

State Meetings

Section 4. The state meetings shall be formed by the presidents of the county meetings as the county meetings were by the town presidents, who shall meet on the first Tuesday of October and choose officers as the county meetings did.

Continental Meetings

Section 5. The continental meetings shall be formed by the state presidents' appointing a sufficient number of faithful persons somewhere near the center of the continent to receive and convey by correspondences all necessary information in the safest and most expeditious manner possible.

ARTICLE III

The main business of all these officers and meetings is to invent the cheapest and most expeditious method of conveying all the knowledge described above to the classes—especially all they need in elections—by furnishing the classes with a monthly magazine, and the town presidents with a weekly newspaper, to contain said knowledge; and when necessary by special meetings, hand bills, and other correspondence. The officers are to receive pay for the whole from the classes until other funds can be established for that purpose, and as soon as can be thought proper, they are to apply to the state legislatures for acts of incorporation, to receive donations, and establish funds for the support of the said society; also, they are to introduce the best regulations possible among them.

ARTICLE IV

If any person belonging to the society should behave unbecoming or be mistrusted of embezzling the society's money, neglecting the duty he undertakes, or in any way trying to injure the society, he may be removed from the society by a majority of the meeting he belongs to, and if he is an officer, another is to be chosen.

ARTICLE V

The president of either meeting shall have the power to call the meeting together at any time when he thinks proper, and in his absence the vice-president may do the same. And they shall be obliged to do so whenever fifteen members request it.

ARTICLE VI, OR, A COVENANT TO BE SIGNED

We, the subscribers, inhabitants of the Town of   in the County of   and the State of   , having considered the foregoing constitution and the ends for which said society is formed, do hereby engage to submit to the regulations and support the honor and dignity thereof, so long as they are conducted agreeable to the laws and constitutions of the government we live under; and we will punctually pay our proportions of the cost of supporting the same. And that we will always be ready to support the constituted authorities in the suppression of insurrections, rebellions, or invasions of the common enemies. Also that we will take pains to inform ourselves as to the true principles and abilities of all those we vote for into any office in the government we live under, and that we will attend on all elections when we can, and put in a vote for those persons we think will serve the public best.

Witness our hands—

OTHER WRITINGS

The following selections originally appeared in the 1798 version of "The Key of Liberty."

ON MERCHANTS

The merchants have organized themselves and have their chambers of commerce and correspondence from one end of the continent to the other. Although they are in many respects a great advantage to the Many, by making vent of our produce and furnishing us with necessaries and conveniences from other countries, yet if we should be drawn into a war by their adventures we should pay very dearly for all the advantages we receive from them. Besides, foreign trade not well regulated is the most dangerous to the interest of the Many of anything we have to fear. Our money may all be carried off from among us for that which will do us no good.

Foreign manufactures may be cheapest at first cost, but not in the long run. Merchants may grow rich on the ruins of our mechanics and manufactories, and bring us unto as bad a condition as we were in in 1786, for the merchants look only to their own interests. And it is evident that a large part of the merchants were in favor of the British treaty and fond of carrying on a trade with that sinking nation, which trade leaves a balance against America of more than four million dollars annually, which will ruin us in a few years unless it is stopped.

The true principles of republicanism and a free government may be taught to youths in some of our colleges and academies, for aught I know. But it is evident that other political principles are admitted in many of them, or we should not be astounded with exhibitions in favor of monarchies—and running down republican principles—as we often are. One thing is pretty certain, that the scholars are taught to keep up the dignity of their professions, for if we apply for a preacher or schoolmaster, we are told the price is so much, and they can't go under, for it is agreed upon, and they shall be disgraced if they take less, let their abilities for the service be what they will.

ON MINISTERS OF THE GOSPEL

The ministers of the Congregational order, and others for aught I know, have formed themselves into societies and many of them are incorporated and have their state and county meetings, which may be of great service or absolutely necessary in their sacred functions. But it is no breach of charity to suppose that they have some political purposes in them. Nor do I deny their right to meddle in politics. But as they receive their support for teaching piety, religion, morality, and things relative to another world, and their hearers, being not all of them capable of discerning between divinity and politics, they ought, whenever they teach obedience to the civil laws or reprove for disobedience, etc., to teach and explain the true principles of our free government as established in our constitutions. Instead of preaching about and praying for officers of government as infallible beings, or so perfect that we ought to submit to and praise them for all they do (when in fact they are all our servants, and at all times accountable to the people), they ought to teach their hearers to be watchful of men in power, and to guard their own rights and privileges with a jealous eye, and teach them how to do it in a constitutional way.

If their principles forbid this, they had better let politics entirely alone, for if they use their great influence to mislead and prejudice their hearers against the true principles of a free government (as many of them have done of late) by praising our executive for making the British treaty, and in short by praising monarchical and despotic government, and running down and blackguarding republican principles and the French nation, they are in fact acting a treasonous and rebellious part, and doing all in their power to destroy the government. Their hearers ought not to attend on such teachings. It is this conduct in ministers that is the principal reason for the neglect of public worship and religious institutions that is so much complained of by the ministers now.

Ministers have it more in their power to turn the minds of their hearers to right and wrong than any other order of men. It had been the general practice of all arbitrary governments to prostitute religion to political purposes, and make a handle of this order of men to mislead, flatter, and drive the people by the terrors of the other world into submission to their political schemes and interests. Consequently, the ministers ought to be watched and guarded against above all other orders, especially when they preach politics.

ON JUDICIAL AND
EXECUTIVE OFFICERS

. . . Whoever takes a view of the conduct and doings of our judicial and executive powers, both state and federal, for a few years back, must perceive a growing uneasiness and aversion in them to be bound down to the strict sense and meaning of our constitution and laws. It is this conduct in them that is the principal cause of all our differences with France, and our contentions among ourselves. It would take volumes to define them; therefore, I shall only attempt here to describe but one example, and that one is but of little consequence. The one I shall attempt to describe is the call of General Hull on the division of militia under his command, including the whole county of Middlesex, to dress themselves in uniform and appear at Concord for a military exhibition.

Neither the laws nor the constitution of Massachusetts empower any officer, not even the governor, to call the militia together in larger bodies than regiments. Nor does it empower them to call even regiments, where it causes more than twenty miles of travel for any company (except upon invasion or insurrection). And there is no law to oblige any solider to get a uniform.

This call at first came out only as a request, and but few if any thought that they were obliged to comply with it. But the ambition of the regimental officers was soon stirred up to a high degree, to see which would appear the most respectable with their regiments and companies. All the arts of flattery were used to obtain their ends. But seeing they were likely to fail in them, they soon had recourse to threatening and falsehoods, declaring that there were orders and laws to oblige the men to dress and go. Although the laws demand only ten shillings for nonappearance at musters, hundreds of them were made to believe that they must pay four times that sum if they disobeyed. Consequently, thousands attended the muster. Some went thirty or forty miles, which took them four or five days, and were at ten or twelve dollars cost for a uniform. Some that did go paid their fines rather than dispute their officers. Others being conscious that there was no law for such things stood trial before the justices, and some of them got cleared. But by far the greatest number of them had both fine and cost to pay. (This much judicial and executive officers can do without any assistance from the legislature.) It is supposed that a fair cost, at least, in uniforming, time, and money was thirty thousand dollars, without any advantage to the public or satisfaction to those who planned it.

For it pleased the Almighty to send a tremendous storm upon them at the very moment they were about to exhibit, which spoiled all their fun. As it was all done without or in opposition to law, the authors of it have great reason to be thankful that it did not rain fire and brimstone upon them instead of cold water.[1]

I should not have swelled my remarks with this narrative, did I not believe that there was more intended than pretended by these events. The pretense was to revive a military spirit and make us appear more formidable to other nations, which appears to me to have a contrary effect. For where a nation pretends to a well-organized and efficient government as we do, for individuals to start up in such a manner to do the business of government proves its weakness. It is the duty of all in a free government to wait for the determination of the legislative power, and punctually obey it. Then they would be general and formidable.

Therefore, I believe that this fuss was more intended to sound the people, and try the strength of the executive and judicial powers over the legislative's, and to set the militia to murmuring so as to form the pretext for a standing army. For if it should once become a law to dress in such costly uniforms and attend such musters, it would be cheaper to support an army than submit to it. I am led to these conclusions by the extraordinary precautions and consultations that were taken in giving out the orders, they being such as may be fairly constructed into positive orders or only requests—so that there was no way for a delinquent to defend his cause but by impeaching the justice that gave judgment for his fine. And if we may judge from the trials of

Hunt and Blunt, a single person had better submit to pay a hundred times ten shillings than seek for a remedy in that way.[2] Consequently, the executive and judicial powers, when united, may take just such sums from individuals and execute just such military enterprises as they please.

ON LAWYERS

The lawyers have established their bar meetings and become the most formidable and influential order of any in the government—though they are neither judicial nor executive officers, but a kind of mule order, engendered by and many times overawing both. This order of men get their living entirely from the quarrels, follies, disputes, and distress of the Many, and the intricacy of our laws. It is from the arts and doings of these men that the judicial and executive officers are furnished with the chief of their business and employ. Consequently, they are bound together by the strongest bonds of union.

Many have been the complaints against the lawyers in years back, and the intricacy of our laws. Much time has been spent and many pains taken by the legislature to remedy the evil. But all to little or no purpose. The sole reason is because we send these fee officers as representatives to make our laws. Unless the people can be brought to calculate more upon the operation of these little selfish principles on mankind, and purge the legislatures of fee officers, they cannot be governed by laws very long.

Thus, we see all the orders of the Few completely organized, and they have of late gotten so monstrously crowded with numbers that it is impossible for them all to get a living by their professions. Being in want of employ, they are aiding all the plans and schemes of the Cincinnati to influence the Many.

I would not be understood to be against the associations of any orders of men, for to hinder them would hinder their improvements in their professions, and hinder them from being serviceable to the Many. There need only be one society more established, or proper means of information among the Many to hinder the associations of the Few being dangerous in politics. In order to promote those means of information among the people, there have been many societies established, known as Constitutional, Democratical, and other names, made up of men of republican principles and great abilities who did all in their power to enlighten the people to their true interests. But the want of the society I have mentioned, or a proper channel of conveying their sentiments to the people—and the joint exertion of the majority of the other orders I have mentioned to hinder their usefulness and prejudice the minds of the people against them— have brought them almost into disuse. But I have no doubt that they will revive again when they think they can do any good . . .

ON LEARNING

No person who is a friend to liberty will be against a large expense in learning, but it ought to be promoted in the cheapest and best manner possible.[3] Which in my opinion would be:

For every state to maintain as many colleges in convenient parts thereof as would be attended upon to give the highest degrees of learning.

For every county to keep as many grammar schools or academies in convenient parts thereof as would be attended to by both sexes, summer and winter. No student or scholar would pay anything for tuition.

For the county schools to pay particular attention to teaching the English language, and qualifying its scholars to teach and govern common schools for little children.

For every town to be obliged to keep as much as six weeks of writing school in the winter and twelve weeks of a woman school in the summer in every part of the town—so that none should be thronged with too many scholars, and no scholar should have too far to travel. Every person to be obliged to send his children to school—for the public is as much interested in the learning of one child as another.

If this method of learning were established, we would soon have plenty of schoolmasters and mistresses as cheap as we could hire other labor, and labor and learning would be connected together, and lessen the number of those that live without work. Also, we should have plenty of men to fill the highest offices of state for less than half we now give. But instead of this mode of learning, the Few are always striving to oblige us to maintain great men with great salaries, and to maintain grammar schools in every town to teach our children the ABCs. All of which is only to give employ to gentlemen's sons and make places for men who live without work. For there is no more need of a man's having a knowledge of all languages to teach a child to read, write, and cipher than there is for a farmer to have the mariner's art to hold the plow.

ON THE BRITISH TREATY
AND THE WAR WITH FRANCE

To describe all the bad effects of this treaty would take volumes. I shall therefore only mention two or three which have a direct tendency to deprive us of a medium of trade and get us into wars, especially one with France.

In one of the articles of said treaty, it is agreed that no higher duties shall be laid on articles imported from Britain.[4] Consequently, we shall be thronged with their manufactures, made by their slaves who by the oppression of their government are obliged to work for a trifle and live upon less. They will undersell, destroy all our manufactories, and carry all our money away from us. And all our future taxes must be collected for our lands, property, and dealings in the country.

In Article X, it is declared that there shall be no confiscations or seizures of private property belonging to subjects of either nation in case of war between the two powers—seizures which the laws of nations declare to be just. This article deprives us of almost our only defense against Great Britain; for the immense sums they have in our funds, banks, and due from our merchants, together with the advantage of our trade to them, would be a greater guard against their making war with us than fifty ships of the line. But this is given up, so that the property of these creditors who have great influence in both nations will be safe in case of war. Thus, they will not be interested in opposing war, but will readily join the Few in both nations to make war for the sake of keeping standing armies to enslave the Many.

But the greatest danger from this treaty is a war with France, and this seems to have been the design of our administration ever since the treaty was in contemplation.

For President Washington's great bull of neutrality (however agreeable it might be to the people that did not know our obligations to France) was a direct violation of our treaties with them.[5] By the treaty of commerce, Articles XVII and XXII, we were bound to give them very great privileges, and to withhold them from their enemies in time of war.[6] Also, by the treaty of alliance, Article XI, we were bound to guarantee their West India islands, a great part of which they have lost for want of fulfilling our obligations.[7] Besides, the cause of France was our own cause. The combination against them was against the rights of man and free government all over the world, which we had just been fighting for ourselves, and probably never should have obtained if France had not assisted us. So that we were solemnly bound by treaty, interest, and gratitude to be on the side of France. All these obligations would gladly have been fulfilled by the people if the administration had done its duty. If instead of sending Jay to make the treaty the administration had adopted Mr. Madison's resolutions, kept on the embargo, stopped the importation of British goods, sequestered the British property in our funds, etc., and let the British make a war on us as soon as they dared, it is more than probable (had this been done) that the war in Europe would have been over before now—King George underground with Louis XVI—England a republic—America in good credit, and in other ways much better off than it is now.[8]

But instead of this, and in order to hinder the legislature from adopting those just resolutions, the government sent Jay to make the treaty—hypocritically and falsely pretending that he was sent only to demand restitution for our plundered property and the western posts—and charged our minister to tell the same lies to France. But instead of fulfilling this declaration by the treaty, Jay abandoned the modern laws of nations which he was bound to support both by our treaty with France and his own proclamation, and gave Britain liberty to seize their enemy's property on board our vessels and to seize provisions going to their enemy's ports. Jay also made many articles contraband that were not so by the laws of nations. This being done, the French only took advantage of the second article of our treaty with them, which states that neither party shall grant any particular favors to other nations, respecting navigation and commerce, which shall not immediately become common to the other party, who shall enjoy the same favor freely.[9] So that the French are not to blame for taking our vessels any more than Britain is.

By the treaty's giving this liberty to Britain to seize American ships, it is supposed that we have lost nearly half the shipping we owned three years ago. This is a true statement of the case. Anybody may be convinced of it if they will only look at the treaties and Mr. Monroe's and Fauchet's pamphlets.[10]

Yet we see these combined orders, treatymongers, and British agents under Cincinnati, who were so horribly frightened a little while back for fear of going to war with Britain, crying out—and are ever ready to tear their hair off to persuade us to go to war with France, who alone has conquered almost all of Europe and is now in its full strength and vigor. But the plain truth is that the treaty and those that made it are the causes of all our disgrace and difficulty. The treaty was unconstitutionally made, and ought to be forever disowned, and all those that made it banished from the continent, and their property confiscated towards paying the damages. But if this can not be done, we had infinitely better give France two or three million dollars than to go to war with them for two years. This may appear by taking a short view of the little wars and insurrections we have had since our independence.

ON THE PITTSBURGH INSURRECTION

The Pittsburgh insurrection would never have happened if it had not been for some unreasonable irritations imposed upon the people by trying to enforce the Excise Law there, before it was put into execution in other parts of the continent. Or if they had known the minds of the people on it in other parts, and after it had broken out, they might have settled for a trifle, if fatherly and kind measures had been used. But as it was managed, it cost the continent upwards of twelve hundred thousand dollars.[11]

ON THE NAME OF WASHINGTON

Great use has been made of this name to deceive the people and make them content with the administration of government. And much time has been spent in our legislative bodies and sacred pulpits in the most fulsome and sickish praises and adulations of Washington, for what he ought to have been banished for—which has deceived thousands and thousands of honest people into their measures.[12] Which was principally done by pretending (in addition to his real services in the war) that he was the cause of all the prosperity we were under. For all are sensible that the times have been very prosperous to the interests of the Many. But this was not in the least owing to the measure of the administration, but to the Republican opposition there too, or principally to the three following causes:

First, the free circulation of money arose principally from the state banks which were erected to oppose the partiality of the Continental Bank, which was chiefly employed in speculation.[13] But this would never have raised the price of labor and produce. That arose from two other causes. One is that all orders of men who live without labor have gotten so monstrously crowded with numbers and made it fashionable to live and dress so high, that labor and produce are scarce. If all of them would go to work and live as prudently as common laborers do, that are not absolutely needed by the public, it would soon make a difference in the price of labor and produce. But the greatest cause is the European wars, which have made all kinds of produce in the greatest demand while we had a free trade, which probably might have continued to this day if the treaty had not been made. But as these good times for the Many are, in proportion, bad for the Few, so all the measures of the administration have been opposed to them. The treaty was made to injure the rights of the Many. And it has already effected this, for the lawyers and all the fee men have had more business within two years back than they had for six years before.

ON PARTIES

Much has been said of late about parties, and many are the names by which they have been described, such as Monarchical and Republican, Aristocratical and Democratical, Royalists and Jacobins, Tories and Whigs, the Few and the Many—all which names appear to me to describe but two sets of men differing about one and the same thing. The causes of their disputes arise from the conceived difference of interests I have been describing, and the unreasonable desires of the Few to tyrannize over and enslave the Many. The glorious revolution that has lately taken place in France has alarmed the Few to a very high degree. When it first broke out, almost all the kings of Europe openly combined to destroy it or restore monarchy and tyranny again in France. So great was their confidence of success that they agreed among themselves how to divide the territory and spoils. But as the Lord is always on the side of a people contending for their rights and liberties, He so inspired France with wisdom and courage that they have already cut and torn their enemies to pieces, so that the European monarchs have all but one been obliged to make peace with the French on their own terms.

But all this has not discouraged that party. They are yet in hopes of effecting by bribery and corruption what they cannot do by force of arms. Their combinations are extended far and wide, and are not confined to Europe and America but are extending to every part of the globe. Gog and Magog are gathered together, to destroy the rights of man and banish liberty from the world. They had nearly effected one of their nefarious plans in France last summer, only by their arts and bribery in elections and for want of the means of knowledge among that great people. For by said arts they had gotten a governing part of the legislature, a large part of the judicial power, and two of the Directory in favor of overthrowing the republic and setting up royalty.

And the hand of providence was never more evident than in

the overthrow of the royalists on the fourth of September.[14] For although there was abundant evidence of the conspiracy, yet it could not have been expected that a bare majority of the Directory, with all the assistance they could get, would have attempted it, from mere principles of virtue and obedience to their oaths to support the constitution—especially when their complicated constitution had not particularly provided for such an affair. But providence had so ordered it that their lives were in danger, and they were compelled to do their duty by self-preservation. Thus, the royalists were overthrown and that great republic not only saved but established on a stronger foundation than ever it stood before.

That there is such an extensive combination in favor of royalty is evident from the great knowledge and great calculations that were made upon it all over Europe and in America long before it took place—for the royal newspapers were full of hints about it. Also its being published in England that twenty of the American senators had agreed to sign the British treaty before ever it arrived here is another piece of evidence of said combinations. Thousands of others might be mentioned.[15]

Therefore, I am strongly led to believe, by the great zeal of our administration to send so many ministers to foreign nations—and the characters they send—and the great opposition made in Congress to granting supplies for that purpose, that they are many of them somewhat engaged in this combination. I also believe that by the great zeal of these parties in America, which appears in newspapers and the warm debates in Congress, that one party or the other will soon govern, or there will be a scratch for it. Therefore, I conclude that it is high time for the Republicans to unite as well as the Royalists . . .

Notes

Index

ABBREVIATIONS

BTR	Billerica Town Records, Town Hall, Billerica, Massachusetts
CCP	Middlesex County, Court of Common Pleas, Files, Massachusetts Archives, Columbia Point, Boston, Massachusetts.
CR	Church Book, Church Records, 1663–1842, First Congregational Church, Billerica, Massachusetts.
Grantees	Registry of Deeds, *Billerica Grantees*, Middlesex County Courthouse, Lowell, Massachusetts.
Grantors	Middlesex County Registry of Deeds, *Billerica Grantors*, Middlesex County Courthouse, Lowell, Massachusetts.
MAB	Manning Tavern Account Book, 1753–1778, Baker Library, Graduate School of Business Administration, Harvard University.
MFC	Manning Family Collection, Lyndon Library, University of Lowell.
MV-B	Massachusetts Valuations for 1771, vol. 132 (Billerica), microfilm, Massachusetts Archives, State House, Boston, Massachusetts.

Manning Probate, 1776	Middlesex County Probate Records, first series (1648–1871), file #14611, William Manning, 1776, microfilm, Massachusetts Archives, State House, Boston, Massachusetts.
Manning Probate, 1814	Middlesex County Probate Records, first series (1648–1871), file #14615, William Manning 1814, microfilm, Massachusetts Archives, State House, Boston, Massachusetts.
Morison, ed., "Manning's 'Key' "	Samuel Eliot Morison, ed., "William Manning's 'Key of Libberty,' " *William and Mary Quarterly*, 13 third series (1956), 202–254.
WMQ	*William and Mary Quarterly*, third series.

NOTES

William Manning and the
Invention of American Politics

1. Merle Curti, *The Growth of American Thought* (1943; 2nd ed., New York, 1951), 141–142.
2. See, for example, Gordon S. Wood, "The Democratization of Mind in the American Revolution," in Robert Horowitz, ed., *The Moral Foundations of the American Republic* (1978; 3rd ed., Charlottesville, Va., 1986), 102–128. For an interesting study of both diffusion and reception in the eighteenth-century countryside, see Richard D. Brown, *Knowledge Is Power: The Diffusion of Information in Early America, 1700–1865* (New York, 1989), esp. 132–159. More pertinent to the reception of political ideas is Bernard Bailyn's study of Harbottle Dorr, in Bailyn, *Faces of Revolution: Personalities and Themes in the Struggle for American Independence* (New York, 1990).
3. Nathan O. Hatch, *The Democratization of American Christianity* (New Haven, 1989), 26–27.
4. Max Farrand, ed., *The Records of the Federal Convention of 1787*, 4 vols. (New Haven, 1911, 1937), I, 299.
5. William L. Saunders, ed., *The Colonial Records of North Carolina*, 10 vols. (Raleigh, N.C., 1886–1890), X, 870a.
6. See J. R. Pole, *Political Representation in England and the Origins of the American Revolution* (London, 1966), esp. 227–249.
7. Farrand, *Records*, I, 58.
8. For an overview of this democratic thinking, but with a different interpretation of it, see Gordon S. Wood, *The Radicalism of the American Revolution* (New York, 1992), 227–366.
9. Henry A. Hazen, "Genealogical Register," in Hazen, *History of Billerica, Massachusetts* (Boston, 1883), 93–94, 174. On the Manning homestead and tavern, see also E. F. Bacheller, "Manning House," in E. F. Bacheller, ed., *Colonial Landmarks* (Lynn, Mass., 1896), 15; William H. Manning, "The Manning Homestead," *Massachusetts Magazine* 1 (1908), 42–43; and Myra Manning Koenig, "The Story of the Manning Manse" (mimeo in authors' possession, n.p., 1950), 6–7.

10. On Samuel Manning and his offspring, see Hazen, *History*, 134, 302–307; Hazen, "Genealogical Register," 93–94; and Lucius R. Paige, *History of Cambridge, Mass., 1630–1877, with a Genealogical Register* (Boston, 1877), 602. In 1679, Samuel Manning ranked near the middle of the third quintile (top 47 percent) of the town's tax list; in 1688, he ranked near the top of the second quintile (top 24 percent). For these lists, see *New England Historical and Genealogical Register* 5 (1851), 173, for the year 1679; and 31 (1877), 303, for the year 1688. In 1733, the first William Manning ranked toward the middle of the first quintile (top 14 percent), as did his son (top 12 percent) in 1755. For the Manning holdings in 1771, see MV-B; and in 1776, see Manning probate, 1776. In 1776, our William (the wealthiest Manning in town) ranked at the middle of the second quintile (top 31 percent). For these lists, see Hazen, *History*, 203–205 (1733); 205–207 (1755); and 247–251 (1776).

These shifts in relative position over the years should not be overemphasized, given the relatively egalitarian distribution of wealth in eighteenth-century Billerica compared with the major seaports and rural centers of Massachusetts. Using similar figures from other years, Edward Cook, Jr., grouped Billerica among those towns which had a "fully developed social structure," but with a broader diffusion of property and power than major rural towns like Springfield and Worcester. See Cook, *The Fathers of the Towns: Leadership and Community Structure in Eighteenth-Century New England* (Baltimore, 1976), 167–168, 177–179. See also Jackson Turner Main, *The Social Structure of Revolutionary America* (Princeton, 1962); and Robert A. Gross, *The Minutemen and Their World* (New York, 1976).

As for political connections, both William's father and grandfather served one term each as selectman. William's father was a commissioned lieutenant in the Billerica militia. Hazen, *History*, 306; ibid., "Register," 94.

11. William H. Manning, *The Genealogical and Biographical History of the Manning Families* (Salem, 1902), 213; Hazen, "Register," 93–94; CR (November 25, 1770), 42; (June 4, 1769), 64.

12. Robert Gross reports that the average age of first marriage for sons born to men in Manning's father's cohort in neighboring Concord ranged between 23.9 and 26.0 years. On these matters, and on the rates and social significance of premarital sex and pregnancy, see Gross, *Minutemen and Their World*, 100–101; and Daniel Scott Smith and Michael S. Hindus, "Premarital Pregnancy in America,

1640–1971: An Overview and Interpretation," *Journal of Interdisciplinary History* 5 (1975), 537–570. On parental power and the timing of inheritance, see Toby L. Ditz, *Property and Kinship: Inheritance in Early Connecticut, 1750–1820* (Princeton, 1986), 103–118.

13. On the younger William Manning's holdings in 1771, see MV-B. In April 1776, he appears to have purchased an additional two acres of land, along with a dwelling house, wood house, and blacksmith shop, from Joseph Osgood of Billerica for £13 6s 8p; see agreement dated April 22, 1776, in the MFC. The younger Manning's growing tavern responsibilities are evident from the changes in the handwriting in the MAB. On the young William's election, see BTR, March 6, 1775. The details of the disposal of the elder Manning's estate—including his voiding of the 1772 will—appear in Manning Probate, 1776.

14. On the struggle over the will, see Manning Probate, 1776. On February 11, 1777, Manning received £81 12s from his neighbor Benjamin Dowse, Jr., in exchange for "40 acres more or less" of land; see *Grantees* 8:380–382. The younger William Manning's purchases of his sibling's land rights are elaborated in the agreement dated May 7, 1777, between William Manning and Jonathan Manning, Timothy Manning, Solomon Manning, and Elizabeth Carlton, in the MFC. In 1790, upon his mother's death, Manning bought his sister's and brother-in-law's rights to her widow's third for £12 10p. Two years later he bought Timothy and Solomon's rights, paying them £18 apiece. Agreement dated April 20, 1790, MFC; *Grantees* 8:366.

15. Cook, *Fathers of the Towns*, 167–168, 177–179. See also Van Beck Hall, *Politics without Parties: Massachusetts, 1780–1791* (Pittsburgh, 1972), 3–23. Hall constructed elaborate indices to measure how all Massachusetts towns ranked in various economic and social-cultural categories. By his calculations, Billerica was almost squarely in the middle in all major categories, neither a frontier village nor a commercialized town. See "Appendices to Van Beck Hall's *Politics without Parties*" (n.p., n.d.), Hillman Library, University of Pittsburgh.

16. Hazen, *History*, 87–102, 178–179, 309; MV-B. In all, 86 percent of Billerica's farms in 1771 (including the Mannings') contained tillage, pasture, and hayland, compared to 76 percent of the farms in the state as a whole. In addition, 93 percent of these so-called complete farms (again, including the Mannings') produced at least 30 bushels of grain per year, considered by one historian as the abso-

lute minimum required to support an average-sized family; the colony-wide figure for all complete farms was 81 percent. These proportions suggest a high degree of local self-sufficiency in Billerica, mediated by an intricate web of barter and commercial exchanges of labor and produce of various kinds. At the same time, the figures suggest that a substantial proportion of Billerica's independent farmers raised enough grain to sell a surplus. In 1771, for example, one-third of Billerica's farms—including the Mannings'—produced one hundred bushels or more of grain. On Massachusetts figures and standards of self-sufficiency, see Bettye Hobbs Pruitt, "Self-Sufficiency and the Agricultural Economy of Eighteenth-Century Massachusetts," *WMQ* 39 (1984), 333–364. The Billerica figures were computed from MV-B.

17. MAB. Like many other accounts from this period, the entries in the Manning book end in 1778 (although some scattered later accounts appear in it as well). The runaway inflation of 1779–1780 utterly defeated the best efforts of many otherwise diligent account keepers to record their transactions. It would appear, however, that Manning closed the tavern in 1778, possibly for good. See below, note 33.

18. Charging interest did not in itself mean that any given exchange was a commercial agreement. Far more important was the nature of the relationship between the parties. Even where interest was charged in the barter networks, payment schedules were very pliable, almost lackadaisical, so long as the people involved remained on good terms with one another.

19. The classic account of these barter networks is W. T. Baxter, *The House of Hancock: Business in Boston, 1724–1775* (Cambridge, Mass., 1945). For other discussions, see Christopher Clark, *The Roots of Rural Capitalism: Western Massachusetts, 1780–1860* (Ithaca, N.Y., 1990), 27–38, 64–74; and Michael Merrill, *Revolutionary America: Agrarianism and Equal Rights in the Early Republic* (Cornell University Press, forthcoming).

20. The term "complex barter" is intended to distinguish these arrangements from the simple, textbook-variety forms of barter, in which people exchange goods without any delay at all, as in a swap meet. W. T. Baxter coined the phrase "bookkeeping barter" to refer to these kinds of relations, but his phrase overestimates the role of formal accounting in their operation. See Baxter, *House of Hancock*, 11–38.

21. MAB, passim.

22. For a powerful elaboration of the theme of lordships and depen-

dency in the postrevolutionary context, see George Brock, "Address to the Yeomanry of Massachusetts," *Independent Chronicle* (Boston), August 31, 1786. Although Manning never cited Brock's address, he almost certainly read it. On the fear of lordships before and during the revolutionary crisis, see Richard Bushman, "Massachusetts Farmers and the Revolution," in Richard Jellison, ed., *Freedom, Society and Conscience: The American Revolution in Virginia, Massachusetts, and New York* (New York, 1976); and Bushman, *King and People in Provincial Massachusetts* (Chapel Hill, 1985), 198–206.

23. BTR, December 28, 1767; February 5, 1773; June 6, 1774. See also Richard D. Brown, *Revolutionary Politics in Massachusetts: The Boston Committee of Correspondence and the Towns, 1772–1774* (Cambridge, Mass., 1970), 200n.

24. BTR, June 6, 1774.

25. BTR, March 6, 7, 1775; October 9, 1775. See Allen French, *The Day of the Battle of Concord and Lexington* (Boston, 1925), 11–15, 50–61, for background on the dispute between General Gage and the towns before the battle at Concord.

26. BTR, March 20, 1775; Hazen, *History*, 234; "Remonstrance of Selectmen of Billerica," in L. Kevin Wroth, et al., eds., *Province in Rebellion: A Documentary History of the Founding of the Commonwealth of Massachusetts, 1774–1775* (Cambridge, 1975), 1964–1965. There is a memorandum dated March 16, 1775, in the Loammi Baldwin Papers, Houghton Library, Harvard University, containing an eyewitness account of the selectmen's meeting with Gage. For the discussion of the Ditson affair in the provincial congress, see William Lincoln, ed., *Journals of Each Provincial Congress* (Boston, 1838), 131–134.

According to local legend, British soldiers first sang "Yankee Doodle" to mock their American adversaries during the Ditson affair. One of the original stanzas would appear to confirm this.

> Yankee Doodle came to town
> For to buy a firelock;
> We will tar and feather him
> And so we will John Hancock.

See Library of Congress, *Report on "the Star-Spangled Banner"* . . . *[and] "Yankee Doodle"*, Oscar G. T. Sonneck, compiler (Washington, D.C., 1909), 129. For a different version of the origins of Yankee Doodle, see J. A. Leo Lamay, "The American Origins of 'Yankee Doodle,'" *WMQ* 33 (1976), 435–464.

27. French, *Concord and Lexington*, 73, 217–218. Manning officially served with Captain Solomon Pollard's (Billerica) Company and was credited with ten days service beginning April 19. See *Massachusetts Soldiers and Sailors of the Revolutionary War*, 17 vols. (Boston, 1902), X, 194–195.

28. This is a modernized rendering from the 1798 version of "The Key," printed in Morison, "Manning's 'Key,' " 211. It is more striking than the revised version of 1799. We have similarly modernized all subsequent quotations from the version edited by Morison.

29. On the *rage militaire* in 1775, see Charles Royster, *A Revolutionary People at War: The Continental Army and the American Character, 1775–1783* (Chapel Hill, 1979), 25–53.

30. William Emerson to his wife, July 17, 1775, in Allen French, *The First Year of the American Revolution* (New York, 1934), 300; Benjamin Thompson, Boston, November 4, 1775, in Historical Manuscripts Commission (Great Britain), *Report on the Manuscripts of Mrs. Stopford-Sackville, of Dayton House, Northamptonshire*, 2 vols. (London, 1884), II, 15, 18; Letter from a Surgeon, May 26, 1775, *Fraley's Bristol Journal*, July 8, 1775, reprinted in Margaret Wheeler Willard, ed., *Letters on the American Revolution* (Boston, 1925), 120.

31. *Massachusetts Soldiers*, X, 194–195. Both Edward Hazen and William H. Manning claimed that Manning served longer, but there is no record of his name on any of the subsequent muster lists. See Hazen, *History*, 244–246; and Manning, *Genealogical History*, 212. Hazen and Manning also incorrectly dated his lieutenant's commission from before the Battle of Bunker Hill, which may account for why they believe he fought there. Not only did his commission come several months after Bunker Hill, but there is no evidence that Pollard's regiment saw any action in the battle, with or without Manning. See Richard Frothingham, *History of the Siege of Boston and of the Battles of Lexington, Concord and Bunker Hill* (Boston, 1849), 309. Wilson Waters, *History of Chelmsford, Massachusetts* (Lowell, 1917), 211–213, gives a history of Manning's reorganized regiment.

32. James Kirby Martin and Mark Edwin Lender, *A Respectable Army: The Military Origins of the Republic, 1763–1789* (Arlington Heights, Ill., 1982), 90–91.

33. Koenig, "Manning Manse," 7–8; *Massachusetts Magazine* 1 (1908), 43; Abram English Brown, *Beside Old Hearth-Stones* (Boston, 1897), 330–331. According to Brown, Manning's descendants showed him a wooden spatula that Sarah Manning had used one morning to

bake bread for a visiting company of New Hampshire militia. We are grateful to Professor Loretta Valtz Manucci for bringing this source to our attention.

Regarding the tavern, the accounts ended in 1778, and any other account book that may have existed has apparently not survived. Moreover, at some point, someone pasted in the book the accounts of debts owed by William to his son Jephtha, dating from 1812— suggestive if not definitive evidence that no other account book ever existed. This, in turn, suggests that Manning closed the tavern for good in 1778. If he did keep it going—or if he reopened it later on—he would seem to have done so without keeping regular accounts, an unlikely proposition.

34. See Oscar Handlin and Mary Handlin, eds., *The Popular Sources of Political Authority: Documents on the Massachusetts Constitution of 1780* (Cambridge, Mass., 1966), esp. 18–51; Samuel Eliot Morison, "The Struggle over the Adoption of the Constitution of Massachusetts, 1780," *Massachusetts Historical Society Proceedings* 50 (May 1917), 353–411.

35. BTR, June 5, 1780; for Billerica's comments, see Handlin and Handlin, *Popular Sources*, 137–138, 635. As in note 36, the final quotation is a modernized rendering of the 1798 version. Later, Manning would be slightly less sweeping in his praise for the Constitution, though he remained an admirer.

36. On the western opposition, see the address of the 1786 Hatfield Convention, in C. O. Parmenter, *History of Pelham, Massachusetts* (Amherst, Mass., 1898), 367–368. On *The Independent Chronicle* and the Boston *Gazette*'s affinities, see Morison, "Struggle over the Massachusetts Constitution," 363, n. 2.

37. On the conventions of the 1780s, see Hall, *Politics without Parties*, 173–184, 204–226. For Manning's views, see Morison, ed., "Manning's 'Key,'" 215, 233–234.

38. Morison reports this bit of oral tradition in his introduction to "The Key." See Morison, ed., "Manning's 'Key,'" 203–204.

39. BTR, March 4, 1782; March 1 and May 6, 1784; March 7, 1785; March 6, 1786; March 5, 1787.

40. On the origins and fate of Shays' Rebellion, see especially Hall, *Politics without Parties*, 166–226. See also George Richards Minot, *The History of the Insurrection in Massachusetts* (1787; 2nd ed., Boston, 1810); Josiah Holland, *History of Western Massachusetts* (Springfield, 1855); Parmenter, *History of Pelham*, 145–163, 366–402; Marion Starkey, *A Little Rebellion* (New York, 1955); and David Szatmary,

Shays' Rebellion: The Anatomy of an Insurrection (Amherst, Mass., 1980). Starkey reported that a person named William Manning was among those sought by authorities for his role in the insurrection, but this was not our William. See Starkey, 220, 248.

41. The most recent estimate of citizen support for the regulation is in Szatmary, *Shays' Rebellion*, 59. On the difficulty of raising troops, see ibid., 80; on legislative reluctance, see Hall, *Politics without Parties*, 215–216.

42. BTR, April 5 and 6, 1781; April 4, 1785; April 3, 1786. Van Beck Hall constructed a table measuring the town's support for procreditor policies, on the basis of nineteen critical votes in the General Court from 1780 to 1786. The Billerica representative voted with the country towns and against the creditors on fifteen of the votes, voted with the creditors only once, and was absent three times. See Hall, *Politics without Parties*, 102–103; William Jenkins, ed., *Records of the States of the United States*, microfilm (Washington, D.C., 1949), Massachusetts, A.1b, reels 10 and 11.

43. BTR, August 17, 1786. On the Groton Regulation, see Samuel Abbott Green, comp., *Groton Historical Series II* (Groton, 1890), 46–48; 55–57; idem, comp., *Groton Historical Series III* (Groton, 1893), 443–447; Seth Chandler, *History of the Town of Shirley* (Shirley, Mass., 1883), 127–133, 702–704; and Lemuel Shattuck, *A History of the Town of Concord* (Boston, 1835), 134.

44. BTR, n.d. [1787]. According to John Farmer, his relation Edward Farmer, Billerica's representative to the General Court, assisted in raising the company, and was one of the justices later delegated to receive the oath of allegiance from the captured Shaysite insurgents after the regulation ended. Farmer, *An Historical Memoir of Billerica* (Amherst, N.H., 1816), 20–21.

45. Isaac Stearns Diary, September 11–13, 1786, Isaac Stearns Papers, Massachusetts Historical Society, Boston; Shattuck, *History of Concord*, 132; *Worcester Magazine*, 4th week of November, 1786; *Massachusetts Centinel*, January 1 and 24, 1787; BTR, September 18, 1786; April 2, 1787. On Bowdoin's resounding defeat and its importance, see Richard D. Brown, "Shays's Rebellion and the Ratification of the Constitution," in Richard Beeman, et al., eds., *Beyond Confederation: Origins of the Constitution and American National Identity* (Chapel Hill, 1987), 113–127.

46. BTR, May 8, 1786; February 25, 1788.

47. Shays' Rebellion Vouchers, Massachusetts Archives, Columbia Point, Boston, Massachusetts.

48. Morison, ed., "Manning's 'Key,' " 243. It is worth noting that Manning dropped this second passage in the 1799 version of "The Key." Perhaps he thought twice about some of his prevarications.
49. BTR, March 11, 1787; Hazen, *Billerica*, 101.
50. KL, 234. Isaac Stearns, a Billerica supporter of the proposed federal constitution, complained to one of his political friends that "the only qualification thought necessary" for election to the state ratifying convention was "to be able to harangue [sic] against the proposed constitution." Stearns to Samuel Adams, December 31, 1787, Stearns Papers, Massachusetts Historical Society. Billerica's delegate, William Thompson, duly voted "no" at the convention. See Jonathan Elliot, *The Debates in the Several State Conventions on the Adoption of the Federal Constitution*, 5 vols. (1836–1845; 2nd ed., Washington, D.C., 1861), II, 179. Cf. Farmer, *Historical Memoir*, 20.
51. Morison, ed., "Manning's 'Key,' " 234.
52. On plebeian democrats and the Bill of Rights, see Sean Wilentz, "The Powers of the Powerless," *New Republic*, December 16 and 23, 1991.
53. Hazen, *History*, 257, 273–277, 315; Farmer, *Historical Memoir*, 21, 27.
54. According to Hazen, the trade carried on the canal from Boston to Billerica never exceeded $200 per year. *History*, 274. Henry David Thoreau, *A Week on the Concord and Merrimack Rivers* (1849; rpt. New York, 1985), 41.
55. Main, *Political Parties*, 85.
56. Hazen, *History*, 275.
57. Memoranda, March 4, 1795, April 1795, Box 3, Folder 1; Agreement between William Manning and L[oammi] Baldwin et al., December 13, 1794, Box 4, Folder 1, Loammi Baldwin Collection, Baker Library, Graduate School of Business Administration, Harvard University.
58. Jacob Abbott v. William Manning, September 7, 1798, CCP.
59. William Manning to Catharine Cummings, July 18, 1787, and April 27, 1792, *Grantors* 8:102, 368, 402. Agreements, William Manning and the Directors of the Union Bank, January 30, 1793; William Manning and Joseph Davis, March 6, 1802; William Manning and Theophilus Manning, December 1, 1808; Jacob Abbott v. William Manning, September 8, 1798, MFC; Jephtha Manning to His Father, William Manning, Dr. [1804–1811], MAB, 62; *Grantees* 9:125, 11:276–279. Jephtha Manning v. William Manning, January 1, 1812, CCP.

60. Land Sold: William Manning (28 acres) to Joseph Jaquith (for £60), February 25, 1794, *Grantors* 8:457; WM (15 acres) to David Rogers (for £40), January 23, 1793, ibid., 9:117; WM (7 acres) to David Levenstone (for £40), October 19, 1796, ibid., 9:245; WM (3.5 acres) to Timothy Manning (for £21), January 10, 1797, ibid., 9:275; WM (4 acres) to Timothy Sprague (for £30 18s), April 20, 1797, ibid., 9:300; WM (11 acres) to Joseph Jaquith et al., (for $268.81), March 1, 1799, ibid., 9:399.

    Land Purchased: William Manning (£8) to John Laws (for 4 acres), November 17, 1790, WM (£50) to David Levenstone (for 50 acres), January 20, 1794, WM ($50) to Thomas Richardson (for 10 acres), April 30, 1796, MFC.

61. See, especially, Richard Hofstadter, *The Age of Reform: Bryan to F.D.R.* (New York, 1955), 23–36.

62. Almost certainly, Manning first learned of the report from the summary in the *Independent Chronicle*, January 28, 1790.

63. E. James Ferguson, *The Power of the Purse: A History of American Public Finance, 1776–1790* (Chapel Hill, 1961), 251–305.

64. For an incisive summary of this line of thought, see Janet Riesman, "Money, Credit, and Federalist Political Economy," in Beeman et al., eds., *Beyond Confederation*, esp. 156–161. Riesman draws special attention to the writings of William Barton and George Logan, and the speeches of William Findley; like Manning, they too thought paper money a good thing, though they differed on the best ways to secure it.

65. Jacob E. Cooke, ed., *The Reports of Alexander Hamilton* (New York, 1964), 8.

66. The essays of "Free Republican" appeared in the *Independent Chronicle* between November 24, 1785, and February 9, 1786. Other readers could have seen the work in the *Massachusetts Magazine*, where it originally appeared. We were able to identify "Free Republican" from marginal notes by James Freeman in his copy of the *Massachusetts Magazine*, now in the possession of the Massachusetts Historical Society. See the issue for February 1784, page 140.

67. Gordon Wood, quoting a similar passage from "The Key," concludes that Manning directed his animus against men of static, proprietary wealth. But by this rendering, Manning's diatribes in both manuscripts against merchants, stock jobbers, and bankers simply fall away, making him appear far less critical of commercial abuses than he plainly was. Cf. Wood, *Radicalism*, 276–277.

68. Manning's reasoning should not in any way be confused with a more

modern class analysis, whether Marxian, Weberian, or some other variety. Samuel Eliot Morison, for example, was completely mistaken when he detected in Manning's work a "lonely American whisper of Karl Marx's cry, 'Workers of the World, Unite!' " (Morison, ed., "Manning's 'Key,' " 207.) The system Manning described did not pit propertyless wage earners against moneyed employers, least of all in the countryside, where the vast majority of the population lived. On the contrary, it set the producing Many, including a wide array of the lower and middling sort—artisans, shopkeepers, wage earners, and independent farmers—against the moneyed Few, a category which covered rentiers and professionals as well as capitalists. Such inclusiveness was entirely appropriate in a world where moneyed men—those with access to large pools of financial assets—had only just begun to command the production and distribution of goods. Moreover, Manning, living in the late eighteenth-century Massachusetts countryside, could see that much of the ability of the Few to gain their fortunes out of the earnings of others derived from their political connections, privileges, and monopolies, a notion which Marx would blithely dismiss as fatuous. See Karl Marx to Joseph Weydemeyer, March 5, 1852, in Alexander Trachtenberg, ed., *Letters to Americans* (New York, 1953), 44–45.

Nor was Manning simply an ambitious, individualistic petty capitalist who more than anything else simply wanted to get rich. Manning endorsed commerce; he appreciated the importance of banks and modern financial institutions to that commerce; and he understood the role played by a ready supply of money in the growth of trade and mass prosperity. But none of this had anything to do with a desire on his part to become one of the fortunate Few, or to open up such opportunities to others. His was a different sort of argument. Most people, he asserted, would always have to labor for a living. The well-spring of national prosperity lay in maximizing the income of the Many who labored, not of the Few who did not. A free commerce, local banks, and a large supply of money were desirable, in his view, not because they expanded the number of opportunities for a few, very enterprising men to get rich, but because they helped to raise the price of labor and its produce, thus to ensure a decent return to the vast majority of laboring people who expected no more than to live by their labor. On the other hand, a restricted commerce, a national bank, and a tightly controlled money supply—all of which were elements of the Hamiltonian plan—would have the opposite effect.

69. Thomas Jefferson, "The Anas (1791–1806)—Selections" and "Notes on Professor Ebeling's Letter of July 30, 1795," in Jefferson, *Writings*, ed. Merrill Peterson (New York, 1984), 661–702; George Logan, *Letters Addressed to the Yeomanry* (Philadelphia, 1791); idem, *Five Letters to the Yeomanry of the United States* (Philadelphia, 1792); idem, *Letters to the Yeomanry on Funding and Banking Systems* (Philadelphia, 1793).

70. On colonial currency finance and state commissioners, see Ferguson, *The Power of the Purse*, 3–24, 184–188, 222–234. The best general account of states' efforts to deal with the outstanding debt remains Merrill Jensen, *The New Nation: A History of the United States during the Confederation, 1781–1784* (New York, 1950), esp. 302–326. See also Allan Nevins, *The American States during and after the Revolution* (New York, 1925), 515–543.

71. On the societies, see Eugene P. Link, *Democratic-Republican Societies, 1790–1800* (New York, 1942). On the Pennsylvania uprising and related events in other states, see Thomas P. Slaughter, *The Whiskey Rebellion: Frontier Epilogue to the American Revolution* (New York, 1986).

72. See, especially, *Independent Chronicle*, January 5, 1795. See also Link, *Democratic-Republican Societies*; Paul Goodman, *The Democratic-Republicans of Massachusetts: Politics in a Young Republic* (Cambridge, Mass., 1964); and Philip S. Foner, ed., *Democratic-Republican Societies, 1790–1800: A Documentary Sourcebook* (Greenwood, Conn., 1976), 255–266.

73. There is an immense literature on the Great Awakening, which can be most conveniently entered through Sydney E. Ahlstrom, *A Religious History of the American People* (New Haven, 1972), 280–329. On the failure of the evangelical churches to institutionalize their gains, see Clarence C. Goen, *Revivalism and Separatism in New England, 1746–1800: Strict Congregationalists and Separate Baptists in the Great Awakening* (New Haven, 1962), 68–114, 208–295, 327; and Steven Marini, *Radical Sects of Revolutionary New England* (Cambridge, Mass., 1980), 19–20.

74. Marini, *Radical Sects*, 40–47. For a provocative criticism of the standard accounts of religious declension during and after the American Revolution, see Douglas Sweet, "Church Vitality and the American Revolution: Historiographical Consensus and Thoughts toward a New Perspective," *Church History* 45 (1976), 341–357. See also William G. McLoughlin, *New England Dissent, 1630–1833*, 2 vols. (Cambridge, Mass., 1971), II, 698–699;

and George Claude Baker, Jr., *An Introduction to the History of Early New England Methodism, 1789–1839* (Durham, N.C., 1941), 5. The Methodists did not venture into the region until the 1790s, but they quickly made up for lost time. By 1800, they claimed more than 8,000 members, a forty-fold increase since the beginning of the decade. James Mudge, *History of the New England Conference of the Methodist Episcopal Church, 1796–1910* (Boston, 1910), 34, 65.

75. Henry Cumings, *An Half-Century Discourse Addressed to the People of Billerica, February 21, 1813* (Cambridge, Mass., 1813), 13; Hazen, *History*, 270; *The Diary of William Bentley, D.D.* (Salem, 1905–1914), II, 39–40.

76. Hazen, *History*, 263–264. There is no evidence of any dispute between Manning and the congregation in the records of Billerica's First Congregational Church, and as late as 1790 his daughter Lucinda was baptized there. CR (January 24, 1790), 101. Manning's second son, Jephtha, did purchase a pew, in the gallery.

77. See the entry for Cumings in William B. Sprague, *Annals of the American Pulpit* (New York, 1865), VIII, 55–64; Henry Cumings, *A Sermon Preached at Billerica, June 28, 1795* (Boston, 1795), hereafter cited as *Sermon [on Natural Religion]*. Cumings' sermon provoked a reply from Ephraim Robbins, who was "at a loss to know whether [in Cumings' opinion] . . . mankind had fallen at all, in a moral view; or whether they had fallen a little." See Robbins, *A Friendly Letter to the Rev. Mr. Cumings, Containing Several Queries upon Certain Observations in His Sermon on Natural Religion* (Newburyport, Mass., 1796), 5.

78. We have not been able to identify the "divine" to whom Manning referred. Nor do we know the name of the "writer" to whom he would refer a bit later in his discussion. But there are striking similarities between what Manning had to say and the comments of Samuel Hopkins, Jonathan Edwards' literary executor, in his influential treatise, *The System of Doctrines Captured in Divine Revelations* (Boston, 1793), 348–349: "It is evident, that sin consists in self love . . . Self love regards nothing but self, as such, and subordinates every being to this; and opposes every thing which, in the view of the selfish person, opposes him, and his selfish interest. He who is under the government of this affection takes all to himself, and gives nothing to any other being, as if he is the greatest, the best, and only worthy and important being in the universe . . . Self love is blindness and delusion itself, as it is a contradiction to all truth,

and the source of all blindness and delusion with respect to things temporal, and spiritual, which have or can ever take place."

79. On the continuing theological differences between Old and New Light divines, see Conrad Wright, *The Beginnings of Unitarianism in America* (Boston, 1955); Joseph Conforti, *Samuel Hopkins and the New Divinity Movement* (Grand Rapids, Mich., 1981); William Breitenbach, "Unregenerate Doings: Selflessness and Selfishness in New Divinity Theology," *American Quarterly* 34 (1982), 479–502; and idem, "The Consistent Calvinism of the New Divinity Movement," *WMQ* 41 (1984), 241–264.

80. See especially, Wright, *Beginnings of Unitarianism*, 135–184. The quotation is from Cumings, *Sermon [on Natural Religion]*, 10.

81. Bentley, *Diary*, I, 275. On the social origins of the New Divinity preachers, see Harry S. Stout, "The Great Awakening in New England Reconsidered: The New England Clergy," *Journal of Social History* 8 (1974), 24, 27–28, 33–36.

82. See Gary B. Nash, "The American Clergy and the French Revolution," *WMQ* 22 (1965), 392–412.

83. Henry Cumings, *A Sermon Preached at Lexington on the 19th of April, 1781* (Boston, 1781), 15–20, 23; idem, *A Sermon Preached before His Honor Thomas Cushing, Esq.* (Boston, 1783), 7.

84. Cumings, *Sermon before Cushing*, 16.

85. Henry Cumings, *Sermon on [Natural Religion]*, 31; idem, *A Sermon Preached at Billerica, December 15, 1796* (Boston, 1797), 22, 24–25, hereafter cited as *[Christmas] Sermon*. The quotation was taken from *[Christmas] Sermon*, 33.

86. Cumings, *A Sermon Preached at Billerica, November 29, 1798* (Boston, 1798), 29, hereafter cited as *[Thanksgiving] Sermon*.

87. See Cumings, *[Christmas] Sermon*, 17, 24–25.

88. See Ahlstrom, *Religious History of the American People*, 423–424; and Oliver Elsbree, *The Rise of the Missionary Spirit in America, 1790–1815* (Williamsport, Pa., 1928), 47–83.

89. Elsbree, *Rise of Missionary Spirit*, 62, 146–150.

90. On Methodist egalitarianism, see Baker, *Early New England Methodism*, 16–25; on the missionary affinities of the Methodists and the New Divinity men, see Elsbree, *Rise of Missionary Spirit*, 151–152.

91. Ahlstrom, *Religious History*, 373. On community, fraternity, and order in eighteenth-century Methodism, see also Russell E. Richey, *Early American Methodism* (Bloomington, Ind., 1991), esp. 11–15.

92. In addition to Baker, *Early New England Methodism*, see Jesse Lee, *Memoir of the Rev. Jesse Lee* (New York, 1823).

93. For detailed treatments of the controversy over Jay's Treaty, see Jerald A. Combs, *The Jay Treaty: Political Battleground of the Founding Fathers* (Berkeley, 1970); and Lance Banning, *The Jeffersonian Persuasion: The Evolution of a Party Ideology* (Ithaca, N.Y., 1978). The quotation is from Thomas Paine, "Letter to George Washington on the Subject of the Late Treaty Concluded between Great Britain and the United States," in *The Complete Works of Thomas Paine: Political and Controversial* (London, n.d. [1875]), 521.

94. William Manning, "Constitution of the Labouring Society" [1797], Houghton Library, Harvard University. This is the title which a later librarian ascribed to the manuscript.

95. On the Adamses and the 1798 repression, see James Morton Smith, *Freedom's Fetters: The Alien and Sedition Laws and American Civil Liberties* (Ithaca, N.Y., 1956), 247–257; and John C. Miller, *Crisis in Freedom: The Alien and Sedition Acts* (Boston, 1951), 29, 120–122, 229.

96. William Manning to Thomas Adams, n.d. [February 15, 1799], MS. Am 880/830, Houghton Library, Harvard University.

97. James Monroe, *A View of the Conduct of the Executive, in the Foreign Affairs of the United States, Connected with the Missions of the French Republic, during the Years 1794, 5, and 6* (Philadelphia, 1797); Joseph Fauchet, *A Sketch of the Present State of Our Political Relations with the United States of North America* (Philadelphia, 1797); Morison, ed., "Manning's 'Key,' " 240–241.

98. The best recent discussion of these developments is David Jaffe, "The Village Enlightenment in New England, 1760–1820," *WMQ* 47 (1990), 327–346. On the rise of the political press, see Donald H. Stewart, *The Opposition Press of the Federalist Period* (Albany, 1969), esp. 3–32.

99. In 1784, for example, Aedanus Burke's *Considerations on the Society or Order of the Cincinnati* (Charleston, S.C., 1783) appeared in the *Chronicle* together with a copy of the Society's constitution and other commentary and reports on its meetings. Manning would also have been able to read the accounts of several town and county conventions held during the year to express concern over various national and local issues. In 1785, the paper reprinted Richard Price's *Observations on the Importance of the American Revolution, and the Means of Making It a Benefit to the World* (London, 1784), and also the first few numbers of "Free Republican." In 1786, the *Chronicle* published the concluding numbers of "Free Republican" and ran Benjamin Austin's fierce, polemical reply to "Free Republi-

can" that eventually appeared in pamphlet form as *Observations on the Pernicious Practice of the Law; Published Occasionally in the Independent Chronicle; By Honestus* (Boston, 1786). Throughout the year, several contributors also debated the appropriate national policy toward the debt, some arguing that the original creditors ought to receive consideration, others that they should not; some insisting that the debt be redeemed at par, others that it be redeemed at its current market value. Still others proposed specific tax plans for retiring the debt as quickly as possible. Two of these contributions, those of "Public Faith" (February 16, 1786) and "Moderation" (March 9, 1786), took positions very similar to those which Manning advanced four years later in his own plan for how to deal with the national debt. From July 1786 through the end of the year, the paper was also full of critical descriptions of and negative comments on the Massachusetts Regulation.

100. Manning Probate, 1814.
101. [John Dickinson], "Letters from a Farmer in Pennsylvania (1767–1768)," in Paul L. Ford, ed., *Writings of John Dickinson* (Philadelphia, 1895). Ruth Bogin makes a similar point in her commentary on "Some Proposals."
102. Cumings, *[Christmas] Sermon*, 27.
103. Cumings, *Sermon before Cushing*, 16.
104. Cumings, *Sermon at Lexington*, 12; idem, *[Thanksgiving] Sermon*, 9.
105. Cumings, *Sermon before Cushing*, 7, 18; Morison, ed., "Manning's 'Key,' " 214.
106. For more on this aspect of New Divinity theology, see Breitenbach, "Unregenerate Doings," *American Quarterly* 34 (1982), 479–502. We have learned a great deal from Breitenbach's incisive reappraisal of the New Divinity movement. We do, however, question the simple and direct connection Breitenbach draws between the New Divinity doctrine of holiness as "universal disinterested benevolence" and the "creation of a mentality fitting New Englanders for participation as individualistic entrepreneurs in a market economy" (Breitenbach, "Unregenerate Doings," 502). No doubt the doctrine served this purpose for some of those touched by New Divinity thinking. But as Manning's case suggests, universal disinterested benevolence could also provide a standard by which to criticize the selfish injustices of the emergent commercial society of the 1790s.
107. MFA, 25, 45–47, 49, 112.
108. L. H. Butterfield, ed., *The Diary and Autobiography of John Adams,*

4 vols. (Cambridge, Mass., 1961), I, 191–192; *American Mercury*, December 31, 1792; William Plumer to Theodore Foster, June 28, 1790, quoted in William A. Robinson, *Jeffersonian Democracy in New England* (New Haven, 1916), 56; and *Connecticut Journal*, April 4, 1799. Most published writing on early American taverns does not rise above the anecdotal. Two exceptions are John D.R. Platt, *The City Tavern* (Denver, 1973); and Kym S. Rice, *Early American Taverns: For the Entertainment of Strangers* (Chicago, 1983). More recently, there has been renewed interest in the subject, open to more exacting cultural analysis. See David Weir Conroy, "The Culture and Politics of Drink in Colonial and Revolutionary Massachusetts, 1681–1790" (Ph.D. dissertation, University of Connecticut, 1987); and Peter Thompson, "A Social History of Philadelphia Taverns, 1683–1800" (Ph.D. dissertation, University of Pennsylvania, 1989).

109. For Manning on almanacs, see "A Proposed Method for Carrying the Foregoing into Execution," Manning Papers, MSS. Am 880/836, Houghton Library, Harvard University. On sheep struck dumb by shearing, see *Isaiah* 53:7; also, *Acts* 8:32.

110. Richard Hofstadter, *Anti-Intellectualism in American Life* (New York, 1963), 151–153. In his misreading of "The Key," Hofstadter also ignored Manning's call for the state governments to maintain colleges that would grant "the highest degrees of learning."

111. For an insightful history of the development of this kind of democratic style in the United States, see Kenneth Cmiel, *Democratic Eloquence: The Fight over Popular Speech in Nineteenth-Century America* (New York, 1990), esp. 55–93.

112. See especially Thomas Paine, *Rights of Man* (1791–1792; Harmondsworth, England, 1984), 146–147, 155–157.

113. For a plebeian spokesman of the contrasting temperament, see Staughton Lynd, ed., "Abraham Yates's History of the Movement for the United States Constitution," *WMQ* 20 (1963), 223–245. See also Cecilia Kenyon, "'Men of Little Faith': The Anti-Federalists and the Nature of Representative Government," *WMQ* 12 (1955), 3–43.

114. Morison, ed., "Manning's 'Key,'" 222.

115. Manning characteristically gave Locke's doctrine his own twist. According to Locke, a "servant"—by which he meant not just those in personal or domestic service but all wage earners—had no more claim to the products of his or her own labor than did a

horse. "Thus the Grass my Horse has bit; the Turfs my Servant has cut; and the Ore I have digg'd in any place where I have a right to them in common with others, become my Property, without the assignation or consent of any body. The labour that was mine, removing them out of that common state they were in, hath fixed my property in them." See *Second Treatise*, 328–330.

116. Richard Hofstadter did the most to draw attention to this sort of political reasoning in *The Paranoid Style in American Politics and Other Essays* (New York, 1965). A thoughtful reconsideration of the entire subject that challenges Hofstadter's approach appears in Gordon S. Wood, "Conspiracy and the Paranoid Style: Causality and Deceit in the Eighteenth Century," *WMQ* 39 (1982), 401–441.

117. See Wallace Evan Davies, "The Society of the Cincinnati in New England, 1783–1800," *WMQ* 5 (1948), 12, 24.

118. Morison, ed., "Manning's 'Key,' " 232.

119. Ibid., 249–250.

120. Ibid., 233, 250, 253. This latter provision, which Manning later dropped, can easily be misunderstood. He might at first glance seem to be calling for an Americanized Committee of Public Safety modeled on the instrument of Robespierre's terror in France. In fact, he had in mind something far more benign—and, arguably, far more likely to be effective. In the late eighteenth-century United States, as two recent historians of impeachment have reported, "literally anyone could bring an impeachment by a report or complaint" (Hoffer and Hull, *Impeachment*, 93). A Laboring Society that "managed impeachments" was not adding to the rights of the people; it was simply, to borrow one of Manning's terms, "improving" upon them.

121. An attempt by French moderates and monarchists, encouraged by Great Britain, to deprive Napoleon Bonaparte of his commands sparked the coup. Aided by the army, members of the Directory (the French national executive) purged the legislature, exiled several leading right-wingers to Guyana, and closed the opposition press. For background, see Georges Lefebvre, *The French Revolution*, trans. Elizabeth Moss Evanson, John Hall Stewart, and James Friguglietti, 2 vols. (New York, 1962–1964), II, 194–201. For the *Independent Chronicle*'s reaction, and the dispatches that almost certainly shaped Manning's view of the affair, see the issues dated November 6–9, 9–13, 13–16, and 16–20, 1797. Thomas Paine, among other democratic luminaries, also welcomed the coup. See

Eric Foner, *Tom Paine and Revolutionary America* (New York, 1976), 252.

122. See Jean-Jacques Rousseau, *A Project of Perpetual Peace*, trans. Edith Nuttal (1761; London, 1927); James Madison, "Universal Peace [1792]," in *The Papers of James Madison: Congressional Series*, William T. Hutchinson and William M.E. Rachal et al., eds., 17 vols. (Charlottesville, Va., 1962–1991), XIV, 206–209; Immanuel Kant, "Eternal Peace: A Philosophical Essay," in *Eternal Peace and Other International Essays*, trans. William Hastie (1795; Boston, 1914). Consider also Paine's famous declaration: "From what we now see, nothing of reform in the political world ought to be held impossible. It is an age of Revolutions, in which everything may be looked for. The intrigue of the Courts, by which the system of war is kept up, may provoke a confederation of Nations to abolish it; and an European Congress, to patronize the progress of free Government, and promote the cooperation of Nations with each other, is an event nearer in probability, than once were the Revolution and Alliance of France and America." Paine, *Rights of Man*, 146–147.

123. A copy of "The Institution of the Society of Cincinnati" can be found in Minor Myers, Jr., *Liberty without Anarchy: A History of the Society of the Cincinnati* (Charlottesville, Va., 1983), 258–266.

124. According to the aggregate figures for Billerica given in MV-B, there were three "servants for life," aged fourteen to forty-five, in the town in 1771. On the actual valuation lists, however, it appears that four Billerica households each included one such servant—those headed by Josiah Bowers, Joseph Munroe, Zebediah Rogers, and William Thompson.

The 1790 federal population schedules list five Billerica households (those headed by Joseph Dowse, David Levenstone, Thomas Rogers, William Thompson, and John White) with one free black each; in 1800, there were four free blacks in Billerica, residing in the households of Joseph Dowse, Thomas Rogers, John Soley, and Mary White; in 1810, there were two, in the households of Joseph Dowse and Josiah Rogers. U.S. Bureau of the Census, Population Schedules of the First, Second, and Third Census of the United States, National Archives, Record Group 29 (microfilm). From these lists, it appears that some of Billerica's free blacks after the Revolution were the same persons who had been slaves before 1780. For details on Tony Clark, see *Massachusetts Soldiers*, III, 582. On slavery and its abolition in eighteenth-century Massachusetts, see Lorenzo J. Greene, *The Negro in Colo-*

nial New England, 1620–1776 (New York, 1942); Arthur Zilver-smit, *The First Emancipation: The Abolition of Slavery in the North* (New York, 1967); and Elaine MacEachern, "Emancipation of Slavery in Massachusetts: A Reexamination, 1770–1790," *Journal of Negro History* (1970), 289–306.

The only brief allusion to the institution of chattel slavery in all of Manning's manuscripts appears in the 1799 draft of "The Key of Liberty." On early American white racism, see Winthrop D. Jordan, *White over Black: American Attitudes toward the Negro, 1550–1812* (Chapel Hill, 1968). On *herrenvolk* democracy, see George M. Fredrickson, *The Black Image in the White Mind: The Debate on Afro-American Character and Destiny, 1817–1914* (New York, 1971). On eighteenth-century connections between slavery and democracy, see Edmund S. Morgan, *American Slavery American Freedom: The Ordeal of Colonial Virginia* (New York, 1975). The New England experience shows that slavery was hardly a precondition for democratization among whites. And Manning's writings show that, at least in the 1790s, plebeian democrats need not have held proscriptive racialist assumptions about free blacks. But the political connections between white plebeian democrats like Manning and southern slaveholders would remain a central feature of American life until the collapse of the Jacksonian coalition in the 1840s and 1850s—connections that placed sharp limits on the meanings and possibilities of American democracy.

125. See, above all, Simon Peter Newman, "American Political Culture in the Age of the French Revolution" (Ph.D. dissertation, Princeton University, 1991). On early journeymen's unions, see Bruce Laurie, *Working People of Philadelphia, 1800–1850* (Philadelphia, 1980); and Sean Wilentz, *Chants Democratic: New York City and the Rise of the American Working Class, 1788–1850* (New York, 1984).

126. See especially Richard Hofstadter, *The Idea of a Party System: The Rise of Legitimate Opposition in the United States, 1790–1840* (Berkeley, 1970).

127. Various historians have cast the emergence of professional parties in the 1820s and 1830s as a political watershed in which the antiparty animus of the eighteenth century finally disappeared. Usually, however, discussion focuses on how politicians supposedly built parties mainly in order to advance their own careers and widen their popular constituencies. The effects of popular pressure from below in this process—as well as the genuinely democratic and populist principles of party men like Martin

Van Buren—have yet to receive their due. So has the earlier history of popular party formations, particularly on the local level, stretching back at least to the 1790s. The crucial discussions of parties appear in Hofstadter, *Idea of a Party System;* and in Michael Wallace, "Changing Concepts of Party in the United States: New York, 1815–1828," *American Historical Review* 74 (1968), 453–491.

128. "The Key of Libberty, Containing Proposals for Taking a Monthly Magazine to be Stiled the Farmers or Labourers Magazine . . . ," 5–6, Houghton Library, Harvard University.

129. Manning, "A Proposed Method for Carrying the Foregoing into Execution" [1806], Manning Papers, MSS. Am 880/836, Houghton Library, Harvard University.

130. Manning, "A Proposed Plan for Carrying the Foregoing into Execution" [c. 1806/1807], Manning Papers, MSS. Am 880/839, Houghton Library, Harvard University.

131. Manning, "A Proposed Plan for Carrying 'The Key of Libberty' into Circulation" [c. 1807], Manning Papers, MSS. Am 880/834, Houghton Library, Harvard University.

132. On Brown, see Smith, *Freedom's Fetters,* 257–270; Charles Warren, *Jacobin and Junto, or Early American Politics as Viewed in the Diary of Dr. Nathaniel Ames, 1788–1822* (Cambridge, Mass., 1931), 106–110; *Independent Chronicle,* June 17 and 20, 1799.

133. *Columbian Centinel* (Boston), March 27, 1799.

134. *Independent Chronicle,* June 17, 1798.

135. Jefferson, *Writings,* 700, 985–990, 1035–1037.

136. Seth Ames, ed., *Works of Fisher Ames,* 2 vols. (Boston, 1854), II, 115. For more on Republican party organization, see Robinson, *Jeffersonian Democracy* (New Haven, 1916), 52–75; and Noble Cunningham, Jr., *The Jeffersonian Republicans in Power* (Chapel Hill, 1963), 133–142.

137. See Robinson, *Jeffersonian Democracy;* David Hackett Fischer, *The Revolution of American Conservatism: The Federalist Party in the Era of Jeffersonian Democracy* (New York, 1965); and James M. Banner, Jr., *To the Hartford Convention: The Federalists and the Origins of Party Politics in Massachusetts, 1789–1815* (New York, 1970).

138. Robinson, *Jeffersonian Democracy,* 63–65; Warren, *Jacobin and Junto,* 226.

139. Robinson, *Jeffersonian Democracy,* 63.

140. On this point see Hofstadter, *The Idea of a Party System,* 150–155, 167–169.

141. Jephtha Manning to His Father, William Manning, Dr. [1804–1811], MAB, 62; Manning Probate, 1814.
142. Morison was aware of this material, but his analysis of it was flawed. See Morison, ed., "Manning's 'Key,' " 206.
143. Manning, "A Proposed Method"; "A Proposed Plan for Carrying the Foregoing into Execution"; "A Proposed Plan for Carrying the Key of Libberty into Execution."
144. [Anon.], *Trial of Thomas O. Selfridge* (Boston, n.d. [1807]).
145. Manning's discussion of family duties captured a more general shift in New England away from the severe Puritan dictates of the seventeenth and early eighteenth centuries toward a more benevolent patriarchal order. For a cogent summary, see the opening chapters of Steven Mintz and Susan Kellogg, *Domestic Revolutions: A Social History of American Family Life* (New York, 1988).
146. William Manning to William Manning, Jr., April 7, 1807, *Grantors* 10:462.
147. Jephtha Manning to His Father, William Manning, Dr. [1804–1811], MAB, 62.
148. William Manning to William Manning, Jr., April 7, 1807, *Grantors* 10:462. Jephtha Manning v. William Manning, January 1, 1812, CCP.
149. *Grantees* 11:276–279.
150. [Theophilus Manning], "His Book" [1798]; Samuel Jacques to [?], March 14, 1801, in Theophilus Manning, Middlesex Canal Accounts, Payrolls, Baker Library, Graduate School of Business Administration, Harvard University. This collection includes Theophilus' payroll records from his time as overseer, as well as a brief mention of the packet line.
    In the 1820s, Theophilus briefly owned the saw-and-grist mill of his late father-in-law, Asa Patten, but he sold it in 1825 to Asa's nephew, Aaron Patten. Hazen, *History*, 282.
151. Manning Probate, 1814.
152. *Grantees* 17:327 and 19:196; Koenig, "Manning Manse," 8–10.
153. Manning, *Genealogical History of the Mannings*, 65; Koenig, "Manning Manse," 10–12.
154. The epitaph was aptly chosen for an orthodox Calvinist democrat like Manning:

> Death is to us from terrors free
> When once 'tis understood
> 'Tis nature's due, 'tis God's decree
> It is and must be good.

155. Hazen, *History*, 280–282; Caroline Ware, *The Early New England Cotton Manufacture* (Boston, 1931), 60–61, 80; Jonathan Prude, *The Coming of Industrial Order: Town and Factory Life in Rural Massachusetts, 1810–1860* (New York, 1983); and Hal S. Barron, *Those Who Stayed Behind: Rural Society in Nineteenth-Century New England* (New York, 1984).
156. Thoreau, *Week on the Concord and Merrimack*, 41.
157. Of course, the popular memory of the Revolution did not disappear altogether. For an insightful, at times poignant meditation on this theme, see Alfred F. Young, "George Robert Twelves Hewes (1742–1840): A Boston Shoemaker and the Memory of the American Revolution," *WMQ* 38 (1981): 561–623.
158. See David Montgomery, *Beyond Equality: Labor and the Radical Republicans, 1862–1872* (New York, 1967), 14–17.
159. For an intriguing example of this sort of reconstruction, see Mark A. Lause, "The Unwashed Infidelity: Thomas Paine and Early New York Labor History," *Labor History* 27 (1986), 385–407. For a more general consideration, see Staughton Lynd, *The Intellectual Origins of American Radicalism* (New York, 1968). On the confluence of American popular democracy and European immigrant ideas in the nineteenth century, see Wilentz, *Chants Democratic*, 363–389; Bruce Levine, *The Spirit of 1848: German Immigrants, Labor Conflict, and the Coming of the Civil War* (Urbana, 1992); and Paul Krause, *The Battle for Homestead 1880–1892: Politics, Culture, and Steel* (Pittsburgh, 1992). On Populism, see Lawrence Goodwyn, *Democratic Promise: The Populist Moment in America* (New York, 1976).

"Some Proposals"

1. Manning's observation about the lack of opposition to Hamilton is misleading—although he may not have been aware of the extent of the opposition when he began "Some Proposals." On February 11, 1790, James Madison introduced an amendment to the Funding Act then being debated in Congress that called for the original holders to receive in federal securities the difference between the nominal and the market value of the outstanding debt. As E. James Ferguson has explained, his proposal "publicly announced a rift in the aristocracy whose united efforts had produced the Constitution" and "brought to focus a residual hatred of merchants, rich men and speculators." See E. James Ferguson, *The Power of the*

Purse: A History of American Public Finance, 1776–1790 (Chapel Hill, 1961), 297–303. Later in "Some Proposals," Manning does discuss some of the plans put forward by opponents of Hamilton's scheme—indicating that he worked on the essay for some weeks after February 6, 1790.

2. "Such-a-one": the original loan certificate forms included a blank space where the name of the creditor was entered.

3. Manning here describes a relationship governed by commercial expectations—repayment is expected to occur unfailingly and with due interest at a stated time. But he also used the principle that a creditor is owed "full value of what he received with interest therefor, and no more" to sustain the claims of the original creditors. The paradigmatic instance of a complex barter transaction—in which two individuals exchange various goods and services with each other at irregular intervals without settling accounts or even striking a balance—relied on interest-free trade credits. But the conventions of flexible repayment schedules that governed such transactions were applicable to other exchanges in which interest was charged. The wealthier members of a community often lent their poorer neighbors money at interest, receiving a mortgage on land as a guarantee of repayment. Also, transactions involving large sums of money (for example, those that might arise between family members in the course of an estate settlement) were often secured by bonds—formal promises to pay a stated sum at a given date with interest. Even though interest was customarily charged in these circumstances, repayment of the debts owed was often governed by the flexible and forgiving expectations of the complex barter networks rather than the strict and unforgiving expectations of a commercial transaction.

4. As written, this sentence would seem to mean, simply, that the people were acquainted with many modes of taxation and collection. But also Manning argues that they had only recently (that is, after or during the later stages of the war) become so acquainted. To be consistent, then, this sentence would have to mean that the people were at first acquainted with only one mode of taxation.

One way of reconciling this apparent contradiction is to interpret this sentence as follows: At first there were many modes of collecting taxes across the continent, but people in each state or locality were familiar with only one. As a result, the central government had difficulty imposing any one system on the whole area. Later, however, people in each locality became familiar with a variety of different taxes and collection systems. Consequently, Congress could more easily impose a single tax on the whole.

5. The "fourteen" Manning is referring to are probably the original thirteen American states along with the continental government, all of which had issued loan certificates and passed laws that affected their value. Alternatively, Manning may have had in mind the thirteen original states plus Vermont, which had declared itself an independent republic in 1777 and was not admitted to the union as the fourteenth state until 1791.

6. Manning here proposes that Congress pay off its foreign creditors with what amounts to barter transactions—purchasing American goods with domestic paper money and then transporting them overseas, where they can be sold to obtain the local currency necessary to pay off creditors in that country.

7. Manning appears to have taken this figure from the summary of Hamilton's report in the *Independent Chronicle*, January 28, 1790. As the summary accurately reported, the domestic debt of the United States—including the principal and arrears of interest on the domestic debt of the national government, plus the combined debts of the states—totaled, according to Hamilton's account, $70,325,000.

8. Manning could have discovered the trade figures reported in the next three paragraphs in any of several sources. Although numerous biases in reporting make accuracy elusive, Manning was basically correct in his assertions about the imbalance of trade between Britain and America. And most of his figures are in line with those gathered by modern historians. See B. R. Mitchell with the collaboration of Phyllis Deane, *Abstract of British Historical Statistics* (Cambridge, 1962), 310–311; and U.S. Department of Commerce, Bureau of the Census, *Historical Statistics of the United States: Colonial Times to 1970*, 2 vols. (Washington, D.C., 1970), II, 1176–1177.

9. Here again, Manning was generally correct about the great imbalance of trade, although the figure of £8 million for 1784 seems greatly exaggerated. See Mitchell and Deane, *Abstract*, 311; and U.S. Bureau of the Census, *Historical Statistics*, 1176–1177.

10. Manning could have borrowed this wording (perhaps indirectly) from David Hume, who used a very similar image in his discussion of balance of trade problems. Hume, however, was arguing against those who, like Manning, explained price fluctuations solely by changes in the money supply. See Hume, "On the Balance of

Trade" [1752], in *Essays: Moral, Political and Literary* (Indianapolis, 1985), 308–313.

11. This exposition draws most heavily on Articles I and VII of the Massachusetts Constitution of 1780. See Oscar Handlin and Mary Handlin, eds., *The Popular Sources of Political Authority: Documents on the Massachusetts Constitution of 1780* (Cambridge, Mass., 1966), 442, 444.

12. This passage refers to the constitutional distance between the citizenry and the new federal government, but may also have evoked the common complaints that governments situated in the seaboard cities were inaccessible to poorer country citizens. On these complaints, see Rosemarie Zaggari, "Representation and the Removal of State Capitals, 1776–1812," *Journal of American History* 74 (1988), 1239–1256.

13. The *Independent Chronicle* reprinted numbers 2 through 14 of "Observer" between October 29, 1789, and February 18, 1790. While "Observer" sounded many Federalist themes—such as the absence in America of both rich and poor, the benefit of funding the national debt at par and allowing it to circulate indefinitely, and the injustice of discriminating against the current holders—his principal concern was to argue the case for uniform property and excise taxes across the nation. His tenth number, which appeared in the *Chronicle* on January 7, 1790, offered empty praise of the agricultural interest as the backbone of the country.

14. Here, and in the next three paragraphs, Manning shows that he was well acquainted with the various funding plans offered by Hamilton's opponents during the debates over the funding plan in the spring of 1790. Of particular interest is the third proposal, which Manning criticizes for failing to provide for an adequate medium of trade. He appears to be referring to James Madison's very similar proposal, delivered on the floor of the Congress on February 11, 1790. See Ferguson, *Power of the Purse*, 297–298, 312.

"The Key of Liberty"

1. The Society of the Cincinnati was organized in 1783 by officers of the American Continental Army, then about to disband. George Washington served as the group's first president-general. Membership was hereditary, passed on through the eldest male line or, in case of failure, through collateral descent. Organized into thirteen state societies (with a branch in France for French officers who had

served in the American cause), the society also established a large permanent fund for the aid of officers' widows and the indigent. In the 1780s and 1790s, the society came under heavy attack for its hereditary structure, its wealth, and its alleged political intrigues. The French branch dissolved in 1792, amid the French Revolution's attack on hereditary institutions. The American society declined after 1800, and revived only in the 1930s.

Freemasonry was imported to the American colonies by English, Scottish, and Irish Masons in the 1730s. A fraternal organization for local notables, freemasonry included in its ranks a large segment of the revolutionary leadership. (Fifty of the fifty-six signers of the Declaration of Independence were members.) In the 1790s, free-masonry had strong Federalist connections; thereafter, Jeffersonians became increasingly prominent in its ranks. See John L. Brooke, "Ancient Lodges and Self-Created Societies: Voluntary Associations and the Public Sphere in the Early Republic," paper presented to the annual conference of the United States Capitol Hill Historical Society, March 1990.

2. The essays by "Free Republican" (Benjamin Lincoln, Jr.) appeared in the *Independent Chronicle* from November 24, 1785, to February 9, 1786.
3. The story of Joseph occupies chapters 37 to 50 of *Genesis*.
4. This image, of course, originated with Jesus. See *Matthew* 7:3–5.

We have not been able to identify with certainty either the "divine" referred to here, or the "writer" mentioned two paragraphs below. Among Manning's contemporaries, the most likely possibility is Samuel Hopkins (1721–1803), or someone closely associated with him. Manning's exhortation on the self in this section of "The Key" is practically a précis of Hopkins' views. "It is evident, that sin consists in self love . . . Self love regards nothing but self, as such, and subordinates every being to this; and opposes every thing which, in the view of the selfish person, opposes him, and his selfish interest. He who is under the government of this affection takes all to himself, and gives nothing to any other being, as if he is the greatest, the best, and only worthy and important being in the universe . . . Self love is blindness and delusion itself, as it is a contradiction to all truth, and the source of all blindness and delusion with respect to things temporal, and spiritual, which have or can ever take place." *The System of Doctrines Captured in Divine Revelations* (Boston, 1793), 348–349.
5. *II Kings* 8:13.

6. The story of Haman is in *Esther*, chapters 3 through 7. Although in his other scriptural references in "The Key" Manning quotes from his King James verbatim, he does not do so here.

7. Here Manning quietly challenged "Free Republican," who had copied his own political taxonomy directly from Montesquieu's *The Spirit of the Laws* (1748). See "Free Republican No. V," *Independent Chronicle*, December 22, 1785. Manning's division of government into two basic types—free and not free—can also be found in the concluding chapter of Thomas Paine's *Rights of Man, Part I* (1791), although Manning never referred to Paine in any of his manuscripts.

8. This commonplace assertion shows Manning working well within a frame of reference usually associated with John Locke. See Locke, *Second Treatise on Government*, ed. P. Laslett (Cambridge, 1960), 395.

9. The following summary highlights the major democratic features of the Massachusetts Declaration of Rights, which led Manning to concur with those who considered the constitution from which it came an exemplary one. His exactness suggests that he kept a copy close to hand. See Oscar Handlin and Mary Handlin, eds., *The Popular Sources of Political Authority: Documents on the Massachusetts Constitution of 1780* (Cambridge, Mass., 1966), esp. 442–444.

10. Impeachment originated as a check on the arbitrary power of monarchs, and its role in a republican government was anything but clear to the revolutionary generation. Should elected officials be liable to impeachment—that is, by a court of some kind? Or should they be removable only by election—that is, by the people at large? And if they were to be impeachable, which tribunal ought to hear the case? In particular, were sitting judges to hear cases against their fellow jurists? Or should a special court be impaneled? Many prominent revolutionaries, including the archrivals Alexander Hamilton and Thomas Jefferson, favored setting up special impeachment courts. For a complete discussion of the debate over impeachment in the revolutionary era, see Peter Charles Hoffer and N. E. H. Hull, *Impeachment in America, 1635–1805* (New Haven, 1984), esp. 70–75, 96–100.

11. *Matthew* 7:12.

12. *Genesis* 3:19.

13. This section is based very closely on the argument in "Free Republican No. V," *Independent Chronicle*, December 22, 1785, which is in turn based very closely on the classic statement of the labor theory

of property in John Locke, "On Property," *Second Treatise on Government*, 338.

14. That is, scarce money meant lower prices for labor and produce. And lower prices for labor and produce advantaged the Few—especially those who lived on money incomes—and disadvantaged the Many.

15. This famous contemptuous phrase originated with Edmund Burke, *Reflections on the Revolution in France* (1790). There is no hard evidence that Manning read Burke's book or Thomas Paine's well-known response, *Rights of Man* (1791–1792). A popular English satiric chapbook, *A Tribute to the Swinish Multitude*, ran through several American editions in 1794 and 1795.

16. *Proverbs* 22:6.

17. The 1780s and 1790s saw important reforms in women's education. There was a marked increase in the numbers of girls attending local secondary schools; various women's academies began to educate young women in some of the basics of Enlightenment learning, to prepare them as better wives and mothers. Yet there were also conflicts, especially in New England, over the best future direction for women's education. Manning was one of the many late eighteenth-century Massachusetts democrats who called for increased attention to the education of girls. According to Kathryn Kish Sklar, the principal opponents of such schooling were members of the local elites, who pressed for Latin grammar schools intended to prepare their sons for college, and preferred to educate their daughters at private finishing schools. See Sklar, "Sources of Change in the Schooling of Girls in Massachusetts, 1750–1810" (unpublished paper, n.d., Department of History, State University of New York at Binghamton).

18. Manning seems to have aimed these remarks in particular against Harvard College, which aside from Williams was the only college in Massachusetts at the time. Blatantly pro-Federalist orations and valedictory addresses were common at Harvard in the 1790s.

19. Cf. Manning's attack and the one contained in Benjamin Austin's polemic, *Observations on the Pernicious Practice of the Law*. Manning almost certainly read Austin's remarks, which originally ran in several numbers of the *Independent Chronicle* in the spring of 1786 as a direct response to "Free Republican," especially "Free Republican No. IX," *Independent Chronicle*, January 26, 1787. See also Sydney Kaplan, "'Honestus' and the Annihilation of the Lawyers," *South Atlantic Quarterly* 48 (1949), 401–420. Manning's distrust of lawyers

was widely shared in postrevolutionary America. See the sample of opinion in Charles Warren, *A History of the American Bar* (Boston, 1911), 211–239.

20. Manning's remarks reflected the long-standing, deep-seated Anglo-American fear of a permanent standing army—a fear that, in the 1760s and 1770s, helped lead to the American Revolution. Manning's reflections about the abiding desires of the Few to build an American standing army voiced a widespread popular apprehension—which was not at all far-fetched. In 1798, amid the quasi-war with France, Federalists talked loosely of the dangers posed by "terrorists," and of the need for a strengthened military. President Adams and the Congress, in turn, approved a massive military buildup in June and July 1798. Those who pushed hardest for the new appropriations (above all, Alexander Hamilton) had in mind a permanent standing army, designed partly to obstruct Republican voting and political organizing. See Richard H. Kohn, *Eagle and Sword: The Federalists and the Creation of the Military Establishment in America, 1783–1802* (New York, 1975), 2–13, 193–273.

21. See Wallace Evan Davies, "The Society of the Cincinnati in New England, 1783–1800," *WMQ* 5 (1948), 3–25; and Minor Myers, Jr., *Liberty without Anarchy: A History of the Society of the Cincinnati* (Charlottesville, Va., 1983), 48–76.

22. The president of the Society of the Cincinnati was George Washington.

23. This passing reference is to the wars with the Indians in the Ohio Valley and Great Lakes regions.

24. In 1795, the Georgia legislature enacted a law selling 13 million acres of the state's so-called Yazoo lands (presently the states of Alabama and Mississippi) to four land companies, at the bargain rate of $500 million—or about a penny and a half per acre. It soon became evident that nearly all of the legislators who had voted for the sale had been bribed by the land companies involved. A political explosion predictably followed, and in 1796 a newly elected Georgia legislature repealed the law and repudiated the sale. But the controversy continued. Immediately after they had obtained the Yazoo lands, the land companies had dumped their titles to second- and third-hand speculators, most of them in New England. After the repeal of the 1795 law, these speculators demanded compensation and mounted a campaign that would last eighteen years. A turning point came in the celebrated case of *Fletcher v. Peck* (1810), where the Supreme Court ruled that the Georgia legisla-

ture's 1796 repeal law violated the contract clause of the U.S. Constitution. In 1814, Congress finally provided $4.2 million to compensate the claimants, and the affair ended.

25. The first American chamber of commerce was established in New York City in 1768, with a charter from King George III. Boston's chamber, like that of several other cities, evolved out of its colonial-era Board of Trade, established to supervise the city's commerce.

26. The Boston Medical Society was formed in 1780 largely to establish fee schedules for physicians. The Massachusetts Medical Society was incorporated by the state legislature one year later.

27. During the 1790s, the Congregational ministers of Massachusetts belonged to twenty-two different district associations. However, a statewide General Association was not formed until 1802.

28. In the various states, restrictions on admission to practice law appeared in the rules of court and by statute, as well as in the rules formulated by bar associations. Bar associations, in Massachusetts and elsewhere, dated back to the mid-eighteenth century, well before the Revolution.

29. Cockades were ribboned emblems, worn in hats to display one's political allegiance. Federalists in the 1790s wore black cockades; Republicans wore either red or the tricolor.

30. "And when his thousand years are expired, Satan shall be loosed out of his prison, and shall go out to deceive the nations which are in the four quarters of the earth, Gog and Magog, to gather them together to battle: the number of whom is as the sand of the sea." *Revelation* 20:7–8. Manning may also have seen the English broadside *A Remarkable Prophecy* (1794), which went through several American editions and predicted that Gog and Magog "will make war against all the nations in the world." See Ruth Bloch, *Visionary Republic: Millennial Themes in American Thought, 1756–1800* (Cambridge, 1985), 162–163.

31. See Albert Gallatin's pamphlet *A Sketch of the Finances of the United States* (New York, 1796), which outlined the mounting debt accumulated by Washington's administration during Alexander Hamilton's tenure as secretary of the Treasury. If Manning did not read this pamphlet, he was clearly aware of its argument.

32. Here Manning correctly cited Article I, sections 1 and 8, of the U S. Constitution, but also silently smuggled in the stipulation in Amendment 10 that all powers not expressly given to Congress are reserved to the states.

33. Article II, section 2, of the Constitution gives the president of the

United States the power to make treaties "by and with the advice and consent" of the Senate, without consulting the House of Representatives. This power, Manning is arguing, cannot have been intended to refer to all treaties—including those that require a new law or appropriation to take effect—without contradicting Article I, section 8, of the Constitution, which gives to Congress the power to make all laws "necessary and proper for carrying into execution" all the powers vested by the Constitution in the government of the United States.

34. This discussion, continuing over the next three paragraphs, details Manning's position in the debate over treaty-making powers that was sparked by the House opposition to Jay's Treaty in 1795–1796.

35. Manning refers here to the vote taken in the House of Representatives on March 24, 1796, on Edward Livingston's resolution to demand that the executive produce all papers related to Jay's Treaty "excepting such of said papers as any existing negotiations may render improper to be disclosed." The actual tally was 62 yea, 37 nay, with 5 absent and the Speaker not voting. *The Debates and Proceedings in the Congress of the United States*, 42 vols. (Washington, D.C., 1834–1856), V, 759–760.

36. As Manning's remarks suggests, protreaty Federalists stressed the danger of war with Great Britain if Jay's Treaty was not approved. Manning mocked these scare tactics. He appears, like other antitreaty men, to have strongly doubted that Britain would risk making war on its most reliable trading partner, the United States.

37. In 1793, the Pennsylvania legislature elected the Swiss-born Albert Gallatin to the United States Senate. When Gallatin, a talented friend of the opposition, attempted to claim his seat, he was challenged and excluded by administration allies, on the grounds that he had not been a naturalized citizen for eight years. Unfazed, Gallatin returned to his home in western Pennsylvania, now more than ever a popular hero. That autumn, the western counties elected him to the House of Representatives, in the face of proadministration charges that, in the interim, he had helped foment the Whiskey Rebellion. Gallatin quickly became one of the most important Republican voices in Congress, and he assumed the leadership of the House opposition when James Madison and William Branch Giles retired from their seats in 1797. Thereafter, he won his greatest fame as secretary of the Treasury under President Thomas Jefferson.

38. Manning refers to Alexander Hamilton's sexual liaison with Mrs.

Maria Reynolds in 1791–1792, which caused a scandal when it was made public in 1797.

Manning's reference, in this same sentence, to "fifteen thousand men," is to the number of troops raised to suppress the Whiskey Rebellion.

39. Gabriel, one of the four archangels, was God's messenger and interpreter. His trumpet blast was supposed to announce the return of Christ.

40. Hamilton's excise tax program first came into force in 1791. In 1794, when foreign affairs turned sour, Hamilton raised the excise tax on distilled spirits, which provoked the Whiskey Rebellion. The stamp tax on legal papers (including those concerned with will probates) was enacted in 1797. The direct tax on dwellings, land, and slaves came the following year, as did the four measures known collectively as the Alien and Sedition Acts.

41. Manning could have discovered these figures in any of several sources. They appear to be only slightly exaggerated. In 1784, Ezra Stiles noted in his diary that 6,853 votes were cast in that year's Connecticut gubernatorial elections. According to newspaper reports, 7,773 votes were cast in the 1796 statewide Connecticut elections, and 7,075 were cast two years later. The latter figures translated, respectively, into a mere 3.2 percent and 2.8 percent of the total state population as reported in the 1800 federal census. See Richard J. Purcell, *Connecticut in Transition, 1775–1818* (1918; 2nd ed. Middletown, Conn., 1963), 188.

42. See the comments in Thomas Jefferson's "The Anas" about monarchial customs in the Washington administration, in Jefferson, *Writings*, ed. Merrill Peterson (New York, 1984), 661–690.

43. In 1791, the year that Hamilton's Bank of the United States (B.U.S.) was established, only three other American banks existed, including the Massachusetts Bank, founded in Boston in 1784. By 1800, there were twenty-nine American banks, including six in Massachusetts; the numbers would continue to spiral upward in the coming years. Many of the newer institutions after 1791 arose expressly to challenge the Federalist hold on banking, which had tightened with the creation of the B.U.S. Manning obtained a mortgage from one of these newer institutions, the Union Bank of Boston, in 1792.

44. Unfortunately, tables issued by the U.S. Bureau of the Census report only total figures for U.S. imports in the 1790s. Figures compiled by B. R. Mitchell and Phyllis Deane show a difference of £3,797,000

between U.S. imports from and exports to Great Britain in 1798.
B. R. Mitchell, with the collaboration of Phyllis Deane, *Abstract of British Historical Statistics* (Cambridge, 1962), 311.

45. In February 1787, the Massachusetts state legislature passed an act for the control of swine that directed towns to select a designated "hog reeve" (or, in Manning's phrase, hog constable), who would be responsible for seeing that all swine were properly ringed and marked, and that they rooted only where they were welcome. Samuel Freeman, *The Town Officer, or the Duty and Power of Selectmen* [*etc.*], 4th ed. (Boston, 1799). According to Alice Morse Earle, newly married men were occasionally appointed hog constable in jest. See Earle, *Home Life in Colonial Days* (New York, 1899), 403.

46. Monthly magazines were nothing new in America. The earliest— Andrew Bradford's *American Magazine* and Benjamin Franklin's *General Magazine*, both published in Philadelphia—began their brief runs in 1740–1741. In all, at least thirty-five additional monthlies appeared through 1789, most of them short-lived. The late 1780s and early 1790s brought some more ambitious monthlies, including Noah Webster's *American Magazine* (1787–1788), Matthew Carey's *American Museum* (1787–1792), and, in Worcester, Massachusetts, Isaiah Thomas' *Massachusetts Magazine* (1789–1796).

47. Beginning in the early 1790s, the emerging antiadministration faction began mounting its own annual festivities on July 4. By mid-decade, specific benevolent associations with Republican affinities (such as New York City's Society of Saint Tammany), along with urban craftsmen's societies, began using July 4 as a day for parades and orations, and for electing officers. By 1800, the Fourth had become a highly partisan Republican holiday—so much so that Federalists did not turn out to celebrate the day, or even to read aloud the Declaration of Independence. For an excellent account of July 4 and the partisan politics of the 1790s, see Simon Peter Newman, "American Popular Political Culture in the Age of the French Revolution" (Ph.D. dissertation, Princeton University, 1991), esp. 122–183.

48. Washington was determined that a great national academy be established so that American notables would no longer have to send their bright, ambitious sons abroad for the best available education. In 1794, he set aside his personal shares in the Potomac Canal Company and the James River Canal Company, to be used to support the academy after his death. Two years later, he tried to

insert a formal proposal about the academy in his famous Farewell Address, but Hamilton persuaded him to drop it as irrelevant to the address's main themes.

49. Manning may have borrowed this reference to the Roman tribunes from "Free Republican No. X," *Independent Chronicle*, February 9, 1787. Characteristically, "Free Republican" linked the rise of the tribunes to "abusive impositions on the wealthy," a notion Manning turned upside down.

50. James Bowdoin, governor of Massachusetts, 1785–1787, a conservative who was aligned with the creditor majority in the Massachusetts legislature.

51. John Hancock, governor of Massachusetts, 1780–1785, 1787–1793, had built on his reputation as a revolutionary leader to become the greatest popular political hero in the state in the 1780s. He had retired from the Massachusetts governorship in 1785, just when the state's fiscal problems reached a critical point. In 1787, however, following the suppression of the Massachusetts Regulation, he agreed to stand against the disgraced Governor Bowdoin, and was elected by a large majority.

52. "The Institution of the Society of the Cincinnati" called for the creation of one general and several state societies. The latter were also empowered to form as many district societies as necessary. There was no mention at all of county or town societies, or of neighborhood classes. The "Institution" can be found in Myers, *Liberty without Anarchy*, 258–265.

Other Writings

1. Samuel Eliot Morison confirmed the main facts of the following anecdote by consulting the files of the adjutant-general's office at the Massachusetts State House in Boston. In 1798, the militia consisted of all able-bodied men aged eighteen to forty-five. All who did not receive special dispensation were expected to provide their own equipment and turn out for drill once a year. The exercises Manning described were part of a Federalist effort to lift morale and discipline within the militia in anticipation of a war with France. The commanding officer of the militia's Third Division was Major General William Hull. Fifteen years later, Hull would win notoriety as the man who surrendered Detroit to the British without firing a shot, during the early action of the War of 1812. See Morison, ed., "Manning's 'Key,' " 229, n. 12.

2. The reference is to the impeachment proceedings undertaken against William Hunt in Massachusetts 1794 and against the North Carolina senator William Blount three years later. Hunt, a justice of the peace in Middlesex County, was impeached and found guilty in the General Court of charges concerning conflict of interest. His punishment was light—a year's removal from office—and in 1796, he won his own seat in the General Court. He went on to become a leading high Federalist in the legislature. Blount stood accused of plotting to maneuver the British into invading the Spanish Southwest, to open up the area for speculation by himself and his business associates. As a Federalist-turned-Republican, however, he was also an object of bitter political animosity from congressional Federalists. His case in part tested how thoroughly Congress would allow impeachment to become a politicized process. Ultimately, Blount was found not guilty of having committed any clear criminal violation.

Manning's point is simply that impeachment proceedings were not particularly effective at keeping selfish, peculating officeholders in line. That he would mention the cases of a Federalist and Republican shows that, on this issue, he was nonpartisan. For details on Hunt and Blount, see Peter Charles Hoffer and N. E. H. Hull, *Impeachment in America, 1635–1805* (New Haven, 1984), 141–142, 151–163.

3. Manning's educational proposals in the following section far outstripped existing school systems in the various states. In 1789, Massachusetts reformed its system with a law that required towns of fifty or more families to provide an elementary school for at least six months a year and required towns of two hundred families to provide a grammar school, with classical languages as part of the curriculum. As most Massachusetts towns already provided some sort of partially free elementary schooling—and as the legislature failed to provide any funds to the towns under the reformed system—the law probably had little impact. New York and Connecticut managed to put more ambitious plans into effect in the 1790s (although New York's quickly fell by the wayside). Neither state plan was as comprehensive as Manning's, which even exceeded Thomas Jefferson's visionary proposal for a three-tier statewide school and academy system for Virginia. For details, see Carl Kaestle, *Pillars of the Republic: Common Schools and American Society, 1780–1860* (New York, 1983), 3–13.

4. Article XV of Jay's Treaty.

5. Washington's Proclamation of Neutrality, issued in April 1793, forbade American citizens from aiding or abetting any of the belligerent European powers, and assured the world that the United States intended to remain impartial. Formally, the proclamation did not suspend the Franco-American treaties of alliance and commerce of 1778 (although Manning, along with much of the opposition leadership, believed it certainly violated the spirit, if not the letter, of those treaties). More important, in issuing the proclamation, Washington dismissed the arguments of Jefferson and others that only Congress had the power to declare neutrality, under the war-making provisions of the U.S. Constitution. Washington's move, backed by Hamilton, was a calculated and dramatic bid to expand executive power over foreign policy—which only confirmed Republicans in their fears that the administration was gradually moving the American republic closer toward monarchy. By likening the proclamation to a papal bull, Manning deployed Protestant America's most common image for the highest form of despotism. Yet this implicit attack on the papacy did not, in itself, negate Manning's professions of religious tolerance.

6. The reference is to Articles XVII and XXII of the Treaty of Amity and Commerce (1778).

7. The reference is to Article XI of the Treaty of Alliance with France (1778), in which the United States guaranteed the French king "the present possessions of the Crown of France in America, as well as those which it may acquire by the future treaty of peace." U.S. Senate, *Treaties and Conventions Concluded between the United States of America and Other Powers Since July 4, 1776* (Washington, D.C., 1871), 243.

   Manning's reference to the West Indies repeats charges made by the French envoy Joseph Fauchet, in the pamphlet translated as *A Sketch of the Present State of Our Political Relations with the United States of North-America* (Philadelphia, 1797). Manning would later mention the pamphlet explicitly. In 1793–1794, the British courted the French colonial slaveholders of Saint-Domingue, who stood opposed to both the French Revolution and the island's rebellious slaves. Over the same period, the British won control of the principal towns and ports of the French West Indian colonies, including Saint Domingue. By 1795, the British had mounted an effective blockade of what remained of France's Caribbean holdings, and sent ships to the mouth of the Chesapeake to prevent the departure of American vessels bound either for France or the French West

Indies. The U.S. government, for its part, refused to allow French warships to resupply in American ports and refused to recognize the legitimacy of French seizures of British ships.

Manning, like other pro-French Republicans, thought the American actions yet another violation of the nation's moral debt and of its formal treaty obligations to France. There is no reason to think that his reflections had much to do with the situation regarding the black insurgents of Saint-Domingue. The French had, in 1794, voted to abolish slavery throughout the French empire; thereafter, the leader of Saint-Domingue's slaves, Toussaint L'Ouverture, declared his allegiance to France and fought fiercely (and successfully) against the British. In this respect, Manning was unafraid about supporting a cause in which a French black general had taken the lead. But only in August 1798—six months after Manning completed this draft of the "The Key"—did the weary British finally agree to leave Saint-Domingue, setting the stage for Toussaint's fateful encounters with Napoleon Bonaparte, the ultimate test for the island's black Jacobins. Before that, Manning's primary concern in these matters appears, as ever, to have been with defending France against the British—and against hostile American Federalists—and not with anything connected to slavery and its destruction.

See C. L. R. James, *Black Jacobins: Toussaint L'Ouverture and the San Domingo Revolution* (New York, 1963); Rayford Logan, *The Diplomatic Relations of the United States with Haiti, 1771–1891* (Chapel Hill, 1941), esp. ch. 2; and J. Holland Rose, "The Conflict with Revolutionary France," in *The Cambridge History of the British Empire* (Cambridge, 1940), 41–51, 52–70.

8. This passage refers to the political and diplomatic crises that directly preceded John Jay's mission to Great Britain in 1794. In December 1793, secretary of state Thomas Jefferson released a report which purported to show that American shipping was well treated by France, Spain, and Portugal but subjected to severe restrictions by the Britain. Fortified by Jefferson's findings—and by continued British harrassment of American merchant shipping—James Madison placed three resolutions before the House of Representatives on January 4, 1794, that took square aim at Great Britain. Continued British raids on American shipping over the winter, especially in the West Indies, deepened the crisis. In March, Congress approved a sixty-day embargo on trade (a move which proved unpopular with France as well as Britain and was not renewed). And it began to consider other retaliatory proposals.

The situation looked disastrous to many Federalists, especially Alexander Hamilton. Not only was Hamilton well inclined toward Britain politically; his entire fiscal program depended on British investment in American public securities and on duties placed on international imports, four-fifths of which came from Britain. Determined to head off further congressional action—and, quite possibly, an Anglo-American war—Hamilton urged President Washington to send a special envoy to London to secure a commercial treaty and thereby end the Republican harrassment once and for all. Washington agreed, but chose chief justice John Jay, not Hamilton, for the job, much to Hamilton's dismay.

9. The reference is to Article II of the Treaty of Amity and Commerce (1778).

10. James Monroe, *A View of the Conduct of the Executive in the Foreign Affairs of the United States* (Philadelphia, 1797); Fauchet, *Present State of Political Relations*.

11. Better known as the Whiskey Rebellion: see Thomas P. Slaughter, *The Whiskey Rebellion: Frontier Epilogue to the American Revolution* (New York, 1986). Manning may have exaggerated the cost of suppressing the rebellion, which, according to one historian, came closer to $800,000. See Broadus Mitchell, *Alexander Hamilton: The National Adventure, 1788–1804* (New York, 1962), II, 312.

12. Although Manning put his own construction on the Federalist cult of Washington, he by no means overstated his point. See Gary Nash, "The American Clergy and the French Revolution," *WMQ* 22 (1965), 392–412; Garry Wills, *Cincinnatus: George Washington and the Enlightenment* (New York, 1984); and Newman, "American Political Culture," 50–121.

13. "Continental Bank" refers to the Bank of the United States, established in 1791. From the moment Hamilton proposed the idea, it offended democratic republicans, who objected to the bank as an unconstitutional extension of executive power and as a potential instrument for political corruption. In addition, plebeian democrats and others criticized Hamilton's policies, including his bank, for making money scarce.

Manning's remarks in favor of the state banks foreshadowed what would emerge as an important aspect of the Democratic Republican coalition. Plebeian proponents of democratic trade provided the movement with its main thrust. They preferred economic policies that helped secure the widest possible distribution of wealth (and, hence, in their view, the highest possible income for the laboring majority). They were joined by merchants and moneyed men (notably state bankers) who favored a more freewheeling financial climate—one which would make capital more easily available and enable merchants and financiers outside the seaboard cities to compete with the established, usually pro-British mercantile houses on a more equal footing in local, regional, and overseas commerce. Victorious in 1801, the coalition would prove more testy into the 1820s and after.

For additional background, see Drew McCoy, *The Elusive Republic: Political Economy in Jeffersonian America* (Chapel Hill, 1980); Edwin G. Burrows, *Albert Gallatin and the Political Economy of Republicanism, 1761–1800* (New York, 1986); and John Nelson, *Liberty and Property: Political Economy and Policy Making in the New Nation, 1789–1812* (Baltimore, 1987).

14. On the Fructidor coup, see Georges Lefebvre, *The French Revolution*, trans. Elizabeth Moss Evanson, John Hall Stewart, and James Friguglietti, 2 vols. (New York, 1962–1964), II, 197–199.

15. The charge that the twenty U.S. senators who voted in favor of Jay's Treaty had agreed to do so even before its terms had been announced appeared repeatedly in the Republican press, along with similar claims reprinted from British newspapers. Manning may have first read the accusation in an essay by "Decius," first published in the New York *Argus*, and reprinted in the *Independent Chronicle*, July 20, 1795.

INDEX